D0382889

Arnold J. Zurcher

The Struggle to Unite Europe 1940-1958

An historical account of the development of the contemporary European Movement from its origin in the Pan-European Union to the drafting of the treaties for Euratom and the European Common Market

WITHDRAWN

Washington Square
New York University Press
1958

341.11
Z96
S

UPLAND COLLEGE LIBRARY
UPLAND, CALIFORNIA

14879

© 1958 by Arnold J. Zurcher
Library of Congress catalog card number: 58-6825
Manufactured in the United States of America

Italy consents, on condition of parity with other states, to limitations of sovereignty necessary to an order for assuring peace and justice among nations; it promotes and favors international organization directed toward that end. Article II, Constitution of the Italian Republic, Dec. 27, 1947.

On condition of reciprocal terms, France shall accept the limitations of sovereignty necessary to the organization and defense of peace. Preamble, Constitution of the French Republic, Oct. 27, 1946.

For the maintenance of peace, the Federation may join a system of mutual collective security; in doing so it will consent to those limitations of its sovereign powers which will bring about and secure a peaceful and lasting order in Europe and among the nations of the world. Article 24, Basic Law of the Federal Republic of Germany, May 8, 1949.

The aim of the Council of Europe is to achieve a greater unity between its Members for the purpose of safeguarding and realizing the ideals and principles which are their common heritage and facilitating their economic and social progress. . . . Article I, Statute of the Council of Europe, May 5, 1949.

[The High Contracting Parties]
Resolved to establish the foundations of an ever closer union among the European peoples,
Determined to ensure the economic and social progress of their countries by common action in abolishing the barriers which divide Europe,
Assigning to their efforts the main purpose of constantly improving living and working conditions of their peoples,
Realizing that the removal of existing obstacles calls for concerted action in order to guarantee stable conditions of expansion, balanced trade and fair competition,
Anxious to strengthen the unity of their economies and ensure their harmonious development by reducing differences between the various regions and the backwardness of the less-favoured,
Desirous of contributing by means of a common commercial policy to the gradual removal of restrictions on international trade,
Purposing to confirm the ties which unite Europe and overseas countries and territories, and wishing to ensure their increasing prosperity in accordance with the principles of the United Nations Charter,
Resolved to strengthen the safeguard of liberty and peace by building up this combination of resources, and calling upon the other peoples of Europe who share their ideal to join in their efforts,
Have decided to set up a European Economic Community.
Preamble of the Treaty Establishing the European Economic Community signed by the plenipotentiaries of the six nations of "Little Europe" at Rome, March 25, 1957.

Contents

Contents

Preface

In this book I have sought to provide a brief historical account of the growth of the European Movement—that label being used somewhat arbitrarily to designate the broad effort of the past quarter century, greatly intensified in the years after 1940, to secure a greater degree of integration of the European continent or a portion thereof. The effort embraces the work both of private citizens and of public agencies. It includes activities that are primarily educational and moral in purpose. It also includes official actions formulated in treaties and public resolutions that have aimed at integration, and the operations of relevant public agencies.

In the arrangement and interpretation of the data I have endeavored to explain this movement not merely in terms of political circumstances and the calculations of statesmen but also in terms of the moral and intellectual contributions of leadership dedicated to the cause of union in Europe. The result, it is hoped, is a narrative that, though concerned with developments of the relatively recent past, nevertheless possesses a degree of historical perspective. It is hoped, too, that the narrative will convey to the reader the conception of a movement that, despite occasional changes of direction and modification of its immediate objectives, and despite the relatively brief period of its existence, possesses a basic unity of purpose—one that has grown systematically and not haphazardly, and advanced perceptibly as respects the complexity and relative sophistication of its concept of union.

The introductory chapters describe what may be called the Movement's first phase. These chapters are concerned with the contribution made before and during World War II by Count Richard Coudenhove-Kalergi, a leader who may properly be regarded as the founder of the movement to unify Europe in the twentieth century. Succeeding chapters deal with the period beginning with the assumption of leadership over the European Movement by Sir Winston Churchill in 1946, and continue the account up to 1949 and the creation of the Council of Europe. Most of the remainder of the volume—by far the largest part—deals with the various efforts subsequent to the formation of the Council of Europe to develop European institutions of a supranational character. Though restricted eventually to the six nations of what is popularly denominated "Little Europe," that is, France, the German Federal Republic, Italy, and the three Benelux states, these efforts constitute the most serious steps yet taken to develop suprasovereign agencies in Europe with jurisdiction over various areas of public authority, especially in the economic field.

The evolution of the concept of the supranational community is traced in detail, beginning with the Schuman Plan, continuing with the abortive European Defense and European Political Communities, and concluding with an examination of the most recent plans of this type. These are the proposals formulated in March, 1957, for supranational communities to harness nuclear power for civilian use and to broaden the Schuman pool into an economic community that would have jurisdiction over a customs union and eventually over an economic union of the "Six."

In reviewing the various phases of the growth of the European Movement, extensive consideration has been given to the constitutional structure of the various institutions that have been erected or proposed, including the Council of Europe and the various community plans. Special attention has been directed to the structure and achievements of the Schuman Plan, the only supranational experiment that has actually reached the operative stage. Particulars of this nature are undoubtedly plentiful enough to satisfy the student of public law and others primarily concerned with juridical and administrative phenomena.

But my main reason for supplying such anatomical details has been to demonstrate the substantive nature of the changing conception of union entertained by Europe's leadership and Europe's rank and file. Such details have also been exploited to gain a clearer impression of the reception given various integrative concepts by political leaders and parties and by diplomatists. In the last two chapters of the volume an attempt is made to summarize and to reformulate the fundamental objectives of European union that Western Europe has arrived at through the influence of the European Movement since World War II. In these chapters I have also attempted to provide a systematic appraisal of public and national reaction to these objectives, extending consideration at this point to nations outside the orbit of the movement whose interests may be affected by it, particularly to the two major powers, the United States and the Soviet Union.

In treating the early history of any movement that is likely to lead to important institutional and cultural changes, it is usually difficult to avoid a certain bias in the selection and interpretation of relevant data. The events chronicled are so recent, and the writer and his generation are so intimately involved, that he cannot enjoy the sense of detachment and observe the degree of objectivity that historical writing requires. The European Movement is no exception to this rule. It is possible, moreover, that I may be especially biased in my attitude because of emotional attachments and intellectual enthusiasms generated by a fairly close personal association with the European Movement during the war years. It may be that such bias, if it exists, has not been wholly surrendered to the requirements of objective historical scholarship. At the same time the reader may be assured that every effort has been made to present this story as dispassionately and as objectively as circumstances have permitted.

Readers should be reminded also that this history is the work of a writer with an American background. There is a possibility, therefore, that my interpretation of the Movement has been colored by an American point of view. As every contemporary observer is aware, America has been closely associated with the development of the European Movement throughout its entire history. Through various universities and such private groups as the American Committee on United Europe, its leading citizens have taken a serious interest in the Movement's progress. It is an interest, moreover, that has been shared by those officially responsible for the formulation of American foreign policy. On more than one occasion, it must be confessed, I have identified myself with these American efforts to encourage European union.

I hope that, despite this background of personal interest in the European Movement and support of American policy favorable to it, I have surmounted the limitations that may thus have been imposed on my judgment and independence as a writer. I have sought to give a clear account of the hospitality that the Movement has enjoyed in America and, indeed, of the part America has actually played in helping to nurture it during the war years, 1943-1945. With equal sincerity I have sought to describe the official American attitude toward the Movement, an attitude that, except for the position taken by President Franklin D. Roosevelt, has been uniformly hospitable and encouraging. I have also tried to identify those occasions when, in my judgment, both official America and her leading private citizens may have been too hospitable and too encouraging toward the Movement—so much so that America's attitude may have been misinterpreted by Europeans as a form of pressure and resented by them as American interference.

In this connection it should be noted that America's interest in the European integration movement has been so great and so constant that it has sometimes stimulated critics, both in Europe and in America, to take the position that the European Movement is inspired by American policy and artificially promoted in Europe by American diplomacy and American money. These critics assert that, while Western Europe lay economically helpless in the years immediately after World War II and Marshall Plan funds were being provided to assist her, European politicians paid lip service to the integrative ideal, only to discontinue such superficial loyalty when a modicum of recovery had set in and dependence on American largesse became less pressing. Such critics maintain that the European Movement is only a passing phase in postwar developments in Europe. Conveniently ignoring the evidence of continuing vitality that the Movement has exhibited between 1955 and 1958, they direct attention to the defeat of the European Defense Community Treaty in the French National Assembly in August, 1954, and identify this event as the point at which the allegedly artificial Movement collapsed.

These mistaken observations about American policy are one of the chief reasons why I have sought to be especially frank and especially thorough in my treatment of American policy toward the Movement, and why I have been quick to identify what might legitimately be regarded as any form of American pressure. My conclusion is—and it is hoped that the pages of this volume will sustain that conclusion—that American policy toward the Movement, though mistaken at times, has been entirely honorable. There is no doubt that, in the main, European union will foster America's basic national interests; but it is also perfectly clear that America favors the integrative movement in Europe because she feels it to be in the interest of Europeans and because the idea appeals to American intellectuals and political leaders as a progressive development.

Nor can any fair-minded person conclude from the record that America inspired and led the European Movement. As the subsequent pages will try to make clear, the European Movement is wholly European in inspiration. Its aims and accomplishments have enlisted some of the best minds in postwar Europe. It is European leaders who have provided institutional elaborations; it is they who have defended the Movement and its objectives on premises that are wholly European and in accord with the interests of the European states directly involved. Finally, it is European politicians and legislatures that have decided whether to implement transnational or supranational European institutions or, as in the case of EDC, to vote against going forward with such institutions.

In an appendix I have included one of the first systematic proposals for European unification developed under private auspices during the war years, 1943-1945. The appendices also contain a reprint of the Statute of the Council of Europe as amended. It is hoped that eventually means may be found to make available between two covers reprints of most, if not all, of the constitutions of the various supranational communities that have been produced or adopted in Western Europe since the advent of the Schuman Plan. Such material, not generally available in the United States, will be of considerable use to scholars.

Many organizations and individuals have rendered invaluable assistance in the preparation of this volume. Limitations of space permit acknowledgment to only a few of them. I wish to record my indebtedness to the Directorate of Information of the Council of Europe in Strasbourg, France, for the many periodical and occasional publications that it has provided and on which I have relied to a considerable extent. I have received these publications regularly since the formation of the Council of Europe in 1949. Acknowledgment is also made of the many useful publications that have been supplied by the Information Service of the High Authority of the European Community for Coal and Steel.

Publications of many private organizations interested in European union have also been immensely helpful. Not all of them can be listed here, but I do wish to identify some of them. For supplying various kinds of published material, I am especially grateful to the European Movement, the European Union of Federalists, the European Parliamentary Union, the United Europe Movement, and the Pan-European Organization. I also owe a debt of gratitude to the American Committee on United Europe, whose publications and meetings throughout almost a decade have been of great value in providing a source of information on the trend toward union in Europe and on America's opinion of that trend. I am proud to have been one of the small group responsible for the formation of this Committee in February, 1949, and to have been a member of its Executive Committee since that date.

Among the many individuals who have been especially helpful I wish to pay tribute particularly to Count Richard N. Coudenhove-Kalergi. This pioneer of European union has contributed immensely to whatever understanding of the movement toward integration in Europe I may display in the pages that follow. Direct association with Count Coudenhove during the years of the second global conflict and the access I have had to the Count's many writings on this broad subject—writings that include not only his published works but many memoranda and occasional papers—have been particularly valuable in tracing the earlier phase of the European Movement.

My son, Arnold J. Zurcher, Jr., provided much useful material in an unpublished honors thesis on the subject of European union that he prepared at Harvard College in 1953. He has also been helpful in providing a firsthand account of the organizational meetings of the Common Assembly of the European Community for Coal and Steel, which he witnessed as a reporter in the late summer of 1952.

For assistance in preparing the manuscript for publication, I wish to record my debt to Miss Gloria Tarshis, Miss Madelyn Perkins, and Mrs. Muriel P. Gaines. Mrs. Gaines has provided assistance of a value it would be difficult to estimate; it consisted not merely in preparation of the manuscript for publication but in various editorial services, including the verification of many references. Finally, I wish to express my gratitude to the Executive Director and staff of New York University Press for the careful editorial supervision they have supplied and for carrying this manuscript through to publication.

It is perhaps unnecessary to add that none of the organizations or individuals identified above have any responsibility for the opinions expressed in this book, or for any of the shortcomings, literary or substantive, that the reader will undoubtedly detect. For these I alone am responsible.

ARNOLD J. ZURCHER

New York,
November 22, 1957

Introduction

One of the paradoxes of our time is the tendency of political organization to run counter to the obvious need for a greater degree of global integration. As the world shrinks under the impact of technology, the necessary corollary trend would seem to be the modification of the conventional independent nation-state and the introduction of a greater number of institutional forms that cut across the boundaries of existing nation-states and effect political and economic integration on a multistate basis. The contrary, however, is the case. Instead of bringing established political units together to form larger units of a transnational or multinational character, the twentieth century is pursuing the opposite course. Indeed, instead of reducing the number of sovereign entities on the political map of the world, we are increasing their number, and increasing it so rapidly that we are taxing the ingenuity of the map makers, who must exploit the available spectrum to obtain necessary color differentiation. The political map of the twentieth century might be said to be undergoing a kind of amitosis.

The trend toward a more intensive political compartmentalization of the planet began with the First World War. In little more than a decade after the close of that conflict, more than a dozen new sovereign entities (including the Dominions of the British Commonwealth) came into being. But really convincing evidence that division and political fragmentation, rather than political unification, were to characterize the twentieth century (or at least the first half of it) was added to the historical record during and immediately after the Second World War. At that time the process of breaking the political globe into sovereign bits and pieces went into high gear, and our century began to complicate in earnest the chromatic responsibility of the professionals who must distinguish Ruritania from Graustark on the map of the world. Once more we witnessed a spurt of nation building, and within another postwar decade more than a score of new sovereign states were created. It is clear, moreover, that particularly in Asia and Africa this divisive political trend has not yet come to a halt. If we continue to teach political geography in our elementary and secondary schools, the eighth-grader of 1965 will undoubtedly have to familiarize himself with even more names of sovereign states and more national colors than the eighth-grader of 1955.

Statistical evidence of the rapidly mounting number of independent states in the world during the past forty years is to be found in the membership of various contemporary organizations that lay claim to universalism. Fifty-four members made up the League of Nations in November, 1923, this total including most of the new states that came into existence following the Treaty of Versailles and the other peace settlements of the period. Thirty-five years later, in 1958, the United Nations claimed a membership of eighty-two states, thirty of which had joined after 1945. In the same year the roster of the Universal Postal Union totaled ninety-six members.

A corollary of this trend toward the fragmentation of the political globe has been the decline and destruction of traditional colonial systems that in previous centuries had provided some degree of integration. The process of state creation has been so rapid, and the demand for expression of national sovereignty so vehement, that they have defeated all efforts to remodel these traditional systems of political and economic integration and, perhaps, make them more acceptable to contemporary ideological and national demands on the part of colonial peoples. Almost overnight these systems have disappeared or else have been so seriously undermined that their destruction in most instances appears inevitable. Thus the system erected by the Dutch in the East Indies vanished within a space of two or three years. So, too, did much of the French imperial system in many parts of the world; and the remainder of the French system is seriously threatened. Much of Britain's historic "dependent empire" has also disappeared, and there is grave doubt whether what the British and "associated peoples" have come to call the "Commonwealth of Nations" can survive as an entity that contributes significantly to the unification of policy on any subject.

It is this trend toward political fragmentation, and the defiance of the integrative requirements of our contemporary world implicit in this trend, that underscores the significance of the theme of this volume: the effort on the part of Europeans to establish institutions that would provide a greater degree of political and economic unity for their continent. Except for the creation of the United Nations, the efforts European leaders have been making to provide viable supranational or transnational institutions constitute virtually the sole example of a serious attempt to meet the integrative needs of our century. It is certainly the only contemporary example of a deliberate, uncoerced, popular effort to modify the traditional nation-state pattern, establish political jurisdictions broad enough to satisfy the political and economic needs of our time, and thus successfully counter the curiously unhistorical centrifugal organizational trend to which we called attention earlier.

In this book we shall have occasion to investigate many other unusual aspects of the movement toward European unity besides its historical uniqueness. In the course of our investigation we shall have occasion to applaud the political wisdom and courage of the leaders of the great nations of Europe as they seek to solve the complicated problem of providing appropriate Continental institutions. Their record in this respect is one that renews faith in the democratic process. We may also come to comprehend, at least in part, the reasons for the paradox of the parochial institutional trend that runs contrary to the integrative needs of our century. And if we come to understand those reasons, we may also begin to appreciate the true psychological, legal, and moral dimensions of the problem with which we shall have to cope if we are to reverse the trend toward national provincialism and, in the relatively brief time history still vouchsafes us, bring the art of the political scientist and the economist abreast of a world that has succeeded in transmuting the elements and is about to move toward the conquest of outer space.

The Struggle to Unite Europe: 1940-1958

1 The Prophet and His Idea

WHEN RICHARD COUDENHOVE-KALERGI, a count of the old Holy Roman Empire, landed at La Guardia Airport in New York early in August, 1940, a refugee from Hitler's Europe, he brought to an end the first phase of a remarkable career in personally promoting one of the major political ideals of the twentieth century. This is the ideal of a politically united Europe. For almost a generation Count Coudenhove had carried on, almost singlehandedly, the struggle to enlist the interest and enthusiasm of European statesmen and the general public in his plan to establish what he called the "United States of Europe," that is, to bring into being a Continent sufficiently integrated politically to permit of the establishment of a central organ of government having jurisdiction over all or most European states at least for certain purposes. The basic objectives of this plan were twofold: to insure a modicum of peace and order and to produce among the nations of Europe an expanded opportunity for achieving a more dynamic economy than that afforded by existing systems of nationalistic commercial policy. In the course of his efforts to realize this ideal before the outbreak of the Second World War, Count Coudenhove had been so closely identified with it that he had become a sort of personal symbol of the entire movement to unify Europe. As Sir Winston Churchill has said in his introduction to Count Coudenhove's latest book, ". . . the resuscitation of the Pan-European idea is largely identified with Count Coudenhove-Kalergi." [1]

In the summer of 1940, as Hitler began to overrun virtually all

[1] *An Idea Conquers the World* (London: Hutchinson, 1953), p. ix.

of Continental Europe and German panzers were reaching the North Sea, a period had to be put to the Count's integrative efforts in Europe itself. A new phase of the campaign for his ideal was about to commence in exile in America and continue for almost a decade when, with the war at an end and a large part of newly liberated Europe groping for practical ideas for the restoration of order, other voices were to be added to that of Count Coudenhove in acclaiming the ideal of a federally unified Continent. In a surprisingly short time—not more than five years after VE Day—the concept of the United States of Europe was to become the most discussed and certainly the most popular of all ideals for the reconstruction of the European Continent, and despite many vicissitudes, that ideal was to achieve major victories in modifying both the political and economic structure of Western Europe. It was also to effect a remarkable change in the outlook of Europe's intellectuals and political leaders and even of the masses as to the future organization of the Continent.

Count Coudenhove had begun his active campaign on behalf of the ideal of a unified Europe almost immediately after the First World War when, disappointed by the outcome of that struggle and fearful of the dangers to peace implicit in the Versailles and other settlements, he had concluded that the only true solution was some such radical departure from precedent as the modification of national sovereignty and the gradual identification of the separate states of free Europe in a common political mechanism. His thinking on the subject first took ordered form in 1923, when he published his book, *Pan Europa,* in Vienna. Three years later he organized his first Pan-European Congress in Vienna and took the initial step to mobilize public opinion. From then on, Count Coudenhove devoted practically his entire time to his ideal. At least until the Second World War, he was the prophet preaching the new day, the day of peace and progress, which he was certain would dawn for Europe if that continent's peoples accepted the formula of political unity. He was also a sort of human catalyst who generated enthusiasm among the many for his plan and who inspired intellectual and political leaders to make serious efforts in its behalf.

In promoting his cause, Count Coudenhove and the associates he gathered around him expanded their private organization in the late 1920's to embrace much of the Continent. Branches of the Pan-European Union were established at various European metropolitan centers, especially in Germany, France, and the United Kingdom, and the patronage and support of many of Europe's leading statesmen and men of letters was sought and successfully enlisted. But the significance of these branches of the Pan-European Union rarely exceeded that of study and discussion groups. Count Coudenhove himself sought chiefly to appeal to diplomatists, intellectuals, and heads of government.[2] Rarely was there any serious concerted effort to influence the broad masses of the public. Apparently the strategy of the time, largely dictated by necessity, was to appeal to political leaders in the hope that they might use their influence and power to establish appropriate public organs of European cooperation and mold favorable opinion. It was a strategy that, by reason of its own inherent limitations, could not go far to popularize the movement for integration. Hence, during the interbellum period, although European union became an ideal to be reckoned with among intellectual circles and in the salons where social and political leaders foregathered, it made little headway in capturing the imagination of the common man. The union of Europe continued to be a concept that appealed to scholars, philosophers, and occasional politicians, as indeed it had for centuries, but the masses of the people and the organs of popular opinion remained largely uninfluenced and uninformed.

Nevertheless, Count Coudenhove's promotional efforts and those of his devoted friends and followers were not wholly without practical effect. Either as a direct or indirect result of the efforts of the Pan-European Union, certain leading political figures became identified with the organization's aims to unite Europe. A few of these political leaders went beyond mere endorsement of the ideal and sought to examine, at least in a superficial way, some of the institutional intricacies and political problems that might arise if a leader of courage and vision should seek to translate the ideal of unity into practical reality.

[2] The description of Coudenhove's efforts to interest Europe's leaders in his unity program provides an absorbing narrative in certain chapters of his latest book, *An Idea Conquers the World,* previously cited. See especially Chapters XIV and XV.

One of these leaders was the British statesman, Sir Winston Churchill. The world is rather well aware of the contribution made by that towering figure to the integration of Europe after 1948, and this volume will comment at length on his role after that date. But few realize how early Churchill's attention was seriously attracted to the idea. Sir Winston's early views on European unity were expressed in various magazine articles of which probably the best known to Americans was an essay on European federation appearing in the popular American periodical, *The Saturday Evening Post.* After praising Count Coudenhove for having revived the ideal of European unity, the British leader suggested in his essay that some form of integration of the Continent was distinctly desirable. On the other hand, the United Kingdom, he felt, must remain in the center of its own Commonwealth and imperial bloc. The British people, he said, would not stand in the way of the development of Continental unity. Unified European organs ought to be developed, he declared, without direct British participation but with British encouragement. Within limits, Sir Winston felt that this idea of Continental unity would be wholly beneficial in increasing the wealth of the peoples of Europe and diminishing their armies.[3]

In later years, Sir Winston occasionally expressed similar views. Proposals to unify Europe should enjoy Britain's sympathetic support and encouragement, but should not count on Britain's direct participation. On the other hand, as we shall see, he and others of his countrymen also expressed views that were susceptible of a different interpretation. As a result, after World War II, when integration assumed the status of a political movement of major proportions, Britain became something of a mystery to her European friends, and the essential dichotomy of her position and the vagueness of the statements made by her political leaders at the time contributed markedly to the discouragement of the Continental supporters of greater unity and hence to the loss of momentum which European integration suffered following the first great surge forward between 1949 and 1952.

[3] "The United States of Europe," *The Saturday Evening Post,* Feb. 15, 1930. Churchill's formula concerning Britain's position toward European union at this time is worth quoting: "But we have our own dreams and our own task. We are linked, but not comprised. We are with Europe, but not of it. We are interested and associated but not absorbed."

Still another fairly tangible result of Count Coudenhove's promotional and educational efforts on behalf of Pan-Europe in the period prior to the Second World War was the response his idea received from certain French leaders. Among these were Edouard Herriot, Louis Loucheur, Léon Blum, Joseph Barthelémy, and especially Aristide Briand, perennial French foreign minister during the twenties and the architect of the ill-fated policy of *rapprochement* and reconciliation with Germany undertaken at Locarno in 1925. Stimulated by the idea of using the theme of European unity to promote his long-range plan of European peace and stability, Briand sought to bring about some form of integration of the Continent under the auspices of the League of Nations. His famous address on behalf of his plan was delivered before the Assembly of the League at Geneva on September 5, 1929. Despite the obvious difficulties of any such plan of integration, concerning which the French leader said he had "no illusions," he declared he was convinced "that among the peoples like those of Europe which possess a certain geographical unity, there must also in the long run be some sort of political federation." Subsequently Briand developed a fairly extensive "Memorandum on European Union," which, though decidedly less optimistic in tone than his earlier address, did at least plot the outline of a kind of European "league of nations" within the bosom of the existing more universal League and rather explicitly recommended various ways for promoting European economic cooperation.[4]

Briand's initiative at Geneva on behalf of the European cause represents in a sense Count Coudenhove's greatest achievement between the two world conflagrations. For the first time in modern European history, a great statesman, at the time perhaps the most respected in Europe, had become sufficiently enthusiastic about the ideal that Coudenhove had been promoting to take it up seriously and try to make it the policy of a major European power.[5] But Briand's plan came at a fateful juncture in European affairs. The

[4] For Briand's activities on behalf of the European cause in the late 1920's, see Edouard Herriot, *The United States of Europe*, trans. R. J. Dingle (New York: Viking, 1930), pp. 49 ff. See also Coudenhove, *An Idea Conquers the World*, previously cited, pp. 152 ff.

[5] Coudenhove describes this development in his *Crusade for Pan-Europe* (New York: G. P. Putnam's Sons, 1943), pp. 116 ff.

Hitlerian forces were on the verge of making their most spectacular gain in Germany; and the economy of the Continent and of the world at large was about to undergo the severest and longest depression in history. Almost simultaneously came the death of Stresemann, Briand's co-worker across the Rhine. Stresemann had been the German political leader from whom Briand and other Europeans expected the leadership that might bring Germany to accept a policy of European reconciliation. Indeed at Geneva, following Briand's address on European unification, Stresemann had clearly endorsed the broad idea, declaring it was not utopian but a practical necessity, especially in the economic field. With Stresemann's death and Hitler's looming shadow, the die was cast in Germany for a nationalistic policy of revenge and aggrandizement.

As was expected, moreover, the Briand plan received a cool reception from the British Labour government of the time. Prime Minister MacDonald and his foreign secretary, Arthur Henderson, both suggested that the plan advocated by Briand was premature. Spokesmen for the Conservative Opposition in Parliament, especially Churchill and L. S. Amery, reiterated the view that the policy of commonwealth and imperial unity, upon which Britain's economic welfare and defense were said mainly to repose, precluded any close British links with a federal system on the Continent. Indeed it was at this point that Churchill wrote the essay in *The Saturday Evening Post* described earlier,[6] in order to state as clearly as possible the prevailing British Conservative views on the "European question."

This general attitude of hostility or indifference exhibited by non-French sources, coupled with the opposition in the French Parliament and even among Briand's partisan colleagues, made it necessary to delete most of the substantive portions of the Briand "Memorandum." What finally emerged from Briand's efforts was an organization called the "Study Group on European Union." It was scarcely a shadow of what had originally been intended. Safely ensconced within the administrative structure of the League at Geneva and subjected to the ministrations of a secretariat and a secretary-general (Sir Eric Drummond) that were openly hostile to any such idea as European union, it was made abundantly clear

[6] See page 6.

that this agency might be allowed to become proficient in the collation of innocuous statistics but in nothing else.

The Briand episode brought to a close that period of a few years in the late twenties when Coudenhove-Kalergi's conception of European union had inspired cautious support and occasional appraisal by the practical politician. By 1930, reaction had begun to rear its head and to threaten any such ideal as European union. In the decade that followed, this reaction was to lead to dictatorship, an intensified and brutal form of nationalism in both economic and political spheres, and finally to the most sanguinary of military conflicts. In such a climate, union could scarcely thrive. Indeed, by the end of the 1930's even the prophet of the unity movement found he could no longer abide in the continent to which he sought to apply his prescription. By 1940, when Hitler invaded France and had virtually completed the conquest of all of Europe between the Soviet Union and the Channel, Coudenhove left Europe for the New World. There as an exile, but as an exile with a great cause and a considerable reputation, he was to undertake a new phase of his persistent effort to win converts to his ideal. There he was to prepare for the day when Europe might again be at peace and conditions become more propitious for making a proselyte of that continent for his cause. At the end of his period of exile, Count Coudenhove was to discover that a large portion of Europe had indeed become more receptive to the cause of union and that this movement would enjoy a new and far more fruitful development than at any time in its history.

2 The European Movement in America

In the land of his refuge, the prophet of European union received a cordial welcome, but the future of his cause seemed dark indeed. An ocean now separated him from the continent for the unity of which he had labored and still wished to labor. Moreover, in Europe only Britain remained outside Hitler's orbit. If the cause of a united Europe, which would also be free, was to have any future at all and gain the ascendancy over the European concentration camp that Hitler's victories had brought about, apparently only Britain remained available to lead the way. Belief that Britain, about to be strafed by Goering's *Luftwaffe,* would eventually muster the force to reconquer Europe required a faith vouchsafed to few in the summer of 1940. American sympathies, to be sure, were clearly on the side of Britain and freedom. But America, when Coudenhove arrived on her shores, was still officially neutral; and to many Americans, perhaps the majority, the military victory that Hitler had secured on the Continent seemed to have answered once and for all the questions hitherto raised by proponents of European union. Europe was indeed united and Hitler's panzers had been the architects. As Coudenhove himself pointed out, it was no wonder in the summer of 1940 "that many Americans found it hard to make a distinction between the theoretical notion of a United Europe and the practical reality of a Europe forcibly held together by Hitler's armies. United Europe without Hitler seemed entirely outside the realm of practical politics." [1]

Nevertheless, despite the forbidding outlook for "the theoretical

[1] *An Idea Conquers the World,* previously cited, p. 233.

notion of a United Europe," America offered the exiled prophet of union a real opportunity for constructive work on behalf of that "notion," and Count Coudenhove seized upon that opportunity and made the most of it. Indeed, in retrospect, it can be seen that the period of Count Coudenhove's American exile probably did at least as much to advance the cause of the union of free Europe as did all of his previous efforts in Europe itself.

The steps that he took to promote his ideal in America assumed several forms. Perhaps of greatest ultimate significance was the effort he initiated to subject the concept of European integration to the objective analyses of the academic disciplines of teaching and research. Within months after Count Coudenhove had landed in America for his enforced wartime stay, the authorities of New York University hospitably opened to him the doors of that famous institution. The university's action was in accord with its own tradition of giving academic refuge to men with great ideas. It was in accord also with the whole broad tradition of concern for new ideas that has characterized the universities since they first came into existence in the Middle Ages.

At New York University, various leading academicians gave generously of their time and effort to assist Count Coudenhove with his teaching and research objectives. Among them were the chancellor of the university, Dr. Harry Woodburn Chase; New York University's well-known vice chancellor and secretary, Dr. Harold O. Voorhis; and the dean of the university's graduate school, the historian Dr. Joseph H. Park. In collaboration with the present writer, Count Coudenhove established at New York University what was undoubtedly the first graduate seminar devoted exclusively to the problems of European federation. This step was taken early in 1942 even before the tide of the Second World War had shifted in favor of the United Nations, and the first lectures and discussions in the seminar took place in the spring term of that year. Enrolled in the initial group were some half dozen mature graduate students, most of them Europeans, who began an intensive effort to investigate some of the economic and legal problems that attempts to unify the Continent would necessarily pose.

Thus, beginning in 1942, and for a number of years thereafter, New York University provided Count Coudenhove and the writer the opportunity to develop the principal center in the world for the sustained and disciplined study of the whole concept of European integration. The special university seminar produced various studies. A few of them were subsequently published and enjoyed distribution among a restricted group of academic and political experts. Among the more important was a collection of essays entitled *Postwar European Federation*,[2] issued in the spring of 1943. Other bulletins and articles followed.[3]

In 1943, work was also begun on what was probably the first major contemporary attempt to draft a comprehensive constitution for an association of European states. Much of the responsibility of the drafting of this work fell upon the writer, although several individuals, including Dr. Fernando de los Ríos, former Spanish ambassador and minister of justice of the Spanish Republic, and Dr. Stephen P. Ladas, a well-known attorney, were intimately involved in its preparation. New York University also published this document, known as the *Draft Constitution of the United States of Europe*, in April, 1944.[4] Because it has been out of print for some time, the ninety-five articles of this *Draft Constitution* are reprinted as an appendix to this book.[5]

In some of his earlier comments on the nature of the proposed union of Europe, Count Coudenhove had likened his ideas to the federal structure of Switzerland. The maintenance of polylingualism in that nation and Switzerland's successful association of cultural traditions that were French, Italian, and German in origin had persuaded him that this republic was the exemplar for all Europe. But the formal constitutional plan now proposed took ground less advanced juridically than Swiss federalism. In essence, the constitutional draft outlined what Switzerland had been before the French Revolution or what the United States had been during the period of the Articles of Confederation, that is, a permanent association of

[2] *Postwar European Federation, Contributions of the Research Seminar for Postwar European Federation* (New York: New York University, Spring 1943), 138 pp.

[3] Coudenhove's account of this academic effort appears in his *Crusade for Pan-Europe*, previously cited, pp. 223 ff.

[4] With an introductory statement by Coudenhove.

[5] See p. 213. Comment on the *Draft Constitution* appeared in *The New York Times*, Apr. 10, 1944.

sovereign states, or what the political scientist calls a "confederation." The plan was not intended for practical application. Its authors sought primarily to stimulate discussion on the very difficult problems that would be posed for the supporters of integration once enthusiasts got away from easy generalities and were confronted by the hard realities of constructing a practical plan of association for Europe's sovereign states.

In September, 1943, Count Coudenhove also published his autobiography, *Crusade for Pan-Europe,*[6] a work that remains essential to an understanding of the background of the federal movement in Europe and of the growth of this ideal in the public consciousness. Several months later, Count Coudenhove and the present writer were responsible for holding the first general scholarly discussion of the topic of European federation under the aegis of a major American learned society. This was a round table held in Washington under the auspices of the American Political Science Association. Comment on this round table, and especially on the state of American opinion that it revealed, was published by the writer in a contemporary issue of the periodical *New Europe.*[7]

Thus by the time the Second World War was reaching its climax and the victory of the United Nations had become reasonably certain, Count Coudenhove had succeeded in initiating several major scholarly efforts to clarify the concept of European union. These are directly or indirectly attributable to the existence of the seminar at New York University. These efforts are rightly considered among the first serious investigations of the many complex problems, political and economic, with which students of the subject of European integration and would-be architects of a European politico-economic structure must cope. Partly as a result of these academic studies, the concept of union had achieved greater detail and had become much more clearly outlined. For the first time in the twentieth century, the slogan "United States of Europe" had become something more than a label for hortatory idealism. Because of the

[6] Cited previously. Certain other works of Coudenhove are suggested for those who wish to become acquainted with his long struggle for his conception of a united Europe. These are: *An Idea Conquers the World,* previously cited; *Die Europäische Nation* (Stuttgart: Deutsche Verlags-Anstalt, 1953); and *Aus Meinem Leben* (Zürich: Atlantis-Verlag, 1949).

[7] "Shall Europe Federate," *New Europe* (Apr.-May 1944), pp. 5-11.

work of the New York University seminar, the concept had been subjected to scientific analysis. Suggestions had been elaborated for some of the institutions that might serve an integrated Europe, and a few of the more serious obstacles to union, both political and constitutional, had been identified and assayed.

Count Coudenhove's second achievement in exile ranks as one of the most important contributions he has made to the promotion of his ideal. This was to convince Americans of all social levels and shades of political belief that the integration of Europe along confederal or federal lines should be one of America's primary war aims. In retrospect, it would appear that he succeeded in this aim beyond his expectations and the fondest hopes of his well-wishers. Indeed, on the American side of the Atlantic, Count Coudenhove became perhaps a more successful prophet on behalf of the United States of Europe than he had been in Europe itself.

In both governmental and journalistic circles, the atmosphere was propitious for such a venture as that of advancing European unity into a war aim of the United States. Because of America's constitutional traditions, the idea of ultimately federating the European Continent seemed like an implied compliment to America herself. Moreover, the scope and grandeur of the notion, and even the very obstacles in the way of achieving it, had the effect of firing American enthusiasm. The situation was well calculated to appeal to that combination of lofty idealism, the shrewd almost intuitive common sense, the not too adult spirit of adventure, and the downright naïveté that appear to be equally involved in the composition of the American outlook on international issues.

In seeking to persuade America, once she became a belligerent, to adopt European unity as one of her war aims, Count Coudenhove enlisted the cooperation of certain leading American citizens whom he had interested in his movement some years prior to his enforced wartime sojourn. These included the late Dr. Stephen Duggan, founder and first president of the International Institute of Education; the late President Nicholas Murray Butler of Columbia University, who was also president of the Carnegie Endowment for International Peace; William C. Bullitt, onetime ambassador to the Soviet Union and to France; and a host of other eminent figures in American life. All of these individuals had exhibited interest in the concept of a united Europe as early as the 1930's and some had expressed the hope that America would officially support such an aim in so far as an expression of such support might be appropriate. Some of them had served earlier on an *ad hoc* committee that Count Coudenhove had formed to popularize the idea of a united Europe with American opinion.

Count Coudenhove now sought to capitalize on this earlier interest by reviving his contacts with these leaders and bringing his cause to the attention of the press and the public at large. His methods were discreet and fully in accord with his status as an alien guest of the American government, but the limitations thus imposed did not deny success to his efforts. The New York press, for example, was wholly sympathetic, both major morning dailies, *The New York Times* and the *New York Herald Tribune,* having given generous space to reporting the Count's occasional public utterances and to the efforts of the New York University seminar on federation. On April 11, 1943, for example, Mr. Emmet Crozier, a feature writer for the *Herald Tribune,* wrote at length on the revival of the European program in America under Count Coudenhove's leadership. It was Mr. Crozier's opinion that because of the Count's activities in America and particularly of the work of the New York University seminar, the cause of European integration had moved "back into the arena of world affairs and demands a hearing at the peace table." [8]

Similar interest was exhibited by other leading newspapers, especially by the *Washington Post,* and articles on Count Coudenhove and his efforts on behalf of unifying Europe were written and published from time to time by some of America's most gifted commentators, among them Anne O'Hare McCormick, Dorothy Thompson, and William Philip Simms of the Scripps-Howard newspaper group. The radio supplemented many private forums in which the Count explained his principal ideas, and through his friend, William C. Bullitt, Count Coudenhove maintained informal liaison with governmental leaders in Washington.

It was these largely unheralded but persistent efforts of Count Coudenhove during the war years, 1940-1945, to acquaint American

[8] *New York Herald Tribune,* Sunday, Apr. 11, 1943, Section II, p. 1.

leadership and opinion with the nature and aims of his cause that helped greatly to prepare the way for official American acceptance of federation or confederation in Europe as a part of the policy of the United States. This acceptance was suggested in both houses of Congress, and especially in the Senate, as early as 1944. Encouragement of the policy of European integration came from many leading lawmakers. Count Coudenhove singles out Senators Elbert Thomas of Utah, Fulbright of Arkansas, Hatch of New Mexico, Burton of Ohio, and Wheeler of Montana as having been especially sympathetic. Although President F. D. Roosevelt was apparently unalterably opposed to the plan and hence to giving it official American endorsement, his successor, President Truman, as we shall see, subsequently became a supporter and lent the prestige of his administration to the idea. As Count Coudenhove tells the story, the idea of European union gradually gained support in Congress and the State Department because of the emphatic endorsement that it was gaining in the general area of American opinion.[9]

Thus the ground was prepared for the benevolent attitude toward European federation exhibited by the American government after hostilities ceased. As we shall see, this endorsement came shortly after the close of hostilities in 1945 when, following a brief period of hesitation due principally to President Roosevelt's opposition, both the executive and lawmaking branches of the American government gave unmistakable indications that European federation or any program of integration had the blessing of the American government. It was a policy that was to be reiterated frequently, especially when Washington was justifying major economic and military programs for the European Continent such as the Marshall Plan and the commitments to NATO. From 1946 onward, the United States stood ready to lend appropriate encouragement to any program of voluntary union among free European nations provided those nations themselves took the initiative in that direction.

Finally we come to Count Coudenhove-Kalergi's third contribution of his American sojourn. This was to continue what he had been doing in Europe for a generation, namely, to urge upon Europeans themselves the desirability of greater economic and

[9] See *An Idea Conquers the World,* previously cited, pp. 253 ff.

political union. This phase of the task seemed all the more urgent because Coudenhove rightly sensed the possibility of a ground swell in favor of his ideal once hostilities had ceased; and he wished to contribute what he could to the leadership of such a ground swell if and when the time came.

Admittedly, for one in exile operating 3,000 miles from Europe the task of persuading Europeans was a difficult one. Nevertheless, the Count maintained at least a semblance of his Pan-European organization in America and encouraged discussion and promotion of ideas for unity among Europeans themselves. The latter objectives were accomplished through various informal group meetings of refugee European scholars and political leaders.

The culminating event in this direction was the Fifth Pan-European Congress, held on the campus of New York University, the host institution, during the spring of 1943.[10] The Spanish Republican jurist, diplomat and scholar, Professor Fernando de los Ríos, then of the faculty of the New School for Social Research in New York, who had formally headed the group to formulate the confederal draft constitution for Europe, led the congress' juridical committee. Two months later, this committee submitted a declaration of basic aims for European unity. These emphasized a common European defense system which could exercise control over armament production, the drafting of a European bill of rights, an economic union of European states, including Europe's colonies, to promote an expanding economy, and eventually the elaboration of a formal European constitution. The latter project was developed almost simultaneously.[11]

Since 1943 there have been many conferences, public and private, devoted to advancing the cause of European union. Most of them have been better qualified and morally more competent to issue recommendations than this congress of exiles in New York. But in 1943 there was no other forum; hence the value of such a conference in America was many times greater than would otherwise have been the case. For in that unofficial gathering of exiled European

[10] Earlier congresses of that organization had been held as follows: 1926, Vienna; 1930, Berlin; 1932, Basel; 1935, Vienna.

[11] See p. 12; for actions and resolutions of the Fifth Pan-European Congress, see Coudenhove, *Crusade for Pan-Europe,* previously cited, pp. 224 ff.

scholars and political leaders and their American colleagues, as history was to prove, was the authentic voice of Europe, a voice that Europe, once freed, was to identify as its own.

Count Coudenhove's activities in America continued for about a year after the conclusion of hostilities in Europe. His primary concern in these post-surrender months was to gauge European opinion on the question of union. He was already thinking of a plan to poll virtually all members of national parliaments in Western Europe on this subject, a plan he subsequently carried into effect and which ultimately provided an affirmative vote of more than 95 per cent from the more than 40 per cent of the 4,200 polled parliamentarians who returned the ballot.[12]

What Count Coudenhove sought to learn from parliamentarians he sought also to learn from the rank and file of the European peoples. He was especially anxious to discover what sort of reconstruction ideas were prevalent among the Resistance movements in France, Italy, and the Low Countries. Some reports filtering into America indicated that the leaders of such movements strongly endorsed the union of the Continent; other reports suggested that either a majority or a strong minority in those movements was pro-Communist and supported the Communist-Soviet Russian aim of maintaining nationalism in Europe and keeping Western Europe divided. It was mainly to ascertain the true condition of opinion in Europe that Count Coudenhove decided to return from his exile in June, 1946. Although he subsequently came back to America on several occasions, his stay was never prolonged. The prospects that seemed to open for the movement in Europe itself and the vigorous sponsorship that now came to it from Churchill and other leaders claimed Count Coudenhove's attention. Once more he was to enter upon an active crusade for his cause in Europe. This time, however, as subsequent chapters will show, it was no longer to be a one-man crusade, but a movement that had the patronage of Western Europe's leading statesmen and that was to have practical political goals.

[12] For a preliminary tabulation of this poll, see Coudenhove, *Europe Seeks Unity* (New York: New York University Press, 1948), p. 59. For the final tabulation, see his *Die Europäische Nation*, previously cited, p. 120.

3 A Prime Minister Assumes Leadership

Even before hostilities had come to an end in 1945, it had already become reasonably clear that the idea of unifying Europe had made greater progress with European opinion than men had previously dared to hope. Indeed, as the Second World War was entering its final phases, observers who had previously been cut off from the Continent by the Nazi occupation were surprised to discover the relative scope and intensity of the appeal that the ideal of unity could hold for the ordinary citizen. Even as early as 1944, information seeping out of the tightly controlled Continent to Count Coudenhove and other exiles in America and to various exile governments in London indicated that the concept of the United States of Europe had become a major aim of large elements of the various Resistance movements and in the platforms of some of the free political parties in France, Italy, and the Low Countries that were maintaining a shadow organization despite the iron heel of the conqueror.[1] For these groups the notion of some form of union seemed to offer a prescription for averting future wars and their attendant miseries.

Even official opinion in Western European states appeared to

[1] In July, 1944, for example, delegates of various national resistance movements had affirmed in a "Declaration of the European Resistance Movement" that "Federal Union alone could ensure the preservation of liberty and civilisation on the Continent of Europe, bring about economic recovery and enable the German people to play a peaceful role in European affairs." Quoted in *Europe Today and Tomorrow*, International Bulletin of the European Movement (Dec. 1953), p. 21.

look with favor upon some form of confederal or federal linkage. This became apparent as the result of the poll described in the previous chapter that Count Coudenhove and his associates conducted among European parliamentarians in 1946. About two-fifths of the 4,200 parliamentarians polled took the trouble to reply, and of these only 3 per cent opposed federation in principle. In some states, notably France, Italy, Belgium, and Holland, more than half of all members of the popular chamber responded in the affirmative.[2] This was a truly astonishing affirmative verdict in view of the fact that there had been no preliminary discussion of the question.

But perhaps the clinching evidence that by 1946 European integration had ceased to be merely a philosophers' dream and was about to enter the realm of practical politics came from that master politician and leader of the United Nations alliance, Sir Winston Churchill. In the midst of the war, on March 21, 1943, he had reiterated his earlier allegiance to the idea of Pan-Europe by declaring in a radio address that, to prevent future aggression and war, the Continent should move forward to the creation of a "Council of Europe" and other appropriate organs, including even common armed forces. Then on September 19, 1946, at a convocation at the University of Zürich, Sir Winston, then but recently ousted from the prime ministership of the United Kingdom by the Labour party, became quite articulate about European unity. Concerned apparently with the key problem of reconciling France and Germany, he indicated that some form of confederation might be used to bring these two nations together and thus avoid in the future the nationalistic schism between these two states that had brought Europe and the world into conflagration twice in the twentieth century.

His address, however, was in no sense limited to a particular objective but covered broadly the whole movement for unity up to that time. He gave voice to the hope of millions, but just redeemed from Hitler's tyranny, that in some form of union there might be a promise of a better day, one giving greater security against economic want, despotism and the scourge of war. Appropriate paragraphs of the address invite quotation:

[2] See Coudenhove, *Die Europäische Nation*, previously cited, p. 120.

What is the plight to which Europe has been reduced? Some of the smaller states have indeed made a good recovery, but over wide areas a vast quivering mass of tormented, hungry, care-worn and bewildered human beings gape at the ruins of their cities and homes and scan the dark horizons for the approach of some new peril, tyranny or terror. . . .

There is a remedy which, if it were generally and spontaneously adopted, would, as if by a miracle, transform the whole scene, and would in a few years make all Europe, or the greater part of it, as free and happy as Switzerland is today. . . .

What is the sovereign remedy? It is to recreate the European family, or as much of it as we can, and to provide it with a structure under which it can dwell in peace, safety and freedom. We must build a kind of United States of Europe. . . .

In his address, Churchill paid a handsome tribute to Count Coudenhove and Briand for their pioneer efforts on behalf of European integration. "Much work," said Churchill, "has been done upon this task by the exertions of the Pan-European Union which owes so much to Count Coudenhove-Kalergi, and which demanded the services of the famous French patriot and statesman Aristide Briand." [3]

Sir Winston's Zürich speech was a turning point in the postwar development of the ideal of European unity; for that occasion marks the initiation of a vast private effort to promote various schemes of integration, most of which had the blessing of Churchill and ultimately of most of the political leaders of the West. Four months after his forensic effort at Zürich, Sir Winston organized the United Europe Movement in the United Kingdom and became its chairman. Another long-time British supporter of European integration, Lord Layton, became the immediate director. It was strongly Conservative in its leanings and failed to attract much Labour support, but it had some of the leading foreign experts in the United Kingdom among its estimated 2,500 members.

Across the Channel, similar groups, of varying political complexions but all devoted to fostering the concept of a more united Continent, came into being almost simultaneously. Counterpart of

[3] *The New York Times,* Sept. 20, 1946.

Churchill's British organization was the French Council for United Europe (*Conseil Français pour l'Europe Unie*), a body that embraced practically all the French parliamentary and governmental supporters of the unification movement and that subsequently contributed leadership and influence favorable to integration quite out of proportion to its limited numbers. Still another supporting organization, chiefly French but with some Belgian membership, was the *Nouvelles Equipes Internationales,* whose leader, M. Robert Bichet, regarded it as an instrument for rallying the Catholic parties of Europe, especially those in the Romance states, to the cause of Continental unity. Socialist influence sought expression in the *Mouvement Socialiste pour les États Unis d'Europe,* whose guiding spirits at the outset were M. André Philip of France and M. Rasquin of Luxembourg. Originally intended to bring most of the national Socialist and Labour parties together to support European integration according to Socialist ideals, it made little headway in persuading British Labour and was soon restricted to certain Socialist groups in France, Luxembourg, and Belgium. Also essentially of Socialist political persuasion was an existing federalist organization known as the European Union of Federalists, originally led by Professor H. Brugmans of the Netherlands and M. Henri Frenay of France. This group approached the dimensions of a mass organization with truly multinational support. In France, Italy, the Netherlands, and Belgium, it claimed a membership of over 150,000. Finally mention should be made of the fact that former premier Paul van Zeeland of Belgium became chairman of a special group interested in the economic questions posed by eventual unity. This was known as the Economic League for European Cooperation.

After launching organized support for united Europe in the United Kingdom, Sir Winston's next step was to bring these pro-integration movements together and fuse them into a working multinational, private organization to work for the establishment of a more unified Europe. This aim was achieved in December, 1947, when an international committee representing virtually all these special movements[4] was set up under the directorship of Mr. Duncan Sandys, Sir Winston's son-in-law. This committee in

[4] Only the European Parliamentary Union, headed by Count Coudenhove, to be discussed later, failed to join.

turn proceeded to organize the first truly Continental demonstration in favor of unity, namely, the Congress of Europe, held at The Hague from May 7th to 10th, 1948.

How seriously the ideal of the United States of Europe, or some form of integration approximating such a concept, had seized upon the popular imagination and the imagination of the European leadership is to be discerned in the composition and the actions of this now historic assembly. More than 750 delegates attended from every corner of free Europe. Many of them were representatives of European parliaments and governments. Practically every major name in the postwar leadership of Western Europe except, of course, the names of the contemporary German leaders, was listed in the roster of those attending. Besides Churchill, the Congress roster contained the names of Alcide de Gasperi of Italy; Paul Reynaud, Jean Monnet, Georges Bidault, Paul Ramadier, Robert Schuman and Léon Blum of France; Salvador de Madariaga of Spain; and Paul-Henri Spaak and Paul van Zeeland of Belgium. Lord Layton and Duncan Sandys were among the leaders of the British delegation along with Churchill. Many others, but slightly less prominent, lent the prestige of their names and their attendance to the meetings. Nor, except for the Communists, were any significant political elements missing from the Congress. Socialists and Labour partisans were present as well as Clericals and Conservatives. It must, however, be admitted that British Labour did not express the degree of enthusiasm exhibited by its copartisans in France and the Low Countries.

The various resolutions regarding European unity that emanated from the several commissions of the Hague Congress had, for the most part, been foreshadowed in Churchill's speeches and in the proposals of other leaders. There was agreement that the time had come for European states to relinquish some of their sovereign rights and to promote the political and economic unity of Europe. The major resolution of the Congress declared that one of the immediate tasks of true European statesmanship was to build a deliberative assembly composed of representatives of the European parliaments that might become a political forum for all of free Europe and that could advise upon measures to bring about progressively the economic and political integration of Europe. Other resolutions advocated the drafting of a European charter of human rights, the establishment of a European court, and the integration of Germany into free Europe. Many of these ideas had been advocated before; but their reiteration, under such auspices as the Congress provided, suggested they enjoyed the broadest support and lent them a degree of urgency such as they had not previously possessed. Before the Congress disbanded, the members of the committee that had called it into being established a permanent private organization to carry on the work of unification that became known as the "European Movement."[5]

European enthusiasm at this stage was matched on the American side of the Atlantic. There the seed that Count Coudenhove had sown during the war years not only sprouted but the resulting growth burgeoned. Particularly did this become apparent after President Roosevelt died and the postwar gulf widened between America's objective and those of her erstwhile ally, the Soviet Union. As early as March, 1947, identical resolutions were introduced by Messrs. Fulbright and Thomas in the Senate and Hale Boggs in the House, the substance of which was that America favored the creation of a United States of Europe within the framework of the United Nations Charter. That resolution was subsequently adopted.[6] Other leaders of opinion, particularly former Senator Burton K. Wheeler, John Foster Dulles, and Senator Alexander Wiley, took strong stands in favor of the concept of unity. Even earlier, toward the end of 1945, President Truman indicated his support for the idea in a periodical article[7] thus, for the first time, shifting the support of the presidency to the European integration movement. Subsequently, after the Marshall Plan came into existence in 1947, virtually every spokesman of official America reiterated the hope, almost as often as an opportunity presented itself, that some form of integration might come into existence in Europe.

[5] In this volume the phrase "European Movement" has also been used to identify all phases of the broad effort to unify Europe.

[6] See *Congressional Record,* April 22, 1947, p. A1905 for introduction.

[7] George Creel, "The United States of Europe," *Collier's,* Dec. 22, 1945, pp. 14 ff. The subtitle of the article reads as follows: "It is an open secret that President Truman looks with favor on formation of a European federation to lift the Continent out of chaos. Here is what's behind his thinking in the matter." An edited version of this article is reprinted in the *Reader's Digest,* Jan. 1946, pp. 47-51.

Probably one of the most extraordinary manifestations of favorable American opinion was exhibited by the formation of the American Committee on United Europe. Incorporated in 1949 under the chairmanship of the former head of the Office of Strategic Services, General William J. Donovan, this committee brought together some of the most important figures in America's intellectual, political, and industrial life. The committee not only conducted a campaign of education among the American public but rendered substantial financial assistance to the private European Movement and auxiliary agencies. It also supported significant research projects. Not since the days of Louis Kossuth had American opinion grown so enthusiastic about an idea that was essentially European and that related to Europe's political structure; and it is unlikely that Americans have ever been so generous, either on a private or public plane, in providing funds for the achievement of a political ideal in another continent.

Once Churchill's interest in European unity and that of other political leaders had been effectively aroused, Count Coudenhove ceased to be the dominant personality in the unity movement that he had been previously. As so often happens, when an idea marches with history and approaches the time when men wish to apply its meaning to their institutional life, the ministrations of the prophet give way to the ministrations of the man of affairs. It was a process with which Count Coudenhove was already familiar, for in the twenties, after enlisting the interest of Briand and other French leaders in his Pan-European movement, he sat on the sidelines while the political leaders took over the promotion of the ideas of that movement at Paris and Geneva. Now at Zürich in 1946, history repeated itself. Like Briand before him, Churchill, at Zürich, acknowledged Count Coudenhove's pioneer work in promoting the ideal of unity in European and world opinion. But once Churchill had spoken he became, by reason of his great prestige as a European and world leader, the acknowledged head of the movement to push Europe in the direction of integration.

For a time, Count Coudenhove directed his talents and energies toward the organization and work of the European Parliamentary Union, which held a series of conferences in Switzerland and northern Italy between 1946 and 1949. At one of these, held at

Interlaken, Switzerland, in September, 1948, a fairly comprehensive plan of federal union, largely the work of the British federalist R. W. G. MacKay, was brought out and received the support of more than 500 members of European parliaments.[8] For a brief interval, moreover, relations between Count Coudenhove's Parliamentary Union and the European Movement were somewhat strained. The situation reflected certain personal differences. Chiefly, however, it reflected the differences between the views of the majority of British leaders and those who followed British leadership as respects the form of European union and the views of certain of the Continentals. The former considered the maximum plan something less than the juridical concept of a confederation. The Continentals, among whom was Count Coudenhove, looked toward the establishment almost immediately of a true federal union with federal organs of government that would seriously limit the national sovereignty of the various European states. Their views had been expressed at the Interlaken conference and the ideal organization for many of them had been the plan of union adopted at Interlaken.

This doctrinal difference was never adjusted. Indeed it continues to this day and, as we shall see, provides the major stumbling block toward the consummation of any suprasovereign institution even though many Continentals favor such an idea. But the personal differences between Count Coudenhove and other leaders of European unity were eventually resolved. In 1952 he joined the European Movement and appropriately enough, in view of his past services to the cause, he was made one of the six presidents of honor of that private organization, joining the galaxy of the five great political leaders of the Movement, Churchill, Blum, Spaak, Adenauer, and de Gasperi.

In time the world will doubtless acknowledge the pioneer work of this prophet of Europe's future even as his colleagues in the European Movement have honored him. In nominating him on several occasions for the Nobel Peace Prize, this writer reiterated his belief that there are few among the statesmen and moral leaders of our time striving to bring about a more just and orderly world whose stature exceeds that of Count Richard N. Coudenhove-

[8] *An Idea Conquers the World,* previously cited, p. 291.

Kalergi. His vision and the effort he has made to implement it have profoundly affected the thinking of this generation and have made a most significant contribution to the realization of humanity's age-old aspiration for a peaceful world.

Some measure of Count Coudenhove's relative importance in developing the cause of European union was suggested on May 18, 1950, when the municipality of Aachen, once the capital of Charlemagne's empire, made Count Coudenhove the first recipient of its Charlemagne Prize. The prize is given annually to that European who, in the judgment of a jury of Aachen's leading citizens, has done the most to advance the cause of Europe's unity. The Charlemagne Prize has since been conferred upon other leaders of the European Movement, including Churchill, Spaak, and Adenauer. That it should have been conferred first upon Coudenhove-Kalergi was tacit recognition of the pioneer nature of his work on behalf of Europe. An appropriate assessment of that pioneer work was given on the occasion of the awarding of the prize in a telegram of congratulation that Chancellor Adenauer sent to Count Coudenhove. In part the chancellor's wire said: "I believe that the City of Aachen could not possibly have chosen for this important prize any personality more worthy and with greater merit among the pioneers of the European idea. Working indefatigably for many years, you have achieved great historic merit in preparing for a union of the European nations." Chancellor Adenauer's appraisal of Count Coudenhove's role in the movement toward European union is likely also to be history's formal appraisal.

4 Europe Becomes Seriously Interested in Union

To INSPIRE enthusiasm for some great ideal is usually not too difficult a feat. This is especially the case when, as in Europe after World War II, the ideal offered hope to a generation that had not yet recovered from the ravages of a catastrophic conflict. Moreover, when those discoursing on the ideal can still afford to consider it in purely general terms, there is little likelihood that the enthusiasm thus generated will wane.

The situation is otherwise, however, when the proponents of the ideal are challenged by the task of harnessing enthusiasm to a practical program of action. Sir Winston Churchill, by 1947 the acknowledged leader of the European unity movement, and the man to whom Europe now looked for leadership, apparently had no clear-cut notion as to just what this practical program of European integration should be or as to what precise institutional forms a unified Europe might assume. Lack of definition in Sir Winston's notion of the future institutional structure of a united Europe undoubtedly was due in part to his fondness for generalizations—for phraseology that evoked in the listener's (or the reader's) mind the distant skyline of a metropolis rather than the harsher outlines and the concrete dimensions of some of the principal edifices of such a metropolis.

In greater measure, however, Sir Winston's apparent unwillingness to be precise about the meaning of such a concept as the "United States of Europe" was due to considerations of policy. In other words, he was undoubtedly being deliberately obtuse. For Churchill shared with other Britishers, many of them equally articulate about the desirability of unifying Europe, a certain dichotomy of outlook on the subject. On the one hand, as objective writers and historians, they were inclined to espouse such a concept. It was a logical concept; it was a concept that enjoyed historical dignity, since some of the most respected minds of the past approved of it; finally, it had the approval of the future also, for it was suffused with the aura of progressivism.

At the same time, when these leaders ceased to be merely intellectual "eggheads" and looked upon themselves as responsible political leaders and the formulators of policy for their "tight little isle," they developed quite a different outlook on European union. Then they were inclined to lose some of their enthusiasm for the noble idea and become somewhat nationalistic and isolationist. Then their tendency was to make allusions to Britain's world interests and to stress her commitments to Empire and Commonwealth, declaring that such interests and commitments precluded British leaders from becoming too intimately involved in any sort of supranational or federalistic European organization. Then, too, they began to make nice semantic distinctions between "unity" and "union" or between "united Europe" and "European union." Forgetting the legal name of their own state and its technical implications for jurists nurtured on Austin, they were wont at this stage to suggest that "united Europe" meant only some sort of international fraternizing by European states, whereas "European union" meant political consolidation. These were nice distinctions that might have seemed novel even to a Noah Webster or to an editor of the *Oxford English Dictionary*, but the nub of all this semanticism was that when the "chips were down," British leaders were quite close in their position to that of some of the more enthusiastic American proponents of European integration; that is, they were in the position of advocating unity for somebody else.

The dichotomy in Sir Winston's own outlook had been mirrored, at least to some extent, in his earlier public pronouncements on the European issue. In 1943, when he had suggested the formation of the Council of Europe, he appeared to have in mind a confederation or league of states that would embrace the whole of the Continent but not the United Kingdom or Soviet Russia. These two, along with the United States, would, he said, find their own interests in harmony with the proposed integration of the Continent, but they would themselves not be a part of such a union. Again, at Zürich in 1946, he expressed similar ideas about the British role. If a "Council of Europe" were formed, Britain, the British Commonwealth, and the United States would, he suggested, be cast in the role of benevolent associates but would not themselves become a part of the proposed organization.

On the other hand, a year later, when Sir Winston assumed the leadership of the United Europe Movement in the United Kingdom, he seemed to have changed his views. Then he reminded his colleagues that Britain was geographically and historically a part of Europe and that if European unity was to become a living force, "Britain [would] have to play her full part as a *member* [italics supplied] of the European family." Moreover, in referring to Britain's overseas commitments and her commitments to Empire and Commonwealth, in this same address to the United Europe Movement, he reiterated the view that any policy Britain might adopt toward Europe must enjoy the support and approval of the Dominions. In conceding this, however, he said he saw no reason why the Dominions would not support Britain in the cause of European unity. "They feel with us," he asserted, "that Britain is geographically and historically a part of Europe. . . ."[1] Hence, although Sir Winston's position in 1947 remained somewhat vague, he did seem to imply that the United Kingdom would participate actively with France and other trans-Channel nations in setting up some sort of permanent multinational European organization.

Such an interpretation was, of course, the one that Continental leaders sought to give the British position, especially after the United Europe Movement had been created in Britain and after Churchill had become involved as the actual leader of the European Movement at the Hague Congress. Nothing suited these leaders better than the suggestion of intimate political association with Britain logically implied by the composition and proceedings of that congress, and they were quite willing to ignore the essential

[1] For Sir Winston's address on this occasion, delivered May 14, 1947, see *The New York Times*, May 15, 1947, p. 16.

ambiguity that British leadership and Sir Winston himself had created by past pronouncements on the issue. Nor was the tendency of the Continent to ignore such ambiguity in the British position entirely unrealistic. Protestations of British leaders that their imperial and world obligations precluded intimate association with the Continent hardly induced conviction in the Continental mind. For the historical record made it quite clear that, especially as respects diplomacy, defense, and trade, Britain had always been bound rather intimately to the Continental states—as intimately perhaps as such states are bound to each other. Moreover, no one had forgotten the grand gesture that Sir Winston had made to France in 1940 on the eve of her succumbing to the Hitlerian invasion. What Sir Winston had offered France was real consolidation of the two states; and though it had been offered in a time of stress and mortal danger, there had apparently been no reservation in Britain about the anticipated permanency of the suggested arrangements, had France accepted. In the light of the record, therefore, French statesmen and their Continental confreres could be pardoned for resolving British ambiguity about British association in a proposed European organization in favor of whatever they wished to believe.

For many French leaders particularly, the wish as respects Britain was father to the thought. For them, British participation was virtually a *sine qua non* of any form of viable European political or economic union—at least of any union in which they cared to have a part. In the postwar French mind, European union was primarily a means of organizing security against the East and more especially against the threat of a resurgent Germany. Without the intimate association of Britain in such a union, this security objective could not be achieved; indeed in the context of such a purpose an association without Britain might be dangerous. In this view, moreover, the French had the concurrence of the leadership of the Benelux nations. They, too, wanted Britain intimately associated with themselves in any scheme to organize the nations of Western Europe in a union superior to any sovereign state. For them, too, it had been the lesson of recent history that, in matters of defense especially, any association of Western European states against a potential aggressor would be lacking its primary instrument if it lacked Britain. A less important but still influential reason for wishing British participation in a European organization was the desire of some of the trans-Channel political parties to have the association of British parties of similar ideological outlook in any possible confederation or federal parliament. This was especially the case with some of the Continental Socialists who felt they had much in common with the British Labour party.

Hence, to repeat, it is not surprising that many of the leaders of France and the Low Countries thought they could safely assume that Britain would go along with them at least for a considerable distance in any integration program. They also thought that in 1948 the time was ripe to launch such a movement even though, at the moment, Churchill was out of power in Westminster and the Labour party was directing British policy. These leaders—men like Spaak, Bidault, Ramadier, and Reynaud—wished especially to exploit the moral unity that the Hague Congress had contributed to the movement for European integration as well as the apparent promise of fairly intimate British association in a European union that Churchill and other British leaders had given at that same congress.

Nor was there much doubt that other Continental states would welcome such an initiative. Peripheral states, particularly the Scandinavian, were likely to follow, especially if Britain led or was journeying with the leaders. Italy was another candidate for membership. Although British association might not seem so essential to the Italian mind as to the French, Italy had her own reasons for welcoming a broad European association. In that country, the leadership to the right of extreme Marxism fervently supported the conception of the political and economic integration of Europe. Such leadership looked to union to help solve many of the nation's economic problems. Union might open the borders of other states to Italy's excess population and possibly open European and colonial markets. Certainly European union would assure Italy, then partially disarmed and essentially weak militarily, of a defense against both her internal and external enemies.[2]

Germany, the other great power on the Continent, although still

[2] For comment on Italy's views, see C. L. Sulzberger, *The New York Times*, Aug. 25, 1949.

mute in international assemblies, had already made apparent her postwar support of the ideal of European union. Pan-European ideas had taken root among certain German parties, particularly those of the Center, before World War II. Her leading politician and chancellor-to-be, Konrad Adenauer, had been a confirmed supporter of European union for almost a generation. German youth, moreover, was perhaps more articulate about this ideal than about any other, and foreign statesmen looking to the educational regeneration of the German spirit saw in a program of European unity a substitute for the militarism and pan-Germanism upon which the two earlier generations of German youth had been reared. Finally, Germany saw in unity practically the only formula by which she might take the road back to acceptance by the West of her independence and equality. There was little likelihood that Germany would reject unity whatever the terms might be, and though she welcomed British participation, that participation was perhaps not as necessary to her as to her former foes on the Continent.

International events and the posture of the international scene in 1948 likewise favored some sort of initiative in the direction of transforming the European ideal into a practical political program. Of first importance in this respect was the current expansionist policy of world Communism and the growing awareness of Western Europe of the true seriousness of the Communist threat. In March, 1948, had come the Communist coup in Czechoslovakia. Lulled by the thesis that the policy of the great Masaryk's political creation was to serve as a sort of "bridge" between East and West and as the midwife of a policy of Western "coexistence" with Communism, Western leadership was largely unprepared for the events in Prague. Western Europe was indeed temporarily overwhelmed by the import of the rapid disintegration of the government of President Beneš, the suicide of the younger Masaryk, and the withdrawal of the model Slavic republic behind the Communist barrier and its absorption by the newly formed Cominform. Earlier, in Fulton, Missouri, Churchill had delivered his now famous Iron Curtain speech and advised that Western Europe was in grave danger from Stalin's legions. Criticized as an alarmist and even as a warmonger by the few who were "fellow travelers" and by the many who still misunderstood the nature of the Soviet menace, Sir Winston had confounded most of these critics. By 1948, they had indeed become aware that the dangers he had identified were all too obvious. Western Europe knew by that time it would be well advised to counter those dangers, and the logical answer seemed to be the unification of as much of free Europe as possible.

The Communist threat, thus exposed, helped moreover to create an intramural situation within the governments of various Western states more favorable to some form of European association. For now the postwar alliance of Communist and other parties, which had characterized the cabinets of several free Continental powers, especially of France and of Italy, came to an end. The Communists were denied further participation in governmental coalitions; and their nearest allies in the political spectrum, the Socialists, began in most instances to make common cause with conservative elements including the centrist clerical parties. Thus it was that the constitutional parties of Western Europe, having coalesced for an intramural struggle against internal Communism, found in the policy of European integration an appropriate extramural focus for withstanding the threat of Communism externally.

Still another factor that promoted the climate of unity in Europe in 1948 was the policy of postwar economic assistance that had just been announced by the United States. General George C. Marshall, then America's secretary of state, had announced the plan that bears his name at the Harvard Commencement in June, 1947. In the following weeks, an *ad hoc* meeting of European diplomats, economists, and other experts had been held in Paris to concert plans for advising America of Europe's economic requirements. Out of those meetings, from which the Soviet Union and its satellite governments had rather conveniently withdrawn, was to grow the formal grouping of sixteen Western European nations to be known as the Organization for European Economic Cooperation (OEEC). At the time of its establishment in April, 1948, this body was expected to serve as a sort of multinational planning agency for Western Europe and perhaps also—so it was thought at the time—as the agency to supervise the disbursement of America's intended largesse. Certainly the creation of this agency by the states of Western Europe, and their experience in working together under its aegis in taking stock of Europe's economic plight and in planning the use of the assistance coming from across the Atlantic, provided more than a symbolic prologue for more serious plans for European cooperation and the elaboration of multinational agencies of a more permanent sort.

Western European states that had been on the winning side in World War II were also inclined to take seriously the professed desire of the Germans for Continental unity to which allusion has been made. By 1948, largely because of the defection of the Soviet Union from the wartime alliance of the victor powers, Germany had become a great prize between East and West. Each side wanted her favor and had begun to bid for it. The West, animated by American policy, was seeking actively for a formula by which Germany, or the western half of it, might be brought within the diplomatic and military framework of the free world.

Churchill, speaking for his own government and the friends of European unity, had been concerned from the first with the contribution that a program of European union might make to the solution of the Franco-German problem. In his address to the United Europe Movement in May, 1947, to which reference has been made above, he asserted that "except within the framework and against the background of a United Europe, this problem [the future of Germany] is incapable of solution." [3] By 1947, few responsible Western statesmen considered such a statement extreme. Hence it was not surprising that in the resolutions adopted in the Hague Congress of the European Movement, a year later, that body should solemnly reaffirm the view that Churchill had expressed earlier and state it as the opinion of all Western Europe. "The integration of Germany in a united or federated Europe," said the Congress, "alone provides a solution to both the economic and political aspects of the German problem." [4]

Finally, among the conditions favoring a militant effort to unite Europe in 1948 was the apparently greater degree of cordiality shown for the idea by the British Labour party government. Originally the leadership of the Labour cabinet had been quite hostile

[3] *The New York Times,* May 15, 1947, p. 16.

[4] *Resolutions, Congress of Europe* (Paris: International Committee of the Movement for European Unity, 1948), p. 6.

to the idea; but the growing awareness of the Communist menace seems to have had its effect here also. At any rate, in a major parliamentary address early in 1948, Mr. Ernest Bevin, the foreign secretary, made some remarks on the subject that were distinctly heartening to the confirmed addicts of integration on the Continent. The conception of the unity of Europe and the preservation of Europe as the heart of Western civilization was accepted by most people, he declared. "No one," he said, "disputes the idea of European unity." And although he was inclined to voice the instinctive British dislike for "blueprints" and "neat-looking plans," he was nonetheless sufficiently imbued with enthusiasm for some sort of unity program, at least on this occasion, to voice the opinion that "the time is ripe for a consolidation of Western Europe." [5]

Just what degree of relevancy for the broader problems of European unity the author of these remarks intended is not quite clear. It is certain, however, that Bevin and his colleagues had been sufficiently impressed by the Soviet threat to wish to broaden a Franco-British alliance against Germany that had been set up by the Treaty of Dunkirk in 1947. This had been accomplished by the Brussels Pact signed March 17, 1948, by the three Benelux nations in addition to Britain and France. The pact provided for what amounted to a permanent military organization under the command of Field Marshal Viscount Montgomery, for a permanent consultative committee consisting of the foreign ministers of the five powers that was to meet every three months, and for eventual cooperation on other fronts, economic, social, and cultural.

If this Brussels Pact organization was not a form of "Western union" of a fairly durable character, it appeared to observers to be an eminently respectable prologue to such a union. Such, indeed, as we shall see, it was now about to become. In any event, because of the seemingly favorable diplomatic factors just reviewed and the formal instrument for furthering European cooperation furnished by the Brussels organization, the more dedicated leaders of the European Movement, especially those who had been at the Hague Congress, decided that the time was propitious for a rapid forward movement. These leaders now took certain steps the pur-

[5] *Parl. Debates,* Hansard, 446 House of Commons Debates, 5s, Jan. 22, 1948, p. 389.

pose of which was to implement the resolutions of the Hague Congress, particularly the resolution advocating the immediate creation of a European Assembly.

The first of these steps took place toward the end of July, 1948, when the Belgian prime minister, Paul-Henri Spaak, already recognized as one of the more persistent champions of integration in Europe, announced in his nation's senate that officially he favored the creation of the recommended assembly and that he had invited the European Movement to submit detailed plans, which he then promised to bring to the attention of the other governments in the Brussels Pact.[6] Several weeks later, representatives of the European Movement actually sent a preliminary memorandum on the proposed assembly to the five Brussels Pact powers. Both Spaak and other leaders of the European Movement made it quite clear that they hoped to use the Brussels organization as a sort of official nucleus for further action in integrating Europe. Almost simultaneously the French government officially endorsed this initiative. Its communiqué declared that it had "considered the Memorandum submitted by the European Movement regarding the convening of a conference to prepare for the creation of a European Assembly. The Government has decided to give this project its active support and to initiate all necessary action." Finally, on September 2, 1948, Belgium and France announced that the proposals of the European Movement for a European Assembly were being placed on the agenda of the next quarterly meeting of the Permanent Commission of the Five Brussels Powers.

The upshot of this initiative was a decision at the Paris meetings of the Brussels powers, on October 25, 1948, to set up a study commission under the presidency of the veteran French statesman and traditional supporter of European unity, Edouard Herriot.

By this time, however, the British, fearful of the trend they had originally appeared to encourage, had become rather articulate about their opposition to the whole development. Prime Minister Attlee thought that the assembly idea should not "be brought

[6] *Creation of the Council of Europe, Account of the Successive Steps Taken by the European Movement to Secure the Establishment of the Council of Europe* (published by the European Movement, place and date unspecified), p. 4.

forward at this stage," and Foreign Minister Bevin had suggested on September 15th that the creation of a European Assembly at this point was "in his opinion like 'putting on the roof before building the house.'"[7] But the movement was too far along to be completely stalled and the British government had perforce to try another tack. This was to suggest the venerable expedient of setting up a semipermanent committee of foreign ministers, similar to the Brussels Treaty structure, in lieu of the Assembly. Although this suggestion apparently did not immediately influence the study commission, which one month later developed still another memorandum on the value of a European Assembly, the situation changed by January, 1949. By that time the study commission had taken the first step to compromise the prevailing Continental position on the one hand and the British position on the other. This effort at compromise took the form of a proposal that the contemplated European organization should consist of two major bodies, a committee of ministers, as demanded by the British, and an assembly of a consultative character.

Even this proposal did not immediately satisfy the British, who reserved judgment, although the other four Brussels powers agreed. Only after further compromises, among which was the requirement that the ministerial committee meet in private in contrast to the proposed consultative assembly, which would have public sessions, did the British government agree to sanction the compromise. This occurred at the conference of the five Brussels foreign ministers in London on January 29, 1949. The British declared they agreed "in principle" to this kind of bicameral arrangement, describing that arrangement in the following formula: ". . . a Council of Europe consisting of a ministerial committee meeting in private and a consultative body meeting in public."[8] During the spring of 1949, further discussions were held in London by the diplomatic representatives of the interested powers; and on May 5, 1949, a treaty, embodying the Statute of the Council of Europe, was finally initialled at St. James Palace at Westminster. Representatives of ten states,

[7] *Creation of the Council of Europe*, previously cited, p. 6.

[8] *The European Movement and the Council of Europe* (London: Hutchinson, 1950), p. 56.

five in addition to the members of the Brussels Treaty organization, signed the treaty providing for the statute. Thus was born the Council of Europe. During the following summer plans were made to place this new machinery in operation at Strasbourg, France, and to hold the first meeting of the Council of Europe at the Alsatian city in the autumn.

5 The Council of Europe

ELATION swept the ranks of the protagonists of united Europe on the morrow of the signing of the Westminster Treaty providing for the Statute of the Council of Europe. For the first time in modern history there was in being a permanent instrument of European cooperation, one that at least symbolized the age-old dream of a United States of Europe. Responsible figures in the European Movement, both statesmen and intellectual leaders, congratulated themselves on what had been achieved. All felt they had assisted in erecting one of the great plateaus of human political progress that would support the foundation for a whole new era. Churchill, to be sure, was somewhat less exuberant than usual, but he felt that the establishment of the Council represented a decidedly progressive step. He also felt that the European Movement, which he and his colleagues had formed, should take credit for the Council's creation. "The European Movement," he said, "has already made swifter progress than anybody versed in political affairs would have thought possible. The success which has so far crowned our efforts should inspire us to press forward together with renewed vigour in this momentous enterprise." [1]

Sober second thought, however, had the effect of dampening much of the enthusiasm. The decline of enthusiasm was especially noticeable in France and other trans-Channel nations among confirmed supporters of a federal or supranational solution for Europe. For them few illusions existed as to what had actually been accomplished. They knew that the Strasbourg creation scarcely justified

[1] *Creation of the Council of Europe*, previously cited, p. 14.

the laudatory adjectives that Sir Winston and the leaders of the European Movement were applying to it and to their efforts in creating it, for what had been created was another intergovernmental organization—a sort of little League of Nations or United Nations for Western Europe. Some of the instruments of this new apparatus might represent an advance over the traditional kind of intergovernmental organization, but the improvement, if any, was purely technical. From a juristic standpoint, the new creation scarcely qualified as a confederal organization. It would undoubtedly serve as an institutional symbol, and if properly exploited it might become an important instrument for advancing European unity, but the Strasbourg structure hardly satisfied even the minimum aspirations of those who were looking toward a United States of Europe.

In some respects, indeed, the advocates of effective political unity for Western Europe—that is, supporters of confederation or federation—could regard what had been fabricated at Westminster as retrogression rather than progress. What had come into being had been strongly colored by the Continental effort to placate official British opinion. The aim had been to bring Britain into a European structure and, in pursuance of that aim, so much had been compromised and so much had been surrendered of what was essential to even a modicum of union, that the final result was far less than the minimum that many Continental advocates of union believed was compatible with their ideals. The psychological impact of what they had wrought through compromise with Whitehall might, moreover, affect adversely the whole area of public opinion. It gave Britain credit for an attitude to which she was not entitled, namely, the reputation of being a "good European" and of believing sincerely in European integration. In the immediately succeeding years, that undeserved reputation was to plague the whole movement toward unity. It was to persuade much of the public and even the European leaders who wanted a strong union that Britain was basically sympathetic to their cause, when in fact she was not sympathetic. As a consequence, it was to inspire a great deal of effort by the friends of supranational union—effort that was foredoomed to failure simply because it was posited on the false assumption that British participation could be secured. Moreover, those who sought to press forward to something approximating federation foresaw that the new Council of Europe, weak as it was, might nevertheless become in the public mind a substitute for the real thing. In other words, large segments of the interested public might be persuaded that their aims for Europe had been achieved, thereby retarding further effort to secure something more effective.

Official Britain's real intentions on the question of European unity had been made quite clear in some of the statements issued by her government just before the Treaty of Westminster was signed. Britain's original intention had been to follow well-established precedent and make the proposed council nothing more revolutionary than a sort of permanent council of European ministers. But because of the attitude of the "strong" Europeans and their emotional attachment to the concept of a "European parliament," Britain found it expedient to make a concession. She accordingly agreed that the Statute of the Council of Europe should provide for a "bicameral" organization. But her concession on this point had not prevented her from carrying out her resolve to make the new apparatus little more than another international "round table." Before the Treaty of Westminster had been signed, Britain had insisted that the Council of Europe, when it came into being, should "resemble a miniature Assembly of the United Nations, since it would in fact represent the United Nations of Western Europe. . . ." Accordingly there could be "no limitations of the sovereignty of the participating countries." In somewhat different language the same opinion had been reiterated on all suitable occasions. In the view of Whitehall, said its spokesmen, ". . . it would be unrealistic and impracticable to attempt to give executive or legislative power to any nongovernmental body," [2] and the Council of Europe must necessarily be "nongovernmental."

The policy, thus stated, had been realized for Strasbourg. The Council of Europe might be bicameral. It would consist of both a Consultative Assembly, where some of the rules of a traditional international body such as equality of voice and the requirement of unanimity for decision would not obtain, as well as a Commit-

[2] Release by the British Embassy, Washington, dated Dec. 6, 1948, pp. 1-2.

tee of Ministers, where those rules would obtain; but there was no doubt that the ruling organ of the Council was intended to be the Committee of Ministers, the Assembly being relegated to a status that, at least on paper, made it little more than an appendage of the ministerial body. Such was the extent of the British "compromise" and such the true dimensions of this body that, in 1949, was to symbolize and institutionalize the concept of a "United States of Europe." It is hardly surprising that the protagonists of strong union, preferably with a federal structure, once they had had an opportunity to take stock of the achievement at Westminster, should have experienced some qualms about the intrinsic significance and ultimate value of that achievement.

The degree of success experienced by Britain in limiting the Council of Europe to her specifications and the dubious nature of the "advance" toward unity inherent in the establishment of the Council will become clearer if we analyze in some detail the structure and powers of the new apparatus.

Charter members of the new Council consisted not only of the original five Brussels Pact nations—Britain, France, and the three states of the Benelux—but five additional states. These were Norway, Sweden, Denmark, Italy, and Eire. After 1950, five additional states were included—namely, Iceland, Germany, Greece, Austria, and Turkey—thus raising the membership of the Council to fifteen states. A sixteenth member, the Saar, had the status of associate prior to 1956.

Of the two organs of the Council in addition to its Secretariat, the first, or Committee of Ministers, is actually a committee of the foreign ministers of the Council's member states and usually meets once a year at the Council's seat at Strasbourg. Deputies of these foreign ministers, themselves often ministers permanently accredited to Strasbourg by their respective governments, may and do hold special sessions of the ministerial committee or they serve in the committee's regular meeting in place of their respective states' foreign ministers. The second Council agency, the Consultative Assembly, also meets regularly at Strasbourg. Nominally there is one annual session lasting a number of weeks, but since 1950 this session has generally been held in two parts with about one month intervening.

Of these two organs, it was the Consultative Assembly that the federalists had hoped to establish as a sort of "parliament of Europe," a hope that the compromise with Britain and the antifederalists had prevented. To be sure, certain concessions affecting this body's composition were made by the antifederalists. These make the Assembly something of a hybrid among confederal or intergovernmental agencies. Thus its membership of 132 representatives (1956) is distributed among national member states on a basis that is roughly proportional to the demographic or political importance of those states. Britain, France, Germany, and Italy each have eighteen representatives. Iceland and Luxembourg, on the other hand, each have only three. Selection of the representatives does not follow the rule, traditional among international bodies, that delegates be appointed by governments since some of the representatives, the Italian for example, are elected by the national parliament. An even more significant departure from the composition of the usual international assembly, of which a good deal has been made by partisans of the Strasbourg experiment, is the fact that each national contingent in the Assembly includes representatives of virtually all the political parties, both governmental and opposition, of the member state. In 1954, for example, Britain had both Conservative and Labour delegates at Strasbourg even though the British cabinet was Conservative. German Social Democrats, as well as members of the parties of the Adenauer coalition, represented Germany in the Consultative Assembly. Sweden's delegation represented four national parties; Denmark's, four; Iceland's, three; and Norway's, three.[3]

These departures in the composition of the Assembly from what is traditional for intergovernmental bodies are not without significance. As we shall see, they have given the Assembly a stature perceptibly greater than normally attributable to an intergovernmental agency. But the liberal attitude toward its composition did not carry over into the Assembly's procedure and powers, which are distinctly those of the usual international body and which identify clearly the extent of the victory of the nonfederalists at Westminster. In respect of these attributes the Assembly's outstanding char-

[3] *Europe Today and Tomorrow* (July-Aug. 1954), p. 21. Published by the European Movement but publication suspended in 1954.

acteristic is its almost complete formal subordination to the Committee of Ministers. In accordance with the British policy and the policy of the nonfederalists, and pursuant to the principles of the compromise that the British achieved at the Paris conference in December, 1948, the decisive body of the Council of Europe is in all matters the Committee of Ministers. According to the Council's Statute, the Committee approves the Council's annual budget, controls the Secretariat, invites states to membership, determines the representation of a member state on the Consultative Assembly and the state's financial contribution, and, under certain circumstances, suspends a member state and that state's representation in the Assembly.[4]

But the most obvious evidence of the Assembly's inferiority and of its subordination to the Committee of Ministers is to be discerned in the fact that when the Assembly was first organized it could not even determine its own agenda, that having required the approval of the ministers in all cases. Even more significant was the fact that only the Committee of Ministers could recommend action to the Council's member governments. No resolution of the Assembly or vote on any matter affecting member states of the Council could become effective unless the Committee of Ministers approved. In determining whether to give or withhold approval the Committee of Ministers proceeded like any other intergovernmental body in that each state member, large and small, was given one vote. In effect this meant that each national foreign minister or his deputy on the Council's Committee of Ministers had a sort of *liberum veto* and could, by his sole vote, kill any action of the Assembly. Moreover, he exercised that veto in secret because the ministerial committee's deliberations were not to be made public. The framers of the Statute were being logical, at least, when they decided that the Assembly of the Council of Europe should be known as the "Consultative" Assembly.

Since 1949, this almost absolute preponderance of the Committee of Ministers over the Assembly has been modified somewhat in the Assembly's favor. Thus a special joint committee of the ministerial body and the Assembly provides for more effective

[4] See appropriate Articles of the Statute of Europe, appendix, p. 224.

liaison between the two. Some discretion has also been confided to the Assembly in determining its own agenda, and the subject matter of the agenda may apparently range over a wider area than was originally contemplated, such subjects as defense having been included from time to time even though the Statute explicitly states that such a topic shall not concern the Council of Europe. In practice, the Committee of Ministers has also waived its power to kill any resolution by a single vote. Instead of vetoing an Assembly resolution, a nation's representative on the ministerial committee may abstain from voting and thus allow those state delegations that favor a policy to recommend it to their respective governments. This latter modification is an important concession: for, as we shall see later,[5] it afforded the constitutional opportunity for having the Council of Europe act as an intermediary in creating regional arrangements of an intergovernmental or supranational character.

Concessions such as these, however, have not changed the constitutional nature of the regime at Strasbourg. In essence it remains what it was when first set up: it is an intergovernmental arrangement, juridically of a stature less than confederal, in which the ruling organ is an assembly of representatives of national governments each of which has preserved its sovereignty entire. In the time-honored manner, these delegates vote in secret and apply the rule of unanimity in all important matters. Their recommendations are recommendations merely; and the governments to which the recommendations are sent must take the usual municipal legislative or executive action required for adherence to a multilateral international treaty. Although in certain details of its composition the Consultative Assembly may resemble a quasi-sovereign federal legislature, the resemblance is superficial and of little substantive importance. Only in a moral sense, that is, in the sense that it is a forum in which public opinion may be molded, is the Assembly other than a quite powerless body.

It was this juridically attenuated apparatus of cooperation that came into being in 1949 as the institutional expression of those seeking a united Europe. For the British, the Council's relative powerlessness spelled a diplomatic success. Britain had succeeded

[5] See p. 70.

in securing a minimum interpretation for the somewhat extravagant gesture that Churchill had made at The Hague a year earlier, and though the British may have compromised with the advocates of a "strong Europe" to the extent of accepting the Consultative Assembly as part of the Council's machinery, they could hope that the Committee of Ministers would assert its constitutional ascendancy in all matters and appropriately discipline and censor the Assembly. Thus that body might be expected to develop into something akin to a permanent but innocuous "talkshop" where grandiose ideas could be formulated one day and forgotten the next. The Council thus appeared to be an ideal arrangement to all those who would "limit" Europe, that is, not only to the British but also to such member states as Norway and Denmark and all others who were inclined to follow the British lead and who felt that Strasbourg was as far as united Europe should go.

Hence, however laudatory the appraisals of the Council of Europe on the morrow of the Westminster Treaty and however emotionally inclined the friends of united Europe may have been to regard the Council as a milestone, the discerning realized that not too much had been gained—at least not much from the formal institutional point of view. Strasbourg was just another intergovernmental agency; it was certainly a far cry from the maximum program, namely, a federal structure for Europe.

Even so, the Continental supporters of such a structure—leaders like Spaak, Reynaud, Bidault, Schuman, de Gasperi, Philip, van der Goes van Naters, and others—who had thought in terms of some sort of semisovereign structure were not wholly disappointed. They believed that the internal needs of European states and the disposition of the international situation made something stronger than Strasbourg inevitable. Hence Strasbourg was a step toward the ultimate goal. Moreover the institution of the new Council of Europe might well assist them measurably toward their goal. Its forum could provide a focal point for debate, become an instrument of education, and give the whole movement an impetus and direction that it had formerly lacked. In short the new Council might become for them a sort of way station along the road to the real goal of federation—an instrument for making the ultimate achievement of that goal more certain.

In their post-Westminster planning, the strong Europeans were inclined to place great reliance upon the Council's Consultative Assembly. Whatever the limitations of this organ in power and prestige, and however far removed from the reality of a "parliament of Europe," the strong Europeans hoped to make this body especially useful to them. Once the Council of Europe had become a going concern, they hoped that the Assembly would "take over" and, contrary to British expectations, become the sounding board for real European unity. To bring about this result, great reliance was placed on the Assembly's composition. Thanks to the fact that the Assembly's membership encompassed virtually all the political parties of the associated states, it was confidently anticipated by the champions of federal Europe that its debates would reflect a genuine public opinion, even an opinion opposed to the policy of the government of the day in certain of the states. Rather naïvely, perhaps, it was therefore assumed that the prevailing sentiment in the new organ would favor a more perfect union. Within a relatively short time, it was felt, this new official European forum might well generate so much enthusiasm for greater unity and point the course so unerringly toward that goal that the opposition, even the opposition of the British, would be overcome. Thus what had not been accomplished at The Hague or at Westminster might eventually be accomplished at Strasbourg.

Such were the hopes—or perhaps the rationalizations—of the advocates of effective integration who had acquiesced in the British position on the structure of the Council of Europe. For them the next round in the battle was now to be fought at Strasbourg, where they planned to exploit the new instrument, and many profederalists sincerely believed that this round would be victorious. The new policy of the strong Europeans was admirably stated by Mr. Ronald W. G. MacKay before the Consultative Assembly itself on September 6, 1949, just after it had organized for the first time. Paradoxically, Mr. MacKay is both a British representative and a convinced federalist. Mr. MacKay declared that he was not asking the Assembly to affirm that it wished to have a political authority "today or next year," but he did want it to affirm that "the aim of our work in this Assembly and in the Council of Europe as a whole is to secure in the future a political authority for Europe with limited functions but real powers so that we shall know the direction in which we are to travel." [6]

The initial session of the Consultative Assembly opened with considerable fanfare on August 10, 1949. The House of Europe in which the Council now operates at Strasbourg had not yet been erected, and the Assembly's first meeting was accordingly held in a building of the University of Strasbourg. Paul-Henri Spaak, the Belgian leader, was elected the first president and in his brief inaugural offered his colleagues an emphatic challenge to work toward more effective integration. "Tangible results," he said, "must emerge from the Assembly's work. . . . Tacit and intellectual consent are insufficient if we are to build Europe. We must have results." [7] Representatives appeared to be well aware of the historical uniqueness of their meeting and of the possibility it offered to advance the cause of integration. Western Europe's leading statesmen were there, and they were only too willing to be heard. Churchill had come to Strasbourg in his capacity as the leader of the British Opposition sent by the Labour government along with Labour representatives. Present too were virtually all those Frenchmen, Italians, Dutchmen, and Belgians who, throughout the immediate postwar years, had given distinguished patronage to Europe's leading idea of reconstruction.

From the session's opening day, the strong Europeans sought to point the new instrument in the direction of their policy of more effective union. Their immediate purpose was twofold. In the first place they wished to make organizational and procedural changes in the Strasbourg structure that would strengthen the Assembly vis-à-vis the Committee of Ministers. To this end they made various recommendations: that the Assembly be permitted to fix its own agenda; that its jurisdiction be broadened; that a committee of liaison be established between the Assembly and the ministers; that recommendations of the Assembly be sent to the member governments of the Council directly rather than through the ministers, provided the Assembly had passed the recommendations by an extraordinary majority; that special committees be established

[6] Council of Europe, Directorate of Information, *The First Five Years* (Strasbourg, 1954), p. 23; cited hereafter as *The First Five Years*.

[7] *Ibid.* p. 22.

to provide more expert aid to the Assembly; and that the Council establish effective liaison with other European organs such as the OEEC and, to avoid duplication, perhaps take over some of the work of established European organizations. Some of the ideas advanced were rather vague both in statement and purpose. Many did not get beyond the stage of mere suggestion in the course of debate. A few, however, notably those directed toward equalizing the position of Assembly and Committee of Ministers, were advanced to the status of formal resolutions and were finally sent to the Committee of Ministers for action.

The second, and more important, purpose of the strong Europeans at Strasbourg in August, 1949, had to do with the long-range constitutional question: that is, the development of an authority with essentially supranational power. Much of the inspiration for this effort and a great deal of the initiative apparently came from the more doctrinaire federalists among the members of the Assembly, but the formal leadership came from the French Socialist, André Philip, who was strongly supported by his French colleagues and particularly by the Conservative, Paul Reynaud. They demanded that the Consultative Assembly proceed forthwith to the "creation of a political authority of a supranational character."[8] Against this renewed effort of the federalists and supranationalists, spokesmen for the British Labour government once again marshaled their arguments and political influence. They reiterated their formal concept of the Council, *viz.*, that it was purely an intergovernmental body and that it should remain so. Even Churchill was inclined to be less generous than usual in the language he used to answer the partisans of federalism, cautioning them not to tamper with the powers of parliaments.

Maurice Edelman, one of the British Labour representatives, sought to soften somewhat the position of his government, which by now seemed rather negative and unyielding. He accordingly elaborated on the value and scope of the functions that might fall to the Council of Europe even when acting in a purely intergovernmental capacity. Without modifying the sovereign position of the member governments by one jot, the Council of Europe, he

[8] C. C. Walton, "The Fate of Neo-Federalism in Western Europe," *Western Political Quarterly*, Vol. 5, No. 3 (Sept. 1952), p. 379.

said, could effectively perform the role of mediator and harmonizer. In that role, it could coordinate the economic plans of governments, trade unions, industries, and other private groups.

Although anything but novel, Mr. Edelman's speech made use of an adjective to describe the suggested future activity of the Council that later achieved considerable vogue and was to acquire special semantic significance. This was the word "functional." Mr. Edelman sought to make the approach of the Council to European problems a "functional" approach, as distinct, perhaps, from that advocated by the federalists and supranationalists who were wont to insist that nothing practical could be done about any problem of multinational scope unless it was handled by a European agency having coercive powers and powers superior to those of any particular government. As used in the ensuing debate "functionalism" acquired somewhat ambiguous connotations. The British obviously intended the word to mean merely an approach to specific international problems on the usual intergovernmental basis of negotiation and treaty. But as the debate progressed others came to use the word to describe the possible establishment of a series of supranational authorities each having a particular purpose or "function." "Functionalism" thus also came in time to be associated with the ideas of those who rejected the intergovernmental approach.

That time, however, was not yet. For the immediate period, discussion at Strasbourg continued to be centered upon the traditional division between the intergovernmental advocates of integration and those who wanted to advance toward a broad federal unity of the Continent. The international situation still favored some policy of pooling the strength of the West; hence the supporters of union continued to have the benefit of that temporary hiatus in nationalistic feeling that was so noticeable immediately following the conclusion of hostilities after World War II. The discussion at Strasbourg, moreover, seemed to lean their way. At any rate, when the Consultative Assembly's initial session ended in September, 1949, it was agreed that the Council of Europe should use its power and influence to develop a European political authority with "limited functions but real powers." Paradoxically, both extreme federalist and conservative British advocates of "intergovernmental functionalism" seemed to find the resolution to their liking and voted for it, and the ambiguity in their minds and in the phraseology was left for clarification to the newly constituted chief committee of the Assembly, the twenty-three-member Committee on General Affairs.

That the end results of the Assembly's deliberations in its first session would prove of advantage to the federalist cause was apparently not doubted, at least by the federalists and neofederalists in that body. Spaak, the president of the Assembly, was jubilant. "I came to Strasbourg," he said, "convinced of the necessity of a United States of Europe. I am leaving it with the certitude that union is possible." [9]

In pursuance of its mandate the Assembly's Committee on General Affairs undertook in the final months of 1949 a fairly careful resurvey of the state of opinion on European integration. As chairman of the committee, the Assembly had designated M. Georges Bidault, at the time French foreign minister; as *rapporteur,* the French Socialist leader, M. Guy Mollet. Both individuals were disposed to favor a somewhat stronger form of integration than that represented by the Council and both were committed to reform within the Council. On the whole, therefore, the strong Europeans in the Assembly had left their program in sympathetic hands.

Among the private organizations to which the Committee on General Affairs turned for comment was the European Union of Federalists, identified earlier in this volume as a constituent unit of the European Movement and probably the private prointegration movement with the largest popular following. As might be expected, the Union was far in advance of any other private organization in its desire to establish federal and supranational institutions for the Continent. In the memorandum that its leaders submitted to the Assembly's Committee, the Union took a firm stand in favor of federal institutions. In their opinion the first session of the Assembly had been disappointing. The Assembly had accomplished nothing of importance. Compromise, they declared, was no longer permissible and the worst possible procedure would be to try to tinker with the machinery of the Council of Europe in the hope that something might be salvaged. The only course was to ig-

[9] American Committee on United Europe, "United Europe: A Statement of Progress" (New York, 1950), p. 22.

nore the Council of Europe and make an entirely fresh start in the direction of integration. Their recommendations were prefaced by this appraisal of the Council of Europe: "The first session of the Council . . . marked at the same time a beginning and an end. It marked the beginning of a real and organic cooperation between the nations of Europe; it marked the end of the illusion that the aim of European unity can be achieved without political machinery on a supranational level. The time has now come to draw the necessary conclusions." [10]

On the other hand, spokesmen for the European Movement, that broad association of private organizations favoring united Europe that Churchill had formed at The Hague two years earlier, were inclined to compromise with the *status quo* at Strasbourg. They felt, or professed to feel, that progress could be achieved within the framework of the Council of Europe itself. The Movement's caution reflected growing realization of the extent of the schism currently opening between Britain and certain Continental states on this European question. Somewhat ambiguously, and probably deliberately so, the Movement recommended that member states of the Council provide for a "political authority" through which they would jointly decide, by democratic methods, a common policy in regard to the protection of human rights, external relations, and economic affairs. The Movement also endorsed "functional institutions" that, under the "direction" of the proposed new authority, would deal with problems of currency, commerce, transport, investment, production, and defense. Suggestions were also made that all the members of the Council of Europe should participate in the "proposed Political Authority," but that it was not "essential that all should participate in every one of the functional institutions." [11]

This final recommendation is especially interesting because, as

[10] European Union of Federalists, "From the Powerless Consultative Assembly to a European Pact" (pamphlet printed for the European Union of Federalists, 39, Boulevard Malesherbes, Paris, by Federal Union, 20, Buckingham St., London W.C. 2), p. 4.

[11] European Movement, "Creation of a European Political Authority and Functional Institutions." Statement approved by the International Executive Committee of the European Movement, Jan. 21, 1950, and sent to the General Affairs Committee of the Consultative Assembly.

we shall see, like the discussion of functionalism in September in the Assembly itself, it foreshadowed, at least in some aspects, the syndicated and geographically restricted institutional form that progress toward integration was to assume during the next phase of the European movement.[12]

What the Assembly's Committee on General Affairs ultimately produced in the way of a report was a disappointment to the advocates of neofederalism who had expected that the Committee's leadership would use its influence to support recommendations for greater unity than Strasbourg afforded. The report was a compromise that reflected an attempt to please all the Assembly's factions and the diverse national points of view of the Committee's own membership. On the actual question of moving toward a stronger union of states, the Committee showed less courage than its parent body. Indeed, the Committee's report was more in the nature of an analysis of the problem of integration than a recommendation of policy. That the General Affairs Committee had not succeeded in making any real progress toward implementing the Assembly's plan for a European political authority "with limited functions but real powers" was made quite clear by the former French prime minister, Paul Reynaud, shortly after the Assembly's second session convened in Strasbourg in 1950. He pointed out that in the preceding year "the Assembly had instructed its Committee on General Affairs to study a structural reform of Europe and to put forward precise and concrete proposals. The Committee had set to work but, whereas the President of the Assembly [Spaak] had, in the words of Danton, called for boldness, the Committee had replied with mere cleverness, for the sake of unanimity." Sarcastically he added that "public opinion would take a vital interest in a debate on federalism but would not get excited about coordination, or exercises in flexibility, let alone an *ad hoc* Committee." [13]

[12] Among other bodies consulted by the General Affairs Committee were the International Confederation of Free Trade Unions, the International Confederation of Christian Trade Unions, the International Federation of Agricultural Producers, the Council of the Federation of European Industries, the International Chamber of Commerce, and the Permanent Commission of the Brussels Treaty Powers.

[13] *Summary of Debates, Consultative Assembly, Second Ordinary Session,* I, 1, Aug. 7-11, 1950, pp. 34-35; cited hereafter as *Summary of Debates.*

Another blow befell the cause of the "strong Europeans" in the Consultative Assembly of November, 1949, when the Council's Committee of Ministers finally acted on the Assembly's recommendations. Apart from a rather general resolution endorsing the action of the United Nations forces in Korea, the ministerial committee supported none of the Assembly's recommendations. Most of them were either ignored or vetoed; or action on them was indefinitely deferred. Nor was any hope held out to the Assembly that the rule of unanimity, governing the Committee's procedure in considering Assembly resolutions, with its corollary of a national veto power, would be relaxed. Neither did the ministers suggest that they would give up or modify their formal control over the Assembly's agenda. In their report the ministers even sought to limit the number of Assembly committees, suggesting that some of them were duplicating the work of other international bodies, for example, the OEEC or the United Nations. Altogether the ministers succeeded admirably in placing a damper upon the hopes of the European federalists or supranationalists. The articulate Reynaud once more provided an appropriate description of the frustrations of those who had hoped for more progress toward union. "The Council of Europe," he said, "consists of two bodies, one of them *for* Europe, the other *against* it." [14] The bitterness of the federalists toward the second house of the Council of Europe was not lightened by the open secret that it was Britain and her Scandinavian allies that had been chiefly responsible for the narrow and obstructionist policy that the ministers had displayed.

Thus by the time the second session of the Assembly approached in 1950, it had become clear to the strong Europeans that the high hopes they had entertained during the first session of transforming the Council of Europe into an effective confederal instrument or into a supranational federal agency had been misplaced. Certainly the results of their efforts in that direction had been wholly negative. The Council of Europe could not be thus transformed because no such transformation would win the support of any large number of states assembled at Strasbourg.

But their failure cooled neither the ardor nor the logic of the

[14] *Unite or Perish,* p. 199.

neofederalists and the supranationalists. They continued to be as vocal as in 1949 about the wisdom of proceeding to erect something more enduring than a mere intergovernmental arrangement. But by the time the representatives had assembled a second time at Strasbourg in 1950, it had become quite clear to them that a new start would have to be made. Just what form this new start should take was not clear. What was clear, however, was that at Strasbourg only a few of the Continental states, clustering around France, would be likely to move forward toward institutional forms of association that provided a greater degree of unity than that supplied by the Council of Europe.

6 Toward the Community of the "Six"

THE SECOND SESSION of the Consultative Assembly of the Council of Europe began on August 7, 1950, under fairly heartening circumstances. Early in March of that year construction had started on the House of Europe, the palace of the Council of Europe, on the Place Lenôtre in Strasbourg, and by a remarkable effort, itself a tribute to French industry, the French hosts had completed the building and made it ready for occupancy on the session's opening day. Five months before, Iceland had become a member of the Council; in May, the Saar had become an associate member; and in July, the German Federal Republic had also become an associate member and was soon to become a full member. Thus when the second session of the Assembly convened, the total membership of the Council of Europe had risen to fifteen. Taking note of this tangible progress, Sir Winston Churchill, serving for a second year as a British representative to the Assembly, delivered one of his characteristically optimistic opinions about the progress of European integration. He reminded his colleagues about the events at the Congress of the European Movement at The Hague, two years before. That meeting, he said, had been "an unofficial gathering of enthusiasts, pleading the cause of reconciliation and revival of this shattered Continent." By contrast, he continued, "we have reached the scene today where we sit as a body with ever growing influence and respect, in our own House of Europe, under the flags of fifteen historic states and Nations." [1]

Sir Winston's colleagues of the extant session were not quite

[1] *The First Five Years,* p. 25.

so enthusiastic—at least not verbally. The disappointments of the previous year had taken their toll. The strong Europeans on the Continent were as resolute as ever in their support of some form of neofederal integration and they seemed as certain of eventual success for their program as in 1949. Their mood, however, was a somewhat chastened one. They were not so sure now, as in 1947 and 1948, that a real "United States of Europe" was just around the corner. On the contrary, most of them were now inclined to believe that some intermediate steps would be necessary, steps that temporarily at least would limit the concept of European union both territorially and substantively and that might serve as a prelude to broader integration. The new mood and the more limited objectives were implicit in the deliberations of the new session. Only occasional references were made to the grand idea of 1948 for a real European parliament and to the idea, advanced so confidently a year earlier, that the existing structure of "Europe," represented by the apparatus at Strasbourg, would be quickly transformed into a real federal union.

Instead of such references, much now was said about "functionalism." Precisely what was meant by this word when it first became popular was none too certain. Apparently its use stemmed from some rather haphazard remarks by a British Labour party representative in the Consultative Assembly's session of 1949, remarks upon which we have already commented.[2] Not relishing the advocacy of federation, which had characterized much of the debate of that session, this representative (Mr. Edelman) had obeyed the instinct of his countrymen, one nurtured on courtesy as well as on policy, to supply at least a semantic alternative for what he disliked. The result had been a rather vague reference to "functional" institutions and the "functional approach" to unity. Thereupon the press correspondents, in their inimitable fashion, falling in love with the neat alliteration, had suggested that thenceforth the Consultative Assembly might devote its unity efforts to "functionalism" rather than to "federalism."

In August, 1950, as debate resumed in the Assembly, this undefined concept of "functional association" gave at least some com-

[2] See pp. 50-51.

fort to the Continental exponents of European unity because it appeared that the British and Scandinavian representatives, though opposed to federation, might conceivably be won over to "functionalism" or "functional unions." Indeed as discussion got under way, a British Labour representative had been quite encouraging as to the possibility of British endorsement of "functionalism." He had reiterated the venerable and always extremely obvious theme that Britain was a part of Europe. He had reminded his colleagues that some months earlier the then British prime minister, Mr. Clement Attlee, had told Parliament that it was ridiculous to try to stand on the conception of the absolute sovereignty of the nation state in the modern world and "that it was possible to move forward to functional unity on European lines." [3] At the same time other British representatives had sounded similar notes.[4] Other national delegates at Strasbourg, notably the Dutch and the Italian, felt that "functionalism" would re-entice the British into a new push toward the integration of the Continent.[5] Whatever meaning "functionalism" might have, it did suggest a piecemeal or syndicated approach to European integration rather than some broader and more embracing approach; to that extent, it was bound to appeal to the more timid and conservative on this matter of European integration and, hence, possibly to the British.

Functional integration, as thus defined, also appeared to provide a solution for another difficulty that had been looming on the diplomatic horizon and now bade fair to grow in stature by leaps and bounds. This was the problem posed by the political renascence of Germany and the advent of the German Federal Republic as a full-fledged member of the postwar European community. Under the leadership of Chancellor Konrad Adenauer, West Germany had made great progress in both the economic and diplomatic fields. She had become an associate member of the Council of Europe just one month before the current session of the Assembly had opened, and it was obvious that she would soon be demanding national equality. When that happened both West Germany and some other members of the Western alliance, fearful of Western

[3] James Callaghan, *Summary of Debates,* I, 1, Aug. 7-11, 1950, p. 10.
[4] See, for example, Robert Boothby, *Summary of Debates,* I, 1, p. 23.
[5] *Summary of Debates,* I, 1, pp. 27, 33.

Europe's weakness before the Soviet, would use the occasion to voice demands for a new German army.

Obviously, if and when that demand arose, it would pose a delicate problem especially for the French. After three invasions of France by the Germans in somewhat more than two generations, the restoration of a German army was a matter not to be taken lightly by any Frenchman. In 1950 the immediate military threat to Western Europe, including France, was Soviet Russia. But even at that time the threat to French security of a rearmed and potentially aggressive Germany was, at least to the French mind, of almost equal importance. Indeed, as events of the next few years were to demonstrate, security against Germany was of greater importance to a great many Frenchmen than security against organized Communism. Even so, whatever their qualms, most French leaders realized that they had to be realistic about the prospect of German remilitarization. They realized that, however fearful their countrymen might be about rearming Germany, France could not well pursue the policy of the ostrich on this unwelcome matter. For these leaders, therefore, the concept of a European army, which various supporters of the European Movement had been suggesting and which, for most such leaders, meant a defense force under multinational federal auspices, offered a possible solution to this perplexing French security problem. By integrating German, French, and other forces into a European army, German rearmament on a purely national basis would be prevented, and as a result the possible threat to France would be mitigated. In other words, a European army, with French and German units combined, would at once be the most audacious of all possible "functional" arrangements and it might also solve the cruel dilemma that France faced vis-à-vis Germany.

One of the first Frenchmen to stress this possible exploitation of "functionalism" was the French Socialist leader and long-time friend of integration, M. André Philip. In the very first days of this new session of the Assembly, he declared that German rearmament was, for the moment, out of the question; but then he added that "it could only take place . . . when a European army had been formed." [6]

[6] *Summary of Debates,* I, 1, p. 16.

For the Germans, too, a European army seemed like the best solution for a revived nation. Chancellor Adenauer sincerely believed that a revival of anything like the old Reichswehr would be a mistake not only for Europe but for Germany. The youth of Germany were currently not disposed toward militarization and the public generally feared that rearmament might lead to a new war and make Germany a new battleground. Moreover, every effort had been made by Germany's former antagonists to demilitarize the country and prevent rearmament. To make matters still more difficult, the German government's opposition, led by the Social Democrats, had already made it clear that it would fight conscription and a new army. Obviously it was going to be difficult for any German leader of the moment, including even Dr. Adenauer, to bring Germany back to the point of accepting conscription for new military levies unless, conceivably, such rearmament might spell both the restoration of German sovereignty and independence and identification, through military contingents, with the ideal of a united Europe.

Having suggested how functionalism might be used to help solve major aspects of the reviving German question, M. Philip had gone further and demonstrated the more generous possibilities inherent in the "functional" approach. Thus he became one of the first to clarify the meaning of this new concept of integration. Some four months before the Consultative Assembly had convened, M. Robert Schuman, French foreign minister, had first brought forward unofficially his idea, destined to have momentous consequences, of pooling the West European markets for coal and steel under a European "supranational" authority. M. Philip now suggested that this Schuman proposal for a "functional" form of integration might well be regarded as a model for all sorts of "functional" experiments of a supranational character. Besides a European army, these functional experiments might be extended, he said, to such areas as power, transportation, exports and foreign trade, labor, raw materials, and agricultural produce. Eventually these separate experiments might lead to a kind of piecemeal integration of the Continent. To prevent abuse and the growth of cartels and economic oligarchy, it would be necessary for "functional unions" or "authorities" to become responsible to a democratically elected assembly. It was therefore the duty of the Consultative Assembly, said M. Philip, ultimately to transform itself into a body that could exercise this democratic control over specialized authorities. If it failed to do so, he felt that the existing session might be the Assembly's last.[7] What effect such supranational functional arrangements, if developed, might have on the Council of Europe was not clear at this point. The Council's organs might be abandoned or, as M. Philip suggested, transformed at least in part. Or it was also possible to contemplate the elaboration of the functional units, the Council remaining *in statu quo*.

But hopes that the new libretto of "functionalism" would recapture British support and the support of those who followed the British position at Strasbourg for an effective program of unity were shortly dispelled. "Functionalism," as the neofederalists on the Continent defined it, obviously was to be a sort of syndicated supranationalism. To be sure, it suggested only piecemeal limitation of national sovereignty, but Britain, and those states that supported her position, would have no more of piecemeal limitation of sovereignty than of the general limitation on sovereignty implied by broad federation. In other words, when "functionalism" was finally defined and ceased to belong to the realm of vague generalities, dear to the orator, it quite plainly became a sort of bit by bit approach to federation, and though this new approach might be more pragmatic than broad "paper" schemes of federation, it meant the same thing to the British. They would have none of it. Their hostility to building a permanent supranational unified structure in Europe, even in defined "functional" areas, and becoming a part of that structure, was as inveterate as ever.

Relatively unchanged, too, were the reasons for the British attitude. Labour, still in power in 1950, was particularly sensitive to any suggestion that the British government place its economic policy in the hands of some supranational authority. Labour was fearful that if British enterprise were to compete directly with Continental enterprise without the protection of national policy, the social gains achieved by Labour since 1945 would suffer. Apparently the coal and steel pool proposal particularly bothered the

[7] *Summary of Debates*, I, 1, pp. 16-17.

British because these commodities involved the very foundation of the British economy; Britain's production of both coal and steel was second only to the combined capacity of Western Europe. What other less obvious economic and political reasons motivated British opposition can only be guessed at, although such guesses can be ventured with some confidence. Some of the formal reasons were sometimes not too meaningful and bordered on the ridiculous. This was especially true of the alleged British objection to a written constitution or to formal plans of government. In reiterating such a reason for their opposition to supranational schemes for "functional" European unity, the British, contrary to their normally correct behavior, did not always avoid a sort of backhanded slap at France by their ill-concealed contempt for the art of the Abbé Sieyès and his penchant for written constitutions.[8]

Thus, as the Strasbourg debates wore on during the late summer of 1950, it became quite clear that even if "functionalism" were to supersede "federalism" as a goal, the British would probably persevere in their original policy of keeping the Council of Europe inviolate. The test of the British attitude on "functionalism" had come even before the session had convened with the announcement of the Schuman Plan. As M. Reynaud had pointed out, this plan was a sample of "functional" cooperation; and the British had indicated that they were opposed. "A functional reform," said M. Reynaud, "had in fact been proposed—the Schuman Plan—which the British Government had proceeded to turn down. The Labour party had rejected the very principle of abatement of one iota of its sovereignty. And yet without such an abatement nothing could be done either in the economic sphere or in the military field." [9]

Optimism, however, is difficult to kill, and among the Continental federalists and neofederalists hope persisted, as the session

[8] In their opposition to written constitutions, the British are probably the pupils of Burke. Nevertheless, a country that produced a Lilburne, an Ireton, a Milton, a Paine, and especially a Bentham, all of whom had a hand in developing the tradition of the written constitution—and a sizable hand too—is hardly in a position to suggest that written constitutions are *per se* alien to Britain.

[9] *Summary of Debates,* I, 1, p. 35.

wore on, that Britain might yet agree to cooperate with some form of supranational functionalism. The European army plan, which as we have noted was very much in the air during this August Assembly session, became the subject of a formal proposal placed on the Assembly agenda by none other than Sir Winston Churchill himself. Even if Churchill was in the opposition at Westminster, it was reasonable to suppose that, in introducing this proposal, he had not departed so far from British policy as to suggest a course of action that Britain, as a nation, whatever the complexion of her government, might not be able to support. Thus the European army proposal offered still another test of British intentions, and further examination of the British attitude on this particular issue of the army seemed to be in order before it could be finally ascertained whether Reynaud had been correct in asserting that Britain would have none of the new "functionalism."

Sir Winston had introduced his resolution for the European army on August 11th, the day after M. Schuman had officially outlined the terms of his plan on coal and steel to the Assembly and placed that too on the agenda. The sanguinary defense of the free world against Communism, then in progress in Korea, had stimulated the Committee of Ministers to seek from the Assembly a joint expression of approval of what the United Nations had undertaken on that battlefront. "No one would doubt what their answer would be," said Sir Winston, but he added that it would be futile to discuss the position of Western Europe in relation to the defense of the free world if Western Europe's military position was itself imperiled.

Under the Council of Europe's Statute, defense questions were presumed to be beyond the Council's competence and not appropriate subjects for debate. Sir Winston, therefore, proceeded to exploit the ministers' Korean initiative as a procedural opportunity for introducing his European army resolution. Closing the existing gap in Europe's defense, said the British leader, would be the surest way of defending Western Europe from the aggressive threat of Soviet Russia and the Communist world conspiracy. The gap could be closed, he said, by uniting Western Europe's military power. His colleagues in the Assembly, concluded Sir Winston, "should declare themselves in favour of the immediate creation of a European army under a united command in which all should bear their part." [10]

In the formal resolution that Sir Winston introduced, he added that the proposed army should be "subject to proper European democratic control" and that it should act in cooperation with the United States and Canada. The day following the introduction of the army resolution the Assembly, after some further discussion of the jurisdictional question as to whether it could entertain such a resolution as Sir Winston's, decided that it could. It thereupon passed the resolution by the necessary two-thirds vote. There were eighty-nine affirmative votes and only five "noes." Some twenty-seven representatives refused to cast a ballot. Before acting upon the resolution the Assembly strengthened the unitary character of the proposed European army by substituting the word "united" for "unified" and by requiring that, in addition to being subject to "proper European democratic control," the army should operate "under the authority of a European Minister of Defence." If any doubt had existed as to the degree of unification proposed and the essentially supranational character of the plan, the demand that the responsible executive authority should be "European" removed such doubt.[11]

But if Sir Winston's action seemed to generate a new spark of hope that Britain would espouse the new model "functionalism," the spark did not glow very long. Only the day after the British Conservative leader had introduced his army resolution, the spark was thoroughly extinguished. Official Britain, speaking through Hugh Dalton of the Labour government, suggested that Sir Winston was speaking strictly for himself and that Britain could not support any such resolution as Sir Winston had proposed. He was quite willing to pay tribute to his countryman's initiative in planning so bold a stroke in Europe's defense and said that the "opening phrases" of Sir Winston's resolution would command assent generally, especially the proposal to sustain the action of the United Nations Security Council in Korea and to cooperate with the United States and Canada in current security measures. But on the army plan, Mr. Dalton was inclined to go slow. He

[10] *Summary of Debates,* I, 1, pp. 59 ff.
[11] *Summary of Debates,* I, 1, p. 71.

said he was not sure how far the proposed plan came within the provisions of the Atlantic Pact or how the European army was to be organized. In any event, he said, the proposal needed further study, a suggested procedure that no one was likely to oppose even if its patent purpose was like that of the time-honored parliamentary maneuver of laying a resolution on the table for consideration after an assembly's adjournment.

In the course of his comments, Mr. Dalton made some observations about the British interpretation of "functionalism." He reiterated the idea that "functionalism" meant merely "intergovernmental" as opposed to supranational units, the latter requiring a surrender of sovereignty. This "intergovernmental" conception of "functionalism" had been used many times, he said, in the development of European organs. It had been especially successful in the evolution of the European Payments Union and its predecessor, the Organization for European Economic Cooperation. Both of these organizations were, in his opinion, illustrations of the good that could be accomplished in integrating Europe by such a limited arrangement as the British had in mind. This qualified method of proceeding toward "functionalism," he insisted, was a "natural method to adopt" and it had a place even for "convinced federalists." [12] Mr. Dalton went on to say that those Europeans in the Assembly who had held that this "intergovernmental method" led nowhere were "too pessimistic."

The British leader's reiteration of his nation's official interpretation of "functionalism" was further confirmation, if any were needed, that Britain would have nothing to do with any kind of supranational concept—not with the plan of M. Schuman as currently elaborated and certainly not with so ambitious a plan as a European army controlled by a European defense minister and a European authority. In effect, Mr. Dalton's speech was a rather elaborate footnote to the more succinct comments made earlier by M. Reynaud about the British rejection of the Continental concept of "functionalism" and Britain's unwillingness to forego sovereignty in order to adhere to a supranational agency.

If doubts still persisted in the minds of the optimists about the finality of Britain's rejection of the concept of a supranational com-

[12] *Summary of Debates,* I, 1, p. 65.

munity, they were dissipated when the second part of the Assembly's 1950 session convened in November, 1950, three months after the plans of M. Schuman and Sir Winston for supranational agencies had been introduced. By that time Britain, and those who sympathized with her, had had an opportunity to use the Council of Europe's Committee of Ministers to negative the army plan. This the Committee had done on the ground that defense did not come within the purview of the Assembly or the Council of Europe as a whole. Having vetoed the plan, the Committee blandly expressed the innocuous hope that the defense of free Europe would be dealt with adequately in the near future by the appropriate governments and competent international organizations.

Thus as the second part of the Consultative Assembly's session drew to a close at Strasbourg, the Continental representatives, especially those from France, Italy, and the Low Countries, had about concluded that if anything was to be done to integrate Europe on a supranational or neofederal basis, action would have to be undertaken without Britain and the peripheral Scandinavian states —at least for the time being. Any sort of formal federation of all Western Europe was clearly out of the picture. That had been proven in the previous session of the Assembly. All that was politically feasible at the moment was some sort of bit by bit integration in which surrender of sovereignty was not too obvious. Paul Bastid, a French representative at Strasbourg, described the situation rather aptly and certainly graphically. He had arrived, he said, at the point where he was ready to try any road that could "give life to Europe," and he knew that "the carefully balanced structure which he would like to see erected was impossible." If Europe was to be made, it was rather obvious to him that it would have to be made "only by dint of random improvisations: it would not be a palace but a conglomeration of sheds." [13]

But it was also obvious that, even as respects the "conglomeration of sheds," the Continental proponents of supranational solutions would have to go forward alone in erecting them. Whatever flicker of hope of British participation might continue to be derived from the vague semantics of British representatives at the Assembly, the hard fact was that the British attitude toward "functional" integra-

[13] *Summary of Debates,* I, 1, p. 291.

tion of any serious nature was as negative as it had been toward the older concept of a formal federation. The British attitude was precisely what Reynaud had said it was earlier in the session's debate—an entirely negative approach. Or as one of the franker British representatives described it, the British approach was a "motionless" approach.

For those Continental representatives at Strasbourg who were serious about supranational functionalism, all that remained was to follow the advice given them in the very first session of the Strasbourg Assembly in 1949 by Eire's prime minister, Eamon De Valera. He had suggested that if certain Continental states could not wait or did not wish to wait for Britain and others, they should consider closer union by agreement among themselves.[14] It was advice that had been echoed by another British delegate, R. W. G. MacKay, who had assured France and others that Britain could not be persuaded to go beyond the *status quo* at Strasbourg and that countries that wanted more had best go forward without Britain.[15] Actually Hugh Dalton, in formally rejecting British participation in both the army and the Schuman plans, had urged establishment of the latter by those interested. He said that if six or more states actually organized the Schuman Plan among themselves, Britain "would be ready to help."[16] Simultaneous advice had been given by some of the Scandinavian representatives, who said they were willing to give encouragement to regional unions among France, Italy, and the Low Countries although their own governments were as loath as the British to part with any of their sovereignty.[17] To make that proposal official at Strasbourg, moreover, the Committee of Ministers had itself offered the suggestion that those states interested in participating in the proposed Schuman Plan go forward without the rest.[18]

The existing situation was perhaps most felicitously described by an articulate French representative, M. Edouard Bonnefous. The British attitude toward either a formal federation or supranational

[14] *The First Five Years*, p. 63.
[15] *Summary of Debates*, I, 1, p. 43.
[16] *Summary of Debates*, I, 1, p. 65.
[17] For example, B. G. Ohlin, *Summary of Debates*, I, 1, p. 47.
[18] *Summary of Debates*, I, 5, p. 239.

functional authorities was to be likened, he said, to the "position of Alpinists who cheer on the leading party of climbers whilst they are prepared to make the ascent if the first party succeeds." M. Bonnefous went on to say that some of the nations, meaning his own and certain other Continental states, were willing to accept the responsibility of making the ascent and he urged them to do so. The Assembly, he said, had already done too much talking. It should now proceed to submit definite proposals to the parliaments of interested nations: it should set up specialized authorities with members chosen from the Assembly. An unduly restricted federation would, he said, be a step backward, a "caricature of Europe." On the other hand, the creation of specialized authorities or communities would constitute a step "forwards towards a united Europe." [19]

The climax of the discussion whether to proceed with or without Britain in erecting supranational functional authorities or communities came with the speech of the French foreign minister, Georges Bidault, on November 23, 1950. M. Bidault had also been the chairman of the Consultative Assembly's Committee on General Affairs, which had been charged with this constitutional problem. "What was troubling the Assembly?" asked M. Bidault. "Was it England?" M. Bidault said that he and all his colleagues knew how much England had done for freedom. "But," he added, "it was inadmissible to say: 'Nothing can be done if England does not wish to do anything.' " The British, he continued, had shown themselves the least intransigent in this entire debate. Moreover, he and his colleagues "could not subordinate the creation of Europe to its acceptance by any one country, however great." He thereupon adjured those who had been afraid to act, to act nonetheless. They should not hesitate, he said. If they did not act, "the peoples would once more take in their own bare hands the fate to which they would have been abandoned." [20]

Concrete action followed the conclusion of this address by M. Bidault, the Assembly proceeding, by eighty-three votes to nine, to draft in final form a resolution as to the policy on special functional authorities or communities. This resolution, which confirmed

[19] *Summary of Debates,* I, 5, pp. 267-268.
[20] *Summary of Debates,* I, 5, pp. 293-294.

earlier tentative recommendations, identifies another major plateau in the evolution of the European Movement. Its particular significance lies in the fact that those states that entertained more advanced ideas on integration were now free to proceed with their plans without objection from their associates in the Council of Europe that were content with things as they were. The latter had formally acknowledged, albeit grudgingly, that the apparatus at Strasbourg was not the final step in the process of integration and that those that wished to press forward should do so with at least the formally benevolent support of the states that were content with Strasbourg and wanted to go no further. For all practical purposes this meant that the six Continental nations, France, Italy, West Germany, and the Benelux, could elaborate their ideas of supranational authority and form what might become a sort of "Little Europe" within the orbit of the "Larger Europe" represented at Strasbourg.

Implied in the resolution, moreover, if not explicitly stated, was the hope that the elaboration of the new "authorities" or "communities," limited to only a few members, was not to be the permanent form of the proposed new Europe. Rather, such elaboration was simply a step that would provide an experimental approach to a federal organization. Some day such an organization, having a variety of functions and embracing all of the states at Strasbourg, might still come into being.

With that thought in mind it was provided in the resolution that member states of the Council of Europe be kept informed of developments during the negotiations of conventions for any specialized community or authority, that any authority that might be organized remain open to accession by all member states of the Council of Europe, and that administrative liaison be maintained between the governmental structure of any specialized authority and the regular organs of the Council. Even more specific on this point was the section of the Consultative Assembly's resolution that asserted in substance that the attainment of the ultimate objective of all "Europeans," namely, a broad European political authority, would be furthered by the prior development of the proposed "specialized authorities." [21] As if to emphasize this essentially

[21] See *Summary of Debates,* I, 2, 3, 4, p. 235; Council of Europe, Directorate of Information, *News Report,* Dec. 13, 1951, and No. 8, Sept. 1, 1951, p. 1.

constitutional change and its acceptance of that change, the Strasbourg Assembly considered a variety of suggestions for the proposed new "authorities." One was for a "political authority" with powers to deal with European security and foreign policy. This was voted down.[22] But two other resolutions, one for a "European authority on agriculture" and one on "European transport," were adopted. Steps were also taken to revive the defunct European army resolution and transform that into a project for a special authority limited to six states.

Only one more step had to be taken to secure official Strasbourg endorsement for this proposed new development in European integration. This was the acceptance of the Assembly resolution by the Strasbourg Committee of Ministers. Such acceptance was secured in the summer of 1951. In supporting the resolution, the Committee of Ministers reiterated the Assembly's views on specialized authorities, declaring the proposed procedure "should permit the Council of Europe to make progress in fields where it would not be possible to obtain the adherence of all Members, either because the questions involved do not interest them to the same extent or because of special difficulties which prevent certain Members from associating themselves with a course of action regarded by the others as desirable." [23] The Committee also stated that the resolution should serve as a guide until such time as the Council of Europe's Statute had been amended to provide for the new "authorities and the proposed liaison with the parent Strasbourg agency."

Thus, by the beginning of 1951, the European Movement was launched upon a new course. A few of the states in the Council of Europe, with the grudging blessing of others, were now going to federate piecemeal, a function at a time. They were going to create specialized supranational authorities or communities. Obviously it was not what the federalists had hoped for, but it was a procedure that might lead to greater things. It was not unreasonable to hope that in the course of time these piecemeal developments might provide the threshold of a United States of Europe to which the more optimistic federalists were committed.

[22] *Summary of Debates,* I, 5, p. 295.

[23] Council of Europe, Directorate of Information, *News Report,* Dec. 13, 1951. For text, see Council of Europe, *News,* No. 8, Sept. 1, 1951, p. 1.

7 The First Supranational Community of the "Six"—Coal and Steel

PROPONENTS of the specialized supranational "authority"—or "community" as it now came to be generally known—for "Little Europe" lost no time in pressing the advantage they had gained as the result of the more benevolent attitude exhibited toward such an idea by the two Strasbourg bodies at the end of 1950. For the time being, their maximum objective was to be the establishment of the projected community for coal and steel and perhaps one or two others like the European army, which had been suggested but which had not yet been too well articulated. Primacy was to be given to the coal-steel plan because its conception was already far advanced. Hence the influence and leadership of the proponents of the supranational communities for "Little Europe" were now placed behind a drive formally to organize this supranational community that M. Robert Schuman had originally proposed.

M. Schuman, in his capacity as French foreign minister, had outlined his proposal for such a supranational venture as early as May 9, 1950, and he had subsequently formally presented his views to the Strasbourg Consultative Assembly. M. Schuman's action had, however, been prefaced by several related efforts, which help to explain the appeal of this plan at this particular time. For example, early in 1950, just prior to the Korean War and the attendant demand for rearmament, the Steel Section of the Economic Commission for Europe had issued a report indicating that markets for steel were drying up and that producers were concerting steps to protect the industry. This of course anticipated, somewhat euphemistically, the revival of the European steel cartel, which had operated before World War II. Some months earlier, in December, 1949, the same economic condition in the industry had led the Economic Committee of the Strasbourg Consultative Assembly to recommend the establishment of a multinational steel authority, consisting of governments of steel producing and steel consuming states. This was to be empowered to define the general policy of the industry, particularly as respects investment, prices, and output. The Strasbourg recommendation had insisted that equilibrium in the industry could not be attained by relying upon isolated national policies that, it was alleged, were usually distinguished by the absence of action; neither, said the report, should reliance be placed upon private cartelization.[1] Recommendations of this committee, clearly reflecting a desire for supranational action, had in turn found their inspiration in the still earlier recommendations of the Westminster Economic Conference, called by the European Movement's International Council in April, 1949.[2] It had been developments such as these that had furnished the prologue for the bold initiative of M. Schuman when he introduced his plan to provide a supranational authority for coal and steel.[3]

Negotiations to develop an acceptable treaty embodying M. Schuman's ideas were initiated at Paris on June 6, 1950, a month after the French foreign minister had informally outlined his ideas, and these negotiations were continued for some months. Besides France, which also represented the Saar, the participating states were Italy, the German Federal Republic, and the Benelux countries. Since the formal suggestion of the project had come from the French government and not from the Council of Europe, the latter organization had no official standing in the conduct of the negotiations. Nevertheless, the Consultative Assembly of the Coun-

[1] André Philip, *The Schuman Plan, Nucleus of a European Community* (London: the European Movement, June 1951), pp. 5-6.

[2] See "Report of Basic Industries Committee," *Conference of Westminster, April 20-25, 1949, General Account and Resolutions,* pp. 17 ff.

[3] In the summer of 1949, the Consultative Assembly at Strasbourg had also discussed the related idea of European charters for private industrial companies and had spent much talk on the perennially popular theme of eliminating frontier restrictions on transport and trade. See *Summary of Debates,* I, 2, 3, 4, p. 182.

cil, having played the large role described in the preceding chapter in encouraging the Six to go forward with M. Schuman's plan, could hardly be ignored. It was accordingly kept fully informed about the ensuing discussions at Paris. Moreover, the Consultative Assembly did not hesitate to spread on the record its own views about the Schuman project. Representatives at Strasbourg discussed freely the proposed constitutional organs of the proposed Schuman Community and the purposes that, in their opinion, the Community should strive to achieve. A forum was thus provided for the states in the Council of Europe not represented at Paris and not favorable to a supranational solution; and indirectly, at least, they were given an opportunity to influence the Paris deliberations. Apparently somewhat fearful of being eclipsed, the debaters in the Consultative Assembly stressed the desirability of keeping membership in the proposed community open to other Strasbourg states than the original six should they wish to join subsequently. The Assembly also concerned itself with establishing formal liaison between itself and whatever organs the proposed Schuman Community might establish. At the conclusion of the Assembly's meetings in Strasbourg in November, 1950, appropriate recommendations were transmitted to Paris. Among these was the specific suggestion that, in constructing a parliamentary council for the Community, the six nations of the Community use their existing representatives in the Strasbourg Assembly instead of providing an entirely different set. With minor changes, this suggestion was, in fact, subsequently adopted at the Paris meetings and the interlocking parliamentary membership thus provides a rather direct form of liaison between Strasbourg and the Schuman Community.[4]

After enduring some rather severe strains, the Paris negotiations ended successfully on March 19, 1951, when the delegates of the six states in attendance initialed the Schuman Treaty. Probably the chief credit for this rather extraordinary feat in international negotiation and diplomacy ought to go to M. Jean Monnet, the French economist. It was he who really had elaborated M. Schuman's initial plan and it was he who provided the technical and intellectual leadership for the Schuman parley. Ratification of the treaty was completed by the six states in little more than a year, Italy having

[4] *Summary of Debates*, I, 2, 3, and 4, p. 237.

been the last to ratify. The Italian chambers completed action on the document on June 16, 1952. On August 10 of the same year, the first steps were taken to "set up shop" in Luxembourg, and on September 10 formal organization of the new European Community for Coal and Steel, to give it its official name, was completed at Strasbourg. Because it is a unique creation, and because it is the first multinational institution to be brought into being as a result of the contemporary movement to integrate at least part of Europe on a supranational basis, we shall examine rather carefully its proposed functions and structure.

Compromises required during the Paris deliberations changed many details in M. Schuman's original plan, but those compromises did not vitiate the plan's primary objective. That was to create a single market for coal and steel for the one hundred sixty million people inhabiting the six participating states. In the treaty, it was contemplated that such a market could be achieved over a five-year transitional period. The first logical step was to be the elimination, among the Six, of all tariff walls and other international restrictions such as quotas, exchange controls, and the like that might affect the distribution of coal and steel. Subsequently, a common customs frontier for these two primary products was to be established between the Six and the outside world.

A second major step needed to achieve the treaty's objective was to make the common market also a free market. To that end, the treaty gave authority to the Community to eliminate private cartelism and private marketing agreements. It also authorized the gradual abolition, in each of the six states, of discriminatory economic policies and practices such as national subsidies to economic constituencies or particular classes of firms, and legally enforced differential prices and wage levels in the coal and steel industries.

To make these changes in the existing legal and economic structure and achieve the prime purpose of a free common market required that discretionary authority be placed in the hands of the Community's agencies that would be clearly supranational; that is, the authority would have to be such that it could not be modified by national governments. In providing this authority, the treaty-makers have understandably sought to define it as precisely as possible. They have also sought to encourage the Community's organs to operate indirectly rather than to apply direct sanctions to person and property. The discretion thus lodged in the Community was also subjected to important limitations designed to protect existing national standards of living. Specific limitations on the Community's powers were incorporated in the treaty to protect less efficient and marginal industries from changes so precipitate or so drastic in nature that such industries might find themselves quite suddenly denied existing markets and the power to compete at all.

The treaty confided to the new Community not merely powers to be used to sweep away or gradually eliminate the legal and natural barriers to maintenance of a free market; it also provided powers of a more positive nature. These authorized organs of the Community to increase opportunities for investment, to encourage efficiency and thereby reduce costs, and to encourage the mobility of labor. In other words, the ultimate objective of this proposed experiment in supranationalism transcends even the concept of a common market and becomes the development of a more progressive and dynamic economy—one that will expand income and raise living standards. Indeed, both at Paris and at Strasbourg, when the Schuman Treaty was being whipped into shape, the point was frequently made that the proposed Community would be a failure unless it succeeded in constantly elevating the plateau of equilibrium between production and distribution and "leveled up" output and wages.

To carry out these obligations of a more positive nature and to encourage a more progressive economy, the Schuman Treaty conferred various appropriate prerogatives upon the Community's organization. The first of these was authority to use certain of its funds to encourage industrial modernization and expansion. When labor becomes surplus because of technological change or for other reasons, the Community may finance a labor retraining program, and it can also finance construction of homes for workmen in areas where there is a labor shortage. Individual governments in the Community retain the power to fix wages and regulate social security benefits, but the Community may make recommendations where wages and pensions are substandard and even impose fines upon industries that, by reducing wages unfairly, are held to be taking unfair advantage of their working force.

More directly concerned with the policy of expansionism are certain treaty provisions to promote investment. Since it was felt that the Community could make better terms on the international capital market than individual firms, the Community was authorized to borrow and then make its own loans to firms within its jurisdiction. It can also guarantee private loans to firms. For the latter purpose and to provide for its own administrative budget, it may collect as much as 1 per cent of the total annual value of production within the Community from the firms contributing to that production.

Structurally the core of the Community's organization is a so-called "High Authority" that is the effective instrument of planning and direction. The High Authority makes all the important decisions within the area of the Community's jurisdiction, sees to it that all decisions are carried out, and does all the staff work. To describe the High Authority as the "executive" of this supranational organization would be somewhat ambiguous, for this organ combines within its jurisdiction virtually all of the policy-making and administrative responsibilities of the Community. To inaugurate this agency, eight of its authorized nine members were chosen by the six national governments of the Community; the ninth member was selected by the eight previously chosen. Once organized, two members of the High Authority are to be replaced or reelected each year, one to be designated by the six governments represented in the Community and one to be designated by the existing members of the High Authority itself.

Attached to this central organ of the Community is a Consultative Committee. Producers, workmen, distributors and consumers are represented on this committee and the total membership approximates fifty persons.[5] The committee is essentially advisory. Before coming to any important decision, it is anticipated that the High Authority will review proposed action with the committee. In some instances, the committee must be consulted before the High Authority may act. The membership of the Consultative Committee is chosen by the Schuman Council of Ministers from a list of candidates furnished by various appropriate private organizations.

Of greater importance in the Schuman structure than the Consultative Committee is the Common Assembly, intended to dis-

[5] Schuman Treaty, Art. 18.

charge the responsibility of making the High Authority accountable according to parliamentary usage. Although such a body was clearly contemplated when the Schuman Plan was broached, the composition and relative importance of the Assembly in the institutional scheme of the Community are traceable, in large part, to the reiterated emphasis that the Strasbourg Consultative Assembly had placed upon the need for responsible administration and democratic accountability. If the Schuman Assembly had no other claim to recognition, its existence could be justified as the embodiment of the concern of Western European political leaders, expressed repeatedly and at a high intellectual level, of the danger inherent in allowing proposed supranational communities to evolve a sort of expert oligarchism that would avoid popular control.

The seventy-eight members of this Schuman Common Assembly may be chosen either by the respective parliaments of the six states in the Community or by popular electorates in each of these states. Apparently the intention is ultimately to have the membership elected popularly. In practice, partly to avoid duplication and partly to preserve the significance of the Strasbourg Consultative Assembly among the organs of an integrated Europe, the national contingents that go to the Strasbourg Assembly are virtually identical with those that attend the Schuman Assembly. A slight difference does exist because the Benelux states, in token of their peculiar importance in the industries involved in the Schuman Plan, have more representation on the Schuman than on the Strasbourg Assembly. Thus Belgium and Holland each have ten members in the Schuman body and only seven each in the Strasbourg body. Luxembourg has four in the new body and only three in the more general European organ. The Schuman Assembly is directed to meet at least once a year to review the action of the High Authority. It may ask questions of members of the High Authority and in other respects acts like a stockholders' meeting or a parliamentary committee of control. It has no legislative power nor initiative in determining policy such as is usually enjoyed by a parliament. Its most decisive prerogative is that of replacing the High Authority. This it may do in the admittedly unusual situation where, having discussed the report of the High Authority for at least three days, it then moves a vote of censure on the High Authority, which is subsequently supported by two-thirds of the Assembly's members.[6] If and when this unlikely event transpires, the High Authority must resign in a body and replacements for its nine members must be approved by the Assembly.

A third body, the Council of Ministers, is designed to preserve, in some degree, the principle of national sovereignty and action in the structure of the Schuman institutions. It was introduced at the behest of the Belgian and other governments that were fearful of too much coercive supranational authority in the Schuman Community, especially as originally proposed by the French. The Council of Ministers, unlike its counterpart in the structure of the Council of Europe, is primarily a liaison agency and has few, if any, decisive powers. Its purpose, according to the Schuman Treaty, is to harmonize and coordinate the action of the High Authority and that of the participating governments.[7] Just what this might involve is not too clear. Apparently it involves more or less regular consultation of the Council by the High Authority. The Council of Ministers' only decisive prerogative comes into play when the High Authority makes decisions affecting the general economy of member states of the Community in time of crisis. In such periods, it is assumed that national considerations will become paramount, and the supranational High Authority may then be reduced to the status of partner or even of a subordinate of the ministerial council when decisions are taken.

Finally, the fifth organ of the Schuman Community is the Court of Justice. Composed of seven judges elected for six years, this tribunal serves as an appellate body and is authorized to provide redress against the High Authority when that body has allegedly exceeded its jurisdiction and violated the rights of states or persons. Both private firms and member states of the Community may invoke the Court's authority. If the Court decides that the High Authority has acted contrary to the stipulations of the Schuman Treaty and hence in a manner that is *ultra vires,* the Court may annul the Authority's action. There is no appeal against the Court's decision.

The Schuman Court may thus exercise a potent veto on the

[6] Schuman Treaty, Arts. 23 and 24.
[7] Art. 26.

High Authority's action. In a formal sense its behavior and power are not dissimilar from those of a major European administrative court, which reviews actions of an administrative nature and determines whether or not they are *ultra vires,* but the Court's powers are in fact more nearly comparable to the powers of review over legislation exercised by courts in America, since the issue likely to come up for review is more political in character than narrowly administrative. The essentially political veto of the Court becomes even more important and more obvious in view of its power, under certain circumstances, to proceed beyond mere "legal" questions and review the economic justification of the High Authority's action. Discretion of that nature seems to inhere in the Court since, under certain circumstances, a state of the Schuman Community may appeal to it with the plea that a decision of the High Authority may cause serious and irreparable injury to that state's economy. If placed in operation on any sizable scale, such a prerogative might carry the Schuman Court to the top of the hierarchy of institutions in the Schuman Plan, and make it superior even to the High Authority.

As already indicated, this first European supranational community set up its administrative offices in Luxembourg on August 10, 1952, and its organization was completed at Strasbourg a month later. Various transitional steps, taken at intervals, brought into being delayed phases of the Community's authority, the culminating step, that providing for a common market for special steels, having been taken on August 1, 1954. In a subsequent chapter,[8] we shall review at length the five-year history of this intriguing creation for supranational action. At this point what is to be noted is the fact that the inauguration of the Community at Strasbourg on September 10, 1952, represents the first milestone along the road to the establishment of a kind of "syndicated federalism" for what was coming to be called "Little Europe." In the Luxembourg Community the proponents of this approach to united Europe now had a "going concern" that could serve as a model for other communities. Eventually they might dare to hope that the road that had opened would lead to a form of integration for Western Europe more effective politically and more sophisticated juridically than the form embodied in Strasbourg's Council of Europe.

[8] See p. 147.

8 The European Defense Community

HAVING SUCCESSFULLY ELABORATED a supranational community to manage the distribution of coal and steel among six European nations, the federal element among the integrationists proceeded to seek the development of the same sort of community for other purposes. For this extension of the supranational concept among the Six the logical candidate was the plan for a European army. The outline of such an army, it will be recalled, had been proposed by Sir Winston Churchill, who, spurred by the threats to European and world equilibrium inherent in the then existing war in Korea and by the Soviet danger in Europe, had offered his resolution for the establishment of a "European army" at the meeting of the Consultative Assembly of the Council of Europe in August, 1950. His resolution had come at almost the same time that M. Schuman had chosen to present his plan for the coal-steel pool.

Sir Winston's concept of a European military force had been formulated in very general terms, and it was not clear to his confreres at Strasbourg whether the military force he had in mind was to be subjected to the control of a supranational authority or involve merely the temporary linking together of various national contingents under a common military command much on the order of NATO. The phraseology he had used in his resolution is susceptible of either interpretation, although the Assembly, in amending the resolution before endorsing it, had rather clearly indicated that it intended to place the proposed army under supranational control.[1] Moreover, others at Strasbourg had suggested the idea

[1] On this point see article by the late Léon Marchal, "The Consultative Assembly . . . and the Political Problem of European Defence," *European Yearbook*, II (1956), p. 105. See also *supra* p. 65.

of a European army both before and after the British leader had proposed it, and some of these other suggestions also envisaged a military instrument of a supranational character. Indeed some days before Churchill had introduced his resolution in August, 1950, André Philip, the French Socialist, had offered a plan for such an army as one means of reconciling his countrymen to the prospect of German national revival and rearmament. M. Philip's idea, moreover, at least implied supranational control. At any rate he had indicated that the proposed army would be "financed by a European fund" and that the funds would have to be "backed by European taxes." [2]

When formally presented to the Strasbourg Assembly, Sir Winston's army resolution, it will be recalled, had been approved in principle by an overwhelming vote, although Hugh Dalton, spokesman of Britain's Labour government, had opposed the plan. Subsequently, the Committee of Ministers at Strasbourg vetoed the concept, alleging that it was outside the jurisdiction committed to the Council of Europe.[3] The ministers' frown, however, did not succeed in killing the plan. At that precise moment in history such an idea, proposed by a leader of the stature of Churchill, had too much appeal to succumb without a struggle, particularly since apparently only one or two members of the Committee of Ministers besides the British representative had opposed the plan, the majority having been inclined to support it.

Europe and the world were therefore not as surprised as they might have been when the army plan was revived almost immediately after its defeat in the Strasbourg Committee of Ministers. This time the sponsors were none other than the French prime minister, M. René Pleven, and his redoubtable foreign minister and champion *par excellence* of European causes, M. Robert Schuman. With them in the lists, and serving as their expert counselor, was that twentieth-century Abbé Sieyès, the drafter of supranational constitutions, M. Jean Monnet.

In a remarkably frank address to the Consultative Assembly on November 24, 1950, M. Schuman left no doubt as to the reasons why he and his colleagues were reviving the army plan and virtually

[2] *Summary of Debates,* I, 1, p. 15; see also Marchal, *op. cit.,* II, p. 103.
[3] *Summary of Debates,* I, 1, p. 5.

defying the Strasbourg Committee of Ministers. Those reasons could be distilled into two—namely, the desire to meet the American demand for German rearmament and the belief that national interests would be better served by an integrated European force, including Germany, than by the revival of a national Germany. The demand for German military contingents and their admission to NATO had been formulated by Secretary of State Dean Acheson at the NATO Council meeting in New York in September, 1950. At that meeting Mr. Acheson had called for the arming of ten German divisions. In the opinion of the French foreign minister this American policy made German military revival inevitable, but he also felt that such revival would be a lesser threat to France if German divisions were brought into a European command under a supranational authority. It was at that point that M. Pleven's government decided to offer, as a countersuggestion, the plan for a European army, which had been voted in principle at the August, 1950, session at Strasbourg.

M. Schuman went on to explain in greater detail why a supranational defense arrangement such as he had suggested was much to be preferred, at least by France, to the alternative of German national rearmament and direct German military participation in NATO. In its existing form the NATO system, said M. Schuman, did not offer France adequate guarantees against a rearmed Germany. The NATO command, he reminded his auditors, was not a supranational force. Its basic characteristic was a single command exercised over a variety of national contingents, each of which retained its identity. Under NATO, in other words, national military organizations were continued and national armies remained intact. Furthermore, said M. Schuman, the NATO system was intended to be temporary.

The European army plan, on the other hand, was intended by its authors to be a permanent arrangement. It was not to be "merely the consequence of a contractual arrangement, to be rescinded when desired." Hence whatever technical difficulties might attend such a plan as the creation of a supranational force, and they were admittedly many, the advantages far outweighed the liabilities, at least in the opinion of the French foreign minister. The nations allying themselves with such a plan would, in M. Schuman's opinion, be well advised to abandon "part of their autonomy in favour of a Commissioner or Minister of Defence under the supervision of a Committee of Ministers."[4] The French leader was certain that forces thus amalgamated under a permanent European command would remove or greatly mitigate the threat to France of a rearmed Germany. Instead of the rivalry between these ancient enemies, there would presumably ensue an indefinite period of essentially enforced cooperation and an eventual merging of national interests.

Here was a forthright plea for a supranational solution of an age-old military problem. It was a plea that added stature to the French contribution to the solution of world political organization. At the same time M. Schuman's plan appeared to provide the best if not the only rational safeguard for France against the time when Germany would once more be in a position to bring to bear upon her political and commercial relations with France her undoubted economic and demographic superiority.

For the leaders across the Rhine a supranational army had an equally potent appeal, if for somewhat different reasons. Chancellor Adenauer had endorsed the concept of a European army when Churchill and others had first proposed it, and he now did not hesitate to accept the Pleven-Schuman-Monnet plan in principle. The cordiality of the German response is explained in part by the national advantages that would accrue to Germany if the army plan were implemented. Most German political leaders in the Adenauer coalition looked upon it as a means of overcoming domestic indifference and outright resistance to remilitarization. But the chief value of the plan to Germany inhered in the fact that if the Germans supported it and joined the proposed European army, they would be able to extract, as a price for their support, an Allied agreement to end the occupation and restore the sovereignty and international equality of the postwar German Federal Republic. Indeed the Germans quickly made it clear that this would be the price of their acquiescence in the French plan for a supranational defense system. This was the major national advantage that the Germans hoped to gain. It was their *quid pro quo* for the special

[4] *Summary of Debates,* I, 1, p. 298.

advantage that France hoped to gain for herself if military integration did obviate the danger of German national superiority.

At the same time the Germans also had a long-range view of the value of military integration in a supranational system that approximated the enlightened views of M. Schuman and the chief French leaders. Chancellor Adenauer had long been a sincere advocate of European integration. He entertained as emphatic a desire as any of his French colleagues to use the device of military merger of national forces to ward off a possible policy of *revanche* in Germany and the prospect of a revival of militarism and its allied policy of national chauvinism. For the German leader, too, the European army was a means of insuring the German people against a revival of German militarism even as it was for the French a guarantee against such a revival. The ascription of mere opportunism to Adenauer in this matter, an accusation frequently made by his political adversaries, hardly does justice to the wisdom and moral stature of this first great postwar leader of Germany.

The first indication of the precise nature of the supranational military agency that the French were planning came on October 25, 1950, when M. Pleven outlined it before the French National Assembly. He declared his government sought "the creation, for the purposes of common defense, of a European army linked to the political institution of a united Europe." He said his plan stemmed directly from the original Churchill proposal and declared that as far as possible there should be a "complete merger of men and equipment" in a European army "under a single European political and military authority." [5] The Assembly was sufficiently impressed to support the French prime minister's outline of the plan by a vote of 343 to 225.[6] This, of course, was merely a vote on the general principle of the plan and not on the plan itself.

On the day this action was taken by the French legislature, the French government also informed London and Washington of the main features of the proposal. Apparently the idea the French were then advocating of employing the division as the basic unit of the proposed multinational army, each division to consist of combat teams from various nations, seemed unwieldy to the military ex-

[5] Quoted in Marchal, *op. cit.*, II, pp. 106-107.

[6] *Europe Today and Tomorrow* (Dec. 1953), p. 23.

perts and it did not win approval from the high command at NATO headquarters. As a result, a few weeks later at a meeting in Brussels, the United States prevailed upon Britain and France to accept the policy of including German contingents directly within the NATO structure.

At this point the Germans, having had the terms changed for them unilaterally, demanded a price for their acceptance of the revised policy that frightened France and caused both Washington and London to reconsider. This price was nothing less than full German rearmament with a national army, revival of the German General Staff, and a complete national complement of war industries. General Eisenhower's visit to Europe in January, 1951, seems to have convinced him that the Germans would demand such a price as a minimum alternative to their participation in a European army and he in turn convinced the Pentagon. When the German attitude also became clear to the French, they reiterated their fears of the policy of direct German involvement in NATO. They besought their allies to reconsider the entire project and revive the plan of a European army or a "European Defense Community," as the project now came to be called. Such reconsideration took place and the project of a Defense Community, bringing together France and Germany and the four remaining members of the Six, now became a firm policy. From that time forward, moreover, neither the United States nor its principal NATO allies wavered officially in their support of a supranational Defense Community until the project was finally rejected by the French in August, 1954.

Among the strongest supporters of the project from this time forward was General Eisenhower, both while serving as head of the NATO command and later after he had become president of the United States. At the same time the British government, somewhat anxious over charges stemming from some Continental sources that both Mr. Bevin, the late Labour foreign secretary, and Mr. Churchill, who had recently returned to power, were fundamentally opposed to the conception of a Defense Community, sought to be even more emphatic in its endorsement of the revived project than the United States. Britain, it declared, would not "merge" its forces in the proposed Community but Britain favored it wholeheartedly, supporting it with "no less vigour than the United States and for the same reasons."[7] The British government went on to express the wish that when the moment became opportune it might be "associated" with the projected Defense Community as closely as possible at all stages of its political and military development.[8]

Steps were now taken to iron out some of the administrative complexities and overcome some of the structural weaknesses detected in M. Pleven's original plan and develop a practical project that would secure the formal support of the governments of the Six and secure also the ratification of their respective parliaments. To that end, negotiations among representatives of the Six were inaugurated at Paris by the French government in February, 1951.[9] Almost a year later, that is, in January, 1952, after several major disputes among the negotiators over the precise form of German participation, disputes that threatened at least once to end in deadlock, the definitive plan for the European Defense Community came into being. One month later, the parliaments of both France and the German Federal Republic endorsed this plan in principle and by sizable majorities. In the case of the French National Assembly this was its second endorsement, the earlier one having been given at the request of M. Pleven when the idea of the Community had first been formulated by his government. Finally the Council of the NATO powers, meeting in Lisbon, gave its seal of approval to the draft of the proposed treaty. The treaty itself was signed by representatives of each of the Six at ceremonies in Paris on May 27, 1952.[10]

Thus by the spring of 1952 the idea of a European army, restricted to be sure to the Six or "Little Europe," but supranational as respects those six, had achieved the status of an official project. The treaty, which representatives of the Six had signed, asserted they had set up "A European Defense Community, supranational in

[7] "Britain and a European Army" in *Background Notes* issued by the British Embassy, Washington, D. C., Dec. 17, 1951 (mimeographed).

[8] *Europe Today and Tomorrow* (Dec. 1953), p. 23.

[9] Actually all European members of NATO were invited to the conference but only Belgium, Luxembourg, Italy, and West Germany accepted the invitation at the outset. Later the Netherlands joined the conference; others invited ignored the invitation or merely sent observers.

[10] For an account of the signing and summaries of the chief provisions of the EDC Treaty and ancillary documents, see *The New York Times,* May 28, 1952, pp. 1, 14.

character, comprising common institutions, common armed forces and a common budget." It further declared the intention of the treaty makers to incorporate those forces into the Atlantic system and operate under a single general staff. Diplomatic representatives of the Six had pledged their best efforts to secure the treaty's adoption by their respective national parliaments. What little more than a year before had been called the vaporings of dreamers had become a practical idea of statesmen and politicians, lauded by them as the keystone of the defense of Western Europe and of the entire free world. Ten months later, as we shall see, a special constituent assembly produced a draft constitution for a so-called supranational political community or limited federation of the Six.[11] Thus the year 1952-53 marks one of the high tides of the movement begun at Strasbourg in 1949 to fashion a limited territorial union of Europe on a supranational basis. Though this tide was to ebb again, the strong Europeans felt that victory was near for their effort to federate Europe on a syndicated basis.

Let us turn now to a closer examination of this project for a supranational defense organization. When M. Pleven had broached his plan, it had been the intention to integrate the various national forces by combining "combat teams" from more than one nation in single divisions of the proposed supranational force. Especially from the French point of view, this plan to integrate at the "regimental level" had the advantage of preventing the formation of actual German divisions. Thus it would have prevented the existence in the future of any large integral units of German troops. Integration at the "regimental level" would moreover have provided for a more intimate intermingling of the troops of different nationalities and thus have made the concept of common European service more meaningful to the average soldier.

For various reasons this plan of integrating "European forces" was deemed unwieldy by the professionals. Hence in the revised plan, which became the actual EDC Treaty, it was directed that integration of the forces should take place at the "divisional" rather than at the "regimental" level. Divisions of two or more nationalities were to be brought together as an army corps. Supply troops and

[11] See pages 99 ff.

artillery were to be of the same nationality as the corps commander. The forces thus assembled in the Community would have consisted of some forty divisions apportioned among the six member states as follows: France, fourteen; Germany, twelve; Italy, eleven; and the Benelux states, three divisions. All such troops were to wear a common Community uniform. In that respect at least they were to be "European." Although administratively less unwieldy than the plan of regimental integration first proposed by M. Pleven, there would still have been serious obstacles to effective liaison among units and commanding personnel. As the military analyst, Hanson Baldwin, has pointed out, at divisional command levels a host of interpreters, liaison officers and staff officers would have been required to insure necessary communication.[12]

The Community plan clearly envisaged a special and essentially inferior status for Germany. In the first place, of the twelve divisions planned as the German contribution to the Community forces, ten were to have been integrated in EDC army corps led by non-German commanders. This was a continuation of the policy envisaged in the combat team plan of troop integration of the original Pleven project, that is, to rearm Germany in such a manner as to discourage the identification of an integral German Army and a German High Command. In the second place, Germany was to be allowed to conscript or train no other troops than those to be supplied for the twelve divisions slated for EDC. All other members of the Community, on the other hand, were to be allowed to continue national forces although this authorization probably had little significance except in the case of France, where such troops were to have been used for occupation duty in Europe and for service in French territory overseas. In case of a clearly ascertained emergency situation the NATO command could even have authorized a member state of EDC to withdraw part of its EDC force for national duty overseas, a discretion that, as we shall see,[13] became the subject of contention later. In the third place, Germany was to occupy a special position toward NATO. As a matter of fact Germany was to be the only EDC member that was not directly a member of NATO. Her association with that body was to be an indirect one,

[12] *The New York Times*, Feb. 7, 1953.
[13] See p. 115.

achieved exclusively through her membership in EDC and the integration of Community troops in NATO. This association was defined in one of the ancillary documents that were signed when the treaty proper was signed. Finally, Germany was to be denied the right to make certain types of weapons including nuclear weapons or weapons useful in bacteriological or chemical warfare. This essentially discriminatory position for Germany in EDC arose out of Germany's defeated and disarmed status and the desire to reassure the French. It was a position that the Germans were then willing to accept without official demur.

As respects its directing and administrative structure, the new Community was to have relied heavily upon the agencies already established for the Schuman Community. The Schuman court was to have been used to decide issues arising out of the EDC Treaty and the operation of the proposed new Community. The Schuman Common Assembly, suitably enlarged by three additional members from each of the three major powers in the Community, would have served as the agency of popular control, and the Council of National Ministers of EDC would have been identical with the body having a similar name in the European Coal and Steel Community.

The only new "European agency" that would have been instituted under EDC was a so-called Commissariat of nine members elected for six-year terms. Comparable to the High Authority of the Schuman project, this agency was to have been the directing body of the new Defense Community. In some instances it could have taken decisions by majority vote and these decisions were to have been binding on the national members. Hence, to that degree it would have been a supranational body in the same sense as the Schuman High Authority. But the scope of the supranational authority contemplated for this new agency would not have been comparable to that of the High Authority, the Commissariat having been greatly limited in its discretion by the powers committed to the Council of National Ministers, the agency whose six members acted as the protectors of the sovereign rights of their respective states. This limitation is hardly surprising in an area as sensitive as that of national defense, perhaps the most characteristic and most jealously guarded of all the sovereign powers of the nation-state. What is surprising is the fact that the treaty makers did succeed in effecting some limitation on the sovereign rights of each of the six states in the Community and in defining a discretion that approximated supranational jurisdiction for the Commissariat.

The limitations imposed by the Council of National Ministers upon the Commissariat are apparent in the various prerogatives confided to the Community. According to the treaty, the members of the Commissariat were to have been given power to formulate and execute plans for organizing the military forces of the Community, to direct the military schools and officer-training institutions, and to decide upon the territorial distribution of troops in accordance with the directives of the NATO command. The Commissariat was also directed to prepare budgets and fix the resulting contributions of each of the six states, procure supplies, let contracts, and exercise control over production of armament, munitions, and military supplies in each of the six member countries. But on most of these areas of jurisdiction the decision of the Commissariat was subject to the requirement that the Council of National Ministers give unanimous approval. Thus the characteristic protection of national sovereignty, that is, the requirement of unanimity, and hence the power of veto by a single state, was preserved for most important decisions within the Community.

In the case of the Community budget, the total sum was to have been fixed by the Commissariat and each nation's contribution toward that budget total was likewise to have been proposed by the supranational EDC agency. But again, in order to be valid, both the total sum budgeted and the individual contributions requested had to be confirmed by the Council of National Ministers, which in effect meant that each country could both veto the entire budget and nullify its own contribution.

The most important supranational power confided to the Commissariat of the EDC Treaty was that of placing orders for matériel within the armaments program authorized by the Community's Council of National Ministers. The purpose was to provide for specialization and a balanced armament manufacturing program within the Community area without regard for national boundaries. Powers were also given to regulate the export and import of such matériel.

Judicial powers relating to military matters confided to the Community Court were also essentially supranational. Normally jurisdiction was to be confined to determination of the limits of discretion confided to functionaries under the treaty, apparently also including the prerogatives of the Commissariat; but, in addition, the Court was to decide questions of damages resulting from actions by the military and to exercise even some of the penal functions committed to military tribunals in Continental countries. In addition, it was to have had jurisdiction of a limited nature over infractions of the military code by military personnel, that is, of military law proper. Also essentially supranational in the new program was the plan to abandon military training schools on a national basis and submit their establishment and curriculum to the jurisdiction of the EDC authorities.[14]

Various ancillary documents were elaborated and signed at the time the EDC Treaty came into being. Their provisions were intimately connected with the treaty and they may therefore be considered an integral part of the entire project. One of the more important of these ancillary documents was the protocol defining the relationship between the proposed Community and NATO. In this the six Community states were assured that any attack on them would be regarded as an act of aggression upon the states in NATO and would be resisted accordingly. A reciprocal guarantee was undertaken by the six Community states. This particular protocol has additional significance since it constituted the avenue through which Germany, the only nonmember of NATO in the proposed Defense Community, would have been included in the guarantee of the North Atlantic Alliance.

Two other protocols signed at the same time as the EDC Treaty were chiefly designed to give France certain guarantees against Germany. The first of these was a three-power declaration in which the United States, Britain, and France agreed that any threat to EDC would be regarded as a threat to their own security and treated as such. In giving this guarantee, they asserted their intention "to station such forces on the Continent of Europe, including the Federal Republic of Germany, as they deem necessary and

[14] See analysis of supranational features of treaty in *Europe Today and Tomorrow* (May 1954), pp. 7 ff.

appropriate to contribute to the joint defense of the North Atlantic Treaty area. . . ." This three-power declaration also included guarantees for the city of Berlin. The second protocol was one between Britain and the six members of the proposed Community in which, on a reciprocal basis, Britain promised to give "military and other aid" to any one of these six states if it were attacked. The protection that France sought to secure through these two protocols was assurance of assistance should the day ever come when the German Federal Republic decided to secede from the Community and leave the French exposed to a German force of superior strength. In conjuring up such a possibility there was never far removed from French speculation the course of events that might ensue if East and West Germany were to be reunited and the German nation once again assume its maximum strength in Central Europe.

Finally the fourth document was the "treaty of peace" or "contractual agreement" between the German Federal Republic on the one hand and the three major wartime allies, the United States, Britain, and France, on the other. Though an indispensable preliminary to the establishment of EDC, this treaty was not signed at Paris on May 27 with the other EDC documents but was signed at Bonn the day before. In this agreement, Germany's sovereign status was formally restored, conditions were removed from her right to rearm, and the three powers that had occupied her territory since 1945 gave up their prerogatives. Probably the principal condition in this peace contract and certainly the essential one for the EDC project was the provision that Germany's newly regained sovereignty would be realized if and when EDC became a going concern with Germany a charter member.[15]

These then were the more important aspects of the supranational conception for the security of Western Europe outlined in the European Defense Community project. To have elaborated the various compromises required to bring about a meeting of minds on a conception as bold as this was indeed an achievement. European statesmanship can point to few developments after World War II of which it may be prouder than its success in formulating

[15] For the essential provisions of these various documents see *The New York Times*, May 28, 1952.

the European Defense Community Treaty and obtaining for it the signatures of the representatives of the six nations involved. The significance of the accomplishment was not lost on the statesmen gathered in the Clock Room of the Quai d'Orsay on May 27, 1952. Secretary of State Acheson was the most articulate. He said he wished to express his "profound conviction that what we have witnessed today may well prove to be one of the most important and most far-reaching events of our lifetime. We have," he continued, "seen the beginning of the realization of an ancient dream—the unity of the free peoples of Western Europe." [16] History was to record that this American statesman's conviction was somewhat premature, but the ultimate fate of his handiwork and that of his colleagues in no way diminishes the stature of the conception that they gave the world. For vision, courage, and the kind of disciplined yet lofty thinking that distinguishes the highest statesmanship, few efforts of recent history match the record of those who created the developed plan for a European Defense Community.

[16] *The New York Times*, May 28, 1952.

9 Federation—a Second Attempt

WITH THE PROGRAM to establish supranational communities now seemingly well under way, the time appeared ripe to the strong Europeans at the end of 1952 for a second attempt to bring into being a multipurpose federal European structure. As was suggested earlier, the grand strategy of such Europeans had been to regard the single- or limited-purpose supranational community as one step, albeit a major one, in the elaboration of a supranational community with more comprehensive aims. Such a community, in turn, would come close to satisfying the substantive as well as the juridical canons of a true federation. Undoubtedly the conception of a united Europe with supranational governmental organs varied with the individual even among the supranationalists, and the passage of time and changing political circumstances had probably produced still further modifications in individual views since 1947. Nevertheless, in its basic features, the conception has remained the same for all those committed to a truly united Europe. What they had continued to envision was a European structure with supranational political organs competent to act in various areas. To be sure, the structure thus envisioned would not now comprehend the "Greater Europe" of 1947 but only the six states of "Little Europe." Hope remained strong, however, that, given time and an opportunity to demonstrate the value of supranational institutions, a federation of "Little Europe" would eventually be broadened territorially into a "Greater Europe" that might embrace all of free Europe.

In moving toward this new multipurpose federal structure, its proponents felt that the next step should be the creation of still another community, to be known as the European Political Community. During a transitional period, the new community might be expected to coordinate the activity of the Schuman Community and of the European Defense Community, the treaty for which, it was then confidently anticipated, would soon be ratified by the parliaments of the Six. In due course the Schuman Community and EDC would be consolidated. A single set of supranational organs would then come into existence and "Little Europe" would possess a respectable federal governmental structure.

Initially the powers of this federation would be only those prerogatives identified in the Schuman and EDC treaties; but to the supporters of effective integration it seemed more than likely that once the new structure was set going it would acquire additional prerogatives because of the demonstrated inadequacy of the authority already committed to the Schuman and Defense Communities. The nature of this reasoning was made rather clear by Chancellor Konrad Adenauer in a notable address that he delivered in New York in April, 1953, under the auspices of the American Committee on United Europe. Directing his remarks toward the pending European Defense Community Treaty, the German leader expressed his conviction that a Political Community, with broad and relevant powers, would become a necessity if the EDC's objective of a common defense program, developed under a single authority, was to be attained. "Having created a European Defense Community," said the German chancellor, "can it be imagined that the six participating countries would willingly send their sons to serve in this European army unless a fundamental unity existed in their foreign policies? The establishment of a six-nation Defense Community must lead to a unification—at least to a *rapprochement*—in the field of foreign policy. Thus the end of this development appears to be the creation of a European Political Community." [1]

Other considerations affirmed the desirability of consolidating existing and contemplated supranational developments. However successful the single-purpose community might be in carrying for-

[1] Address by Dr. Konrad Adenauer, Waldorf-Astoria Hotel, New York, Apr. 6, 1953, p. 12; text published by the American Committee on United Europe.

ward its limited objectives, observers were well aware of its inherent structural and administrative liabilities. Much of the regulatory discretion over political and economic matters, the exertion of which might some time prove essential to the attainment of the objectives of the Schuman and Defense Communities, remained with the nation state. Neither of these communities, or any similar single-purpose structure that might be created in the future, operating in isolation, was ever likely to be given power really commensurate with the responsibility placed upon it. The obvious remedy was to consolidate existing authority at the supranational level, eventually augment it, and then vest the resulting powers, together with the responsibility of achieving transnational objectives, in a single set of federal political and administrative organs.

Especially pointed in this respect were the comments of the French M.R.P. leader, M. Pierre-Henri Teitgen. "A single Europe," said M. Teitgen, "was their [the federalists'] goal, but behold they had already made two Europes: the Europe of the Coal and Steel Community, with its little Government and its little Parliament; and the Europe of the Defense Community, also with its little executive and its little parliament. Were they going on along this particular road to construct a third Europe, and a fourth? A transport Europe, with its little executive and its little parliament, and then an agricultural Europe also with its little organisms? It would no longer be Europe; it would be anarchy." M. Teitgen went on to reiterate the obvious remedy, a "single Europe." To achieve such a Europe, he said, its friends need "*absolutely* a single authority" [italics in original].[2] For M. Teitgen, too, the time had come for taking the final step envisioned when the first single-purpose community had been broached in 1950, viz., the elaboration of a single federal authority.

Closely related to M. Teitgen's argument as to the timeliness of proceeding to integrate the Communities into a single structure was another that appealed especially to those concerned with the principle of popular control. In the opinion of such persons, the autonomous, single-purpose communities inevitably brought about an oligarchic type of administration that discouraged formal efforts

[2] *Europe Today and Tomorrow* (Nov. 1953), p. 8.

at democratic control. Nor did they discern an effective remedy for this trend toward oligarchy either in the Common Assembly of the Schuman Community, already in existence, or in the somewhat larger assembly contemplated under EDC, even though these might eventually be consolidated into a single body to supervise both Communities. Either as separately conceived in the respective treaties or operating eventually as a single body, they failed to satisfy the criteria of a truly democratic instrument. Aside from the fact that their jurisdiction was too limited, there was the far more serious criticism that neither of these bodies received its mandate directly from the people at the polls. Like the representatives of the Consultative Assembly at Strasbourg, members of both the Schuman and EDC assemblies were the creatures of national legislatures and governments. For those seeking to institutionalize democratic control of policy and administration within the structure of a more unified Europe, nothing would suffice short of a representative legislature, at least part of whose members would be elected directly by the people.

Here then were some of the reasons, both fundamental and tactical, why, in the autumn of 1952, those who had created the single- or limited-purpose community for "Little Europe" felt that the time had come to inaugurate within that territorial area a second effort toward federation—comparable in its objective to one the federalists had made in the Strasbourg Assembly in 1949-1950, which had then proved to be abortive.

Anticipating some such development, Dr. de Gasperi and certain of his colleagues had insisted upon including in the final draft of the Defense Community Treaty an article that would spell out the formal steps to be taken if a more comprehensive "political" community, approximating a "federation," were to be elaborated. This was the now famous Article 38 of that treaty. Under its terms the role of a constitutional assembly to plan for such a federation was to be discharged by the popular assembly that EDC was to bring into existence, an assembly that, it will be recalled, was to be a slightly enlarged version of the Schuman Assembly. This assembly not having come into existence, it was decided, in September, 1952, that the responsibility for drafting a treaty for the proposed Political Community, or federation of the Six, should be entrusted to the

Common Assembly of the existing Schuman Community. Accordingly this body became invested with the task. Since the proposed EDC Assembly was to have had 87 members, or 9 more than the Schuman Assembly, that number of delegates was added to the Schuman Assembly. These delegates came from Italy, the Federal Republic of Germany, and France. Thus enlarged, the Schuman Assembly, officially designated for this task the "Ad Hoc Assembly," formally began its work on September 10, 1952. On that day, instructions to the Ad Hoc Assembly to draft a treaty for a European Political Community were issued by the foreign ministers of the Six at a meeting in Luxembourg. The Assembly was requested to present a draft within six months, that is, by March, 1953. Ministerial instructions to the Assembly emphasized the desirability of a plan that would maintain close liaison between any new supranational structure among the Six and the organs of the Consultative Assembly at Strasbourg.

Some of the Ad Hoc Assembly's spadework had already been done by a special committee that had been appointed by the Strasbourg Assembly in July, 1952. This had been informally advised by certain American specialists and by representatives of the private European Movement.[3] To expedite the detailed work of preparing a preliminary draft of a treaty, the Assembly appointed a working constitutional committee of twenty-six under the leadership of Herr von Brentano of the German Federal Republic. Actual responsibility for drawing up the plan of the proposed Political Community fell to this committee, and during the next few months it carried forward the work of compromise and draftsmanship with surprising speed. Toward the end of January, 1953, it met for a four-day period at Strasbourg to discuss major issues that had arisen and on which it wished to seek the advice of the Ad Hoc Assembly. Then, on March 6, the committee formally presented to the Assembly the draft of the proposed treaty. Four days later, on March 10, 1953, this draft was adopted by the Assembly by a vote of 50 to 0.

Although virtually every political element except the extreme Right and Left was represented in the national delegations of the

[3] See Robert R. Bowie and C. J. Friedrich, *Studies in Federalism* (Boston, 1954), pp. xxv ff.

Ad Hoc Assembly, the majority of all represented political faiths consisted of confirmed federalists or, at any rate, of believers in a supranational solution for Europe. This explains in part the unanimous endorsement that those present and voting in the Assembly gave the committee's work. It helps also to explain the celerity with which the committee completed its work.

But the unanimity indicated in the vote of endorsement must not obscure the existence of a strong opposition at Strasbourg. Actually some 37 members of the Ad Hoc Assembly did not indicate their opinion on the draft treaty either because they were absent or because, though present, they did not choose to vote. According to the record, five members of the Assembly formally abstained from voting. Three of these were French Socialists led by Guy Mollet, chairman of the French Socialist party and subsequently a French prime minister. Though Mollet was normally a strong supporter of supranational integration, he and his two dissenting colleagues felt that the draft treaty was so drawn that it would prevent Britain's adherence. They were opposed to going forward with any supranational solution among the Six that, in their opinion, would discourage future British adherence or association and thus deny France the protection that might arise from a direct tie with Britain if and when—as Mollet feared—Germany might become the strongest member of the federation. Another French non-Socialist delegate abstained for essentially the same reason. Three supporters of General de Gaulle simply boycotted the voting because they opposed the principle of international federation, and the entire German Social-Democratic element in the Ad Hoc Assembly likewise refused to have anything to do with the proceedings, nominally on the ground that support of the new Community would necessarily imply support of the European Defense Community. To that organization, of course, the German Socialists were unalterably opposed.[4] In the course of time, as we shall see, the influence of these various opposition elements grew and contributed not

[4] A description of the ratification proceedings and an analysis of the opposition appear in Basil Karp, "The Draft Constitution for a European Political Community," *Report from Strasbourg* (May 1954). This article, appearing originally in *International Organization,* was republished by the American Committee on United Europe.

a little to the shelving not only of this new federal plan for Western Europe but of the European Defense Community and, at least temporarily, of the whole idea of supranationalism.

As respects the purely governmental aspects of this limited federal structure, the chief innovations were the provision for a popular parliamentary body and for a limited form of responsible government. The proposed parliament of the Community was to have been bicameral, and the members of one of the houses, to be known as the Senate, were to have been chosen by the parliaments of the Community's constituent states,[5] a procedure for which numerous precedents already existed among "European assemblies." The contemplated Senate was to have had 87 members.

In the case of the new Community's other, or lower, parliamentary body, which was to have had the title of Peoples' Chamber, the drafters of the treaty took advanced ground and came close to satisfying, in several respects, the criteria of a truly democratic "parliament of Europe." In this chamber, representatives were to have been allotted to each constituent state of the Community. France was to have had the largest number (70) because of her overseas position, and the states of the Benelux were to have had more than might have been allotted them under the principle of strict demographic proportionality. But though allotted to the individual member states as national quotas, these representatives were to have been elected directly by the people. The treaty suggested that they were to represent "the peoples united in the Community," and elections were to have been held on a Community-wide basis according to a qualified system of proportional representation. It was presumed, although somewhat wistfully, that the political parties engaging in these prospective elections would eventually command a following that would be "European" and not merely national in character, and that such parties would champion causes and advocate policies that transcended national boundaries. The Peoples' Chamber was to have had a membership of 268.[6]

In the composition of the Peoples' Chamber, moreover, there was also reflected the belief that popular loyalty to such an ideal as

[5] *Draft Treaty Embodying the Statute of the European Political Community* (cited hereafter as *Draft Treaty European Community*), Art. 16.

[6] See *Draft Treaty European Community*, Arts. 11-15.

European integration demanded tangible democratic institutions upon which such loyalty could be focused and in which the ideal of a European community might be given practical political and administrative expression. Like Bismarck when he created the German Reichstag, those who planned the proposed Peoples' Chamber believed that only through some sort of representative popular forum could proponents of the new political structure enlist for that structure the interest and loyalty of the rank and file.

The experts preparing for the European Political Community apparently hoped that the composition of the proposed Peoples' Chamber would go far to satisfy those critics that believed the existing supranational communities had been developed without adequate democratic safeguards. As a further contribution to the satisfaction of this aspiration, the drafters of the treaty sought to lay the foundation for a system of parliamentary control and make the prospective Peoples' Chamber the focus of such a system. In this effort, however, they were not too successful. Partly because of the limitations resulting from persisting national loyalties, and partly because it was feared that a "responsible" executive, along traditional lines, might imperil the stability of the federation, the planners compromised on this institution.

A status equivalent to that of a prime minister in a "responsible" parliamentary system had been intended for the president of the European Executive Council, the official name of the proposed federation's executive body. But instead of making it possible for partisan political forces in the Peoples' Chamber to determine who this leader should be—a procedure more or less characteristic of all contemporary parliamentary regimes—it was stipulated that he be elected by a majority vote of the Senate or less popular chamber.[7] The obvious explanation for this requirement was the belief that members of the proposed Senate, because of the way in which they were chosen, would be more amenable to the control of the nations of the Community and could be depended upon to rebuff popular majorities in the lower house if a particular state's interests were threatened. Since the president of the Community himself was to choose the remaining members of the executive, the Senate, for

[7] *Ibid.*, Art. 28.

all practical purposes, would have controlled the complexion of the entire Community executive. This conclusion is reinforced by the fact that the Senate was intended to have the additional power of ousting the incumbent president and electing a new one, this action being equivalent to a vote of no confidence in the previous administration and requiring the resignation of the entire Executive Council.

A limited power to force resignation of the Executive Council was apparently intended to inhere also in the Peoples' Chamber, but the prerogative was hedged about by restrictions intended to safeguard the integrity of the executive and to prevent irresponsible action by the Chamber. Thus in order to express its disapproval of the Executive Council's policy and force the appointment of a new Council, the Peoples' Chamber was to have been required to muster a vote of censure consisting of at least three-fifths of its entire membership.[8] Under such restrictions it was hardly likely that "responsible government" in the proposed new federation could have acquired any real significance comparable, for example, to the significance attached to that institution, as an instrument of popular control, in such leading regimes as the French and the British.

Except for this somewhat complicated procedure for instituting a system of parliamentary democracy, the political and administrative structure planned for the new Community would have exhibited little change from the pattern developed in the earlier communities. The instrumentalities identified in the pending EDC Treaty and those already in operation in the Schuman Community would simply have been replaced by the appropriate organs of this proposed "Community of Communities." When the anticipated process of consolidation had been completed there would thereafter have been only one set of federal organs for the Six, that is, the bicameral parliament, already identified, consisting of the Senate and the Peoples' Chamber and the federal executive, also previously identified, to be known as the "European Executive Council." The three auxiliary organs would have consisted of a federal

[8] *Draft Treaty European Community,* Art. 31. If a motion of no confidence received less than a three-fifths majority, the Executive Council was expected either to resign or dissolve the Peoples' Chamber and order new elections.

Court, an Economic and Social Council, and a Council of National Ministers. Apparently only the existing directing agency of the Schuman Community, that is, the High Authority, was to have been continued and to have enjoyed a somewhat ambiguous existence under the proposed executive council of the new federation as "an administrative body having the character of a board." [9]

When proposals to establish the new "Community of Communities" were broached, supporters inclined toward a federation hoped that the promised federal system would encompass several prerogatives in addition to those already spelled out in the Schuman and EDC treaties. These hopes were not realized. In the draft treaty for the Political Community supranational authority remained at about the level that had been developed in plans for the first two communities. To be sure, the new treaty was quite discursive in describing the proposed Political Community's power to tax and to engage in foreign relations, but when the relevant phraseology has been properly discounted, the net accretion of new power intended was miniscule.

Actually the fiscal prerogatives of the new European parliament were largely limited to such powers of budgeting, taxing, and securing contributions from member states as had already been defined in the two earlier supranational treaties. In order better to promote the various economic and security objectives for which the new federal structure was created, the treaty directed the Community to "ensure that the foreign policies of member states are coordinated." To that end, the proposed Community executive was authorized to act as the "common representative" of the Six in international matters whenever the Council of National Ministers of the new Community unanimously directed it to act in that manner.[10] Moreover the role of representative did not necessarily entail any discretion to determine the policies to be pursued. Such a discretion was not likely to be given very often if indeed it was given at all.

The response made in the draft treaty to the hope originally entertained of broadening supranational jurisdiction so as to develop the long-sought common Western European market was somewhat

[9] *Ibid.*, Art. 63, para. 2.
[10] *Ibid.*, Art. 69.

more generous than that made to satisfy the desire for a common foreign policy. Indeed Article 82 of the draft treaty was quite explicit on this subject, stipulating that it would be the responsibility of the new Community to "establish progressively a common market among the Member States based on the free movement of goods, capital, and persons." The draft treaty further declared it to be the responsibility of the Community to "foster the coordination of the policy of the Member States in monetary, credit, and financial matters" in order to achieve the aims of such a market. Relying on the precedents created by the Schuman Plan, the drafters of the treaty also made plans for a so-called "readaptation fund" to be financed by contributions, loans, and a 5 per cent tax on armament production, the proceeds of which were to be used for the modernization of industry and to help workers bear the shock of temporary unemployment and displacement.

But the authority of the proposed federal organs to act in this sphere, however seemingly generous, continued to be so hedged about with special restrictions that it probably could not have become very significant even if the Community had been established. In the first place a moratorium on any legislative action was to have been observed for one year after the treaty went into effect. Thereafter, for a period of five years, the federal executive might have developed proposals for legislation, but they would have needed the unanimous support of the Council of National Ministers in which each member state of the Community had an equal voice. After six years the federal parliament might have proceeded with legislative proposals in this area, coming from the executive, provided the Council of National Ministers approved the proposals. To become law, such proposals would have required the support of a simple majority of the Peoples' Chamber and a two-thirds majority of the Senate. Even then, however, any member state of the Community might have negatived the action, at least temporarily, by appealing to a special Community arbitral tribunal to suspend the application of the legislation on the plea that it would cause "fundamental and persistent disturbances" to its economy.[11]

Thus, although political instrumentalities for supranational action

[11] *Draft Treaty European Community,* Chapter V.

had been set up in the draft treaty and the concept of a common market had been rather clearly formulated, it had apparently not yet become possible to free the desired supranational discretion from national leading strings and allow it to operate without encountering an arbitrary national veto. But these limitations, serious as they undoubtedly were, should not be allowed to obscure the accomplishment inherent in the draft treaty. Whatever its drawbacks, the treaty was a great step forward in the development of the public law of a future federal Europe. In it had appeared a comprehensive and detailed plan for establishing over a large portion of that continent a single set of political organs that for certain purposes would have enjoyed a discretion clearly beyond the control of the national state. For the first time in recent history, moreover, such a plan appeared to be a feasible one from the standpoint of practical politics and to enjoy some prospect of being adopted. At any rate, practical politicians had formulated it, endorsed it, and recommended that it become a part of the political structure of Europe. Hence whatever the ultimate fate of the treaty and of the federal plan of government that it formulated, the mere fact that responsible political leaders and experts in public law could have conceived of such a plan, worked out the compromises necessary to elaborate it, and presented it to the world as a potentially viable system of government constitutes an enduring achievement in the art of statecraft. It remained now to determine whether a plan, conceived under such auspices and having such recommendations, would win the approval of public opinion among the Six, and whether the exigencies of the extant political situation in each of these states in the months after March, 1953, would promote a temper favorable to ratification.

10 Federation Fails a Second Time

AMONG THE CONSIDERABLE MAJORITY of the Ad Hoc Assembly that on March 10, 1953, had voted to accept the draft treaty for the Political Community, enthusiasm over the prospect of securing limited federation among the Six had reached a high pitch. This time, unlike the situation that had obtained in 1949 and 1950 when the first abortive attempt to federate had been launched, the six states of "Little Europe" already had one supranational community in actual operation and another apparently far along toward adoption. Moreover, their representatives had just endorsed overwhelmingly a plan to amplify, coordinate, and unify these two communities into a kind of super-supranational community that both politically and in a juridical sense could claim to be a respectable federal structure. Understandably the mood in the House of Europe at Strasbourg where this action had taken place was an optimistic one. Whatever the tribulations that might lie in store for the draft treaty, now that it was really to be submitted to the parliaments of the six states for ratification, few of "Little Europe's" leaders appeared to doubt that the outcome would be favorable. Paul-Henri Spaak, who by 1953 had become one of the most stalwart champions of the cause of union and who had served as the Ad Hoc Assembly's chairman, gave voice to this prevailing mood. In his concluding remarks to his colleagues at Strasbourg, he described their vote on the draft treaty as a decisive step toward union. He thereupon exhorted them to go back to their respective parliaments and not relax their efforts in favor of the treaty until "the United States of Europe has been born from a divided Continent." [1]

[1] *The New York Times*, Mar. 11, 1953.

But the tide that had produced the Schuman Community and the EDC Treaty and that had carried the whole supranationalist movement in Western Europe to the high point of the action on the Political Community on March 10 now began to ebb. Even before the meetings at Strasbourg had been brought to a close M. Bidault, France's foreign minister at the time, had sounded a note of caution if not of gloom. In accepting the draft treaty for the new federal Community on behalf of his colleagues among the Six he reminded the treaty's proponents of the "inevitable division of labour between men with bold and independent minds," such as those who had been directly involved in drafting the treaty and "governments whose honour and impediment it is to carry the responsibility."[2] To be sure, at a meeting of the foreign ministers of the Six, held at Baden-Baden on August 8, most of the basic assumptions upon which the draft treaty rested were restated and the world was assured once more, albeit somewhat falteringly, of the unanimity that prevailed among the six states in their desire to set up a supranational Political Community. But the resolutions adopted at the Baden-Baden meeting suggested that the whole idea of such a community had reverted once more to the stage of generalities and that the ministers had already found it necessary to discard the carefully formulated phraseology of the Strasbourg document.[3]

Subsequent meetings of the foreign ministers' deputies at Rome in September, 1953, and of the ministers themselves at The Hague, three months later, merely confirmed the trend away from the Strasbourg plan for the Political Community and the growing opinion in Europe that the governments of the Six would never ratify that plan. At The Hague the meeting dissolved in what one journalist described appropriately as a "blaze of ambiguity."[4] None of the Six wanted a transnational authority that was "veto-proof" against the action of any one state. Some wanted to make the Council of National Ministers in the proposed Community virtually a third house, thus insuring a national veto upon the action of the Community par-

[2] Quoted in Karp, "The Draft Constitution for a European Political Community," p. 16, cited in preceding chapter.

[3] See Resolutions in *Council of Europe News,* Vol. 3, No. 9 (Sept. 1953), pp. 1-2.

[4] *European Review,* No. 38 (Dec. 1953), p. 8.

liament. Others wished to have the Community executive chosen directly by the national governments. Proposals were also made to limit the authority and circumscribe the procedure of the Community and its organs. In other words, each of the Six, with the possible exception of the Federal Republic of Germany, had begun to shy away from a supranational structure.[5] Although none of the foreign ministers wanted to assume responsibility before world opinion for overtly rejecting the draft treaty for the Political Community, it was becoming clear, only nine months after the Ad Hoc Assembly had so enthusiastically endorsed that document at Strasbourg, that none of the foreign ministers of the Six felt his national parliament would accept it.[6]

The second thoughts of the Six about the Political Community and the mounting objections of their foreign ministers toward that project but reflected the tenor of the much more important and more passionate debate then being conducted among the Six concerning EDC. The treaty for that institution, it will be recalled, had been signed by the governments on May 27, 1952. By March, 1953, when the draft treaty for the Political Community was signed at Strasbourg, EDC had thus been awaiting ratification by the various parliaments for some ten months. Not only was the fate of the Political Community tied to the fate of EDC in the sense that both relied for their acceptance upon a public opinion favorable to supranational institutions; the Political Community's very *raison d'être*, as we noted earlier, was logically dependent upon the prior acceptance of EDC and its establishment as a going institution. Unless the Defense Community became a reality, there was scarcely any need for the proposed Political Community since whatever the

[5] *The New York Times*, Sept. 23, 1953; see also revealing comment of M. Dehousse on the tendency of the foreign ministers to ignore the draft treaty altogether, in his speech to 2nd Congress of the European Movement at The Hague, Oct. 8-10, 1953, in *Europe Today and Tomorrow*, No. 32 (Nov. 1953), pp. 5-6.

[6] After the December meeting of the foreign ministers, a committee headed by Professor Walter Hallstein of the German Foreign Office was instructed to continue work on the Political Community. The committee subsequently prepared a report to be considered by the foreign ministers at a meeting which was scheduled to be held March 30, 1954 at Brussels. However this meeting was postponed indefinitely and work on the project has apparently been suspended. See *Council of Europe News*, Vol. 4, No. 4 (Apr. 1954), p. 1.

latter's long-range aspects, its immediate purpose was to serve as a sort of umbrella agency for EDC and the Schuman pool and to provide instruments of popular and judicial control for those two supranational projects. Discussions about the future of the Political Community *per se* had, therefore, become virtually academic as soon as the draft treaty to create it had been formulated. The question of the moment concerned the fate of EDC. The answer to that question would resolve the future of both EDC and the Political Community and, for the time being at least, of the whole revived federal movement in Western Europe.

At the time the Six signed the EDC Treaty, the prospects for ratification had been reasonably promising. The Korean War, which had been one of the principal inspirations for Churchill's proposed "European army" and hence of EDC, remained in a condition of stalemate, and the Cold War with the Soviet Union had not yet been relaxed, Stalin's demise still being some months in the future. In America Dean Acheson, President Truman's secretary of state, and the Pentagon were quite as insistent as they had been at any time in the past that the defense of the West required German rearmament, and they had become convinced that the safest and most acceptable way to encompass such rearmament was through an association of French and German forces in a supranational community like EDC. Indeed EDC had by now become a seemingly indispensable objective of American foreign policy, and such it was to remain throughout the final months of the Truman administration and into the subsequent administration of President Eisenhower. As an earnest of its support of the EDC plan, it will be recalled, the United States had made certain commitments when the Six signed the EDC Treaty. The most important of these commitments had been its pledge, offered jointly with Britain and France, to come to the defense of EDC if any member of the Community were attacked, and to station troops on the Continent indefinitely.

Britain's position on EDC at this point remained somewhat murky. Some of her spokesmen continued to look at it askance while others approved. Moreover the government itself occasionally shifted its position. Because of her alleged commitments to the Commonwealth and her world-wide political responsibilities, Britain early took the position officially that she could not merge her forces or any part of them in a European army. At the same time, once the six Continental states had indicated a clear desire to go forward with EDC, official Britain had taken the position that she favored such a plan among the Six and that she would assist it whenever she could short of joining it. In pursuance of this policy,[7] when the Six signed the EDC Treaty in May, 1952, Britain joined with the United States and France in a pledge to keep some troops on the Continent for an indefinite period and to assist EDC member states if they were attacked. Independently of the United States, Britain had promised to render military and other aid, on a reciprocal basis, to each national member of the proposed Defense Community.

Among the six proposed member states the German Federal Republic was undoubtedly the most enthusiastic supporter of the EDC plan. For the Germans, EDC was to be the price of readmission to the society of sovereign nations, and despite the objection of German youth to a renewal of conscription and the die-hard opposition to EDC of the German Social Democrats, wise old Chancellor Adenauer, a confirmed pro-European in any case, had made it clear he was not going to miss this opportunity to secure a restoration of Germany's sovereignty and to redeem Germany's status among the free nations.

Almost as prone to support the Defense Community concept were the nations of the Benelux, the Netherlands, Belgium, and Luxembourg. Although small local Communist aggregations in these states opposed ratification and some opposition also existed on the extreme Right, resistance to the treaty was negligible. No one seriously doubted that sizable majorities could be obtained for the treaty in the parliaments of these junior members of the Six.

In these four states steps to secure parliamentary ratification of the treaty were taken almost as soon as the treaty was signed, and during the course of about a year and a half after May, 1952, their parliaments had joined their governments in supporting EDC. Chancellor Adenauer's struggle with the German Social Democrats and even with certain elements in his own coalition was an epic one. All sorts of roadblocks were thrown up, not the least of which were the various efforts to use the West German Constitu-

[7] See p. 93.

tional Court to defeat the chancellor's policy. Various actions were commenced in that tribunal to declare invalid procedural and substantive aspects of the EDC Treaty and its related documents that were alleged to violate sections of the Bonn Basic Law, West Germany's constitution. To quiet certain constitutional objections, the German government found it necessary to secure the necessary special majorities in the Bundestag and the Bundesrat to amend parts of the Basic Law, especially those relating to Germany's disarmament. In the end, however, the chancellor triumphed. President Heuss completed the last formal step attesting Germany's ratification of the EDC documents on March 31, 1954. Between January and April of the same year, the parliaments of the Netherlands, Belgium, and Luxembourg also completed ratification.

Italy, the fifth prospective EDC member, was something of a question mark and was inclined to "drag her feet" on the matter of treaty ratification. Some of her leaders sought to demand as a price for such action an improvement in Italy's status among the nations of the West, seriously disadvantaged by the Mussolini adventure. On occasion, therefore, when ratification was discussed, her government toyed with the idea of demanding some concession from the nations that had defeated her in World War II—for example the return to Italy of Trieste, then uppermost in the Italian mind. Moreover, Togliatti's Communists and Signor Nenni's Communist-oriented Socialists constituted a formidable opposition, especially when augmented by the nationalistic Right, part of which, at least, was also disinclined, albeit for different reasons, to make Italy a member of a federation. Nevertheless, no Western observer seriously doubted that the late Dr. de Gasperi, then prime minister, would bring Italy into the Defense Community when the time came for action. That time, however, appeared to depend upon France's future behavior toward the treaty. Though disposed to support EDC, Italy's leadership was disinclined to precede France to a favorable decision on the project.

But to those who were waiting for France to lead the way to ratification it soon became evident that they might have to wait a very long time indeed. France, it developed, was in no hurry to proceed with the treaty. This seems paradoxical since it was the French who had originated the Community project. Their political leadership had initiated it and provided the first draft of a treaty. But as the history of the next two years was to make all too obvious, the French had no real love for what they had proposed. Unquestionably they had originated the scheme. Nevertheless, even those Frenchmen who were least affected by petty considerations of purely national advantage were inclined to regard the EDC experiment in supranationalism primarily as a gesture that had to be made to the West because of political necessity. They feared that if they did not make the gesture, the *Wehrmacht* or its equivalent might once more come into being across the Rhine—a development far worse for France than even EDC. The French had therefore offered EDC as the lesser of two evils. In their heart of hearts most Frenchmen believe that the safety of their country requires the disarmament of Germany, and that belief was shared by the greater part of those Frenchmen who had proposed EDC.

This fundamental, almost visceral, antipathy to the rearming of Germany was bound to cause trouble for EDC in any French forum. Moreover, in the case of the tribunal in which the decision to ratify had to be taken, that is, the French National Assembly, EDC was to encounter a forum in which, as French leaders themselves admit, it is notoriously difficult to secure a working majority for any positive course of action. When to this inherent institutional weakness was added the factor of the virtually intuitive antipathy to the cause for which affirmative action was being sought, the result was a legislative outlook for EDC that was far from favorable. Certainly it was apparent to even the most superficial observer that any effort of the French government to corral a majority for the EDC Treaty in the French National Assembly would find the party groups in the Assembly even less tractable than usual.

That the road to ratification in the French parliament would be a rocky one for EDC, and that, indeed, it might not lead to the hoped-for objective were possibilities sensed by even the less astute before the ink was dry on the French signatures on the EDC Treaty. When the Pleven government signed that treaty, the French prime minister and his associates had apparently persuaded themselves that the British and American military pledges, signed concurrently, would be sufficient to stem the fears of eventual German superiority that had been voiced by almost every party group in the French

National Assembly. Especially did the government think that such pledges would reassure the more moderate elements in the Assembly, such as the Radicals and Socialists, upon whose favorable attitude, along with a similar attitude on the part of the clerical MRP, the parliamentary fate of EDC appeared primarily to depend. It quickly became obvious, however, that this assumption of M. Pleven and his government was incorrect. Edouard Herriot, venerable leader of the Radicals and himself a long-time supporter of united Europe,[8] became the spearhead of a campaign directed against ratification that accumulated considerable support among his own party members and others.[9] Especially averse to ratification was Edouard Daladier, earlier a partisan associate of M. Herriot and himself prime minister in the early thirties. Their denunciation of the treaty was quite as vitriolic as any that came from the Gaullist Right or from France's large Communist contingent.

As these denunciations of the proposed treaty grew in volume and bitterness it became obvious that not only had the government failed to allay fear of Germany but that the public generally was poorly informed of the nature of the proposed commitment and of its advantages. The latter condition especially lent encouragement to those less responsible elements in the Assembly who were intent upon exploiting the opposition to the treaty merely to embarrass the government or for reasons essentially demagogic.

The resulting rather gloomy outlook for EDC in the Assembly caused the successor of the Pleven cabinet, which was headed by Antoine Pinay and in which the treaty's great friend, Robert Schuman, was still foreign minister, to decide in the late summer of 1952 to postpone formal submission of the document to the Assembly at least until after the American elections in November. Shortly after these had taken place, the Pinay cabinet itself went into the discard, and in the new cabinet of M. René Mayer, Robert Schuman was supplanted as foreign minister by Georges Bidault. The latter, though a member of M. Schuman's party and certainly not unfriendly to European union or EDC, was hardly expected to share the enthusiasm for that concept that was understandably exhibited by M. Schuman, one of the concept's principal creators. On their

[8] See his *United States of Europe,* cited earlier, p. 7.

[9] *The New York Times,* Oct. 22, 1952.

inauguration both the new foreign minister and the new prime minister officially reaffirmed their belief in EDC. At the same time, they expressed their conviction that if any part of the EDC opposition in the Assembly were to be placated, and if France were ever to adopt EDC, various concessions would have to be made by Germany and other prospective EDC associates and by Britain and the United States.

Just what sort of concessions the French had in mind was shortly made known. Six of them took the form of requests for modification of the treaty and were identified as "protocols." Some of the protocols appeared to alter the substance and purpose of the proposed treaty. They promised France a status within EDC superior to that of her associates and rather obviously discriminated against them. In one of the protocols, for example, France sought the right to shift officers at will between the forces she might have committed to the Community and those reserved for overseas duty. France demanded this discretion because of her allegedly unique overseas responsibilities, although it appeared to violate the intention of the treaty that the forces committed to the European army were to be permanently detached from any national army and fully integrated within the European command.

Other modifications sought by the French would have permitted them to withdraw forces from the European organization, when an emergency required such action, without the formal agreement of the NATO command, the latter condition having been stipulated in the original treaty if such a privilege were sought. Again the plea was France's special overseas responsibilities. France also sought to perpetuate a voting strength in the Community's Council of National Ministers equal to Germany's, although according to the treaty, after an initial period, voting strength in the Council was to have depended upon the magnitude of the actual contribution of troops and resources. Because they might have to withdraw forces for overseas duty the French felt that the Germans would soon outnumber them and they wished to safeguard their legal position against such an eventuality. Other protocols were less important. They involved such privileges as that of training officers in the command schools that the Community was to operate and assuring French suppliers that they would provide all the armament and supplies of the French forces to be integrated in EDC. As formulated by the French, the very purpose of the proposed protocols, namely, to protect the "unity and integrity of the French Army and the French Union," indicates how far France had already departed from the spirit, if not the letter, of the proposal to establish a supranational or federal army.[10]

Among France's five intended associates in EDC the six protocols aroused considerable criticism. The Germans especially felt that France had already acquired an unwarranted position of relative superiority in the original plan, and that further concessions, however plausible they might be as a means of conciliating French parliamentary and public opinion, would result in such serious discrimination against France's contemplated partners that it would be almost impossible to secure ratification of the treaty in those states.[11] Indeed, spokesmen of France's national partners in the EDC project insisted that the protocols actually annulled the treaty and that if France persisted in demanding them as a condition of her acceptance of the treaty, it would become necessary to submit the protocols with the treaty to their respective parliaments and request ratification of both. Needless to say, no one was hopeful of securing ratification under such circumstances.

So great was the criticism that at a conference of the Six, during which the protocols were considered, held at Rome on February 25, 1953, M. Bidault, the French foreign minister, felt it necessary to assure the German chancellor that France did not intend to go back on her original agreement. The protocols, insisted M. Bidault, were intended to be merely interpretative; they were not to be considered formal modifications of the original treaty. These assurances by M. Bidault were accepted at face value by the Rome conference although apparently with some reluctance. The conferees agreed that the protocols would be redrafted to make them consistent with the "spirit and essence" of the treaty. It was also agreed that, irrespective of the protocols and their ultimate disposition, the signatory states should proceed with the ratification of the original treaty.[12]

[10] The substance of the protocols appears in *Europe Today and Tomorrow*, No. 29 (Aug. 1953), p. 8.

[11] See Chancellor Adenauer's views in *The New York Times*, Feb. 23, 1953.

[12] *The New York Times*, Feb. 26, 1953.

Ratifications subsequently secured by Germany and among the Benelux states were accordingly completed before any action on the protocols acceptable to France had been undertaken. As a matter of fact, though compromises were offered, it shortly became quite clear that, short of accepting the protocols as proposed, there was no means of satisfying France, and against such a concession France's intended EDC partners were adamant. Hence there was really no middle ground for compromise. The French protocols represented a major alteration in the original plan and France's associates were determined not to accept that change since it involved formal amendment of the treaty and discrimination against them. France, on the other hand, became quite as determined that her associates would have to accommodate themselves to changes in policy implicit in the protocols if EDC were to be submitted to the French National Assembly for ratificatory action. As time wore on, it became ever more certain that France would never forego the advantages over her associates that she sought in the protocols. How completely she had identified her policy with acceptance of the protocols became evident in the summer of 1954, when Pierre Mendès-France, having become prime minister, proceeded to write the final chapter in the French EDC story. As we shall see,[13] the concession that Mendès-France said would be necessary to secure French ratification of EDC was simply the original protocols carried as far as their logic permitted, that is, to the point of abrogating completely EDC's supranational character.[14]

Acceptance of the protocols or of the amendments of the treaty that they implied was but part of the price that the French began to demand at the beginning of 1953 for acceptance of EDC by their parliament. Another, and even more important, concession that France regarded as necessary for favorable action by her parliament did not appear in the protocols. This was a more substantial pledge of military assistance from Britain and more intimate association of Britain with the Defense Community than Britain had offered in the declaration that she had executed at the time the Six had signed the EDC Treaty.[15] Here, indeed, we come to the

[13] See p. 123.
[14] See p. 124.
[15] See p. 92.

heart of the French objection to proceeding with EDC, and we identify the condition that had to be satisfied before all others if France was ever to ratify. The nationalistic arguments of de Gaulle's followers in the Assembly could probably be defied successfully, and the Communists' devious and hypocritical objections to the treaty could be disregarded. But after February, 1953, no French prime minister who entertained any hope of carrying the moderate parties in the Assembly with him on EDC felt he could disregard the argument of many of the members of those parties that, without virtual British membership, EDC might one day become a German trap for France. From this time forward, therefore, the French government, in its effort to secure parliamentary ratification for EDC, in addition to its insistence on the substance of the "protocols," constantly emphasized the necessity of securing a more reassuring EDC tie to Britain.

The campaign to win over the British to a more intimate tie to EDC was undertaken by the Mayer-Bidault government on February 12 when both the French prime minister and the foreign minister made a visit to London. Subsequently, the result of the visit was described as "very unsatisfactory."[16] In substance, what the French sought was a closer political association of the British with the proposed EDC, one short of outright membership that would require a transfer of sovereignty and that the French knew by now the British would not stomach. They sought instead an association that would provide an "organic" link—one not unlike that arranged between Britain and the Schuman pool,[17] but involving closer cooperation and perhaps a greater degree of responsibility by Britain for common decisions than was afforded under the Schuman arrangement. Agreement on a form of British association with EDC was in fact reached in April, 1954, but it did not satisfy the French.[18]

As respects the French desire for an amended British pledge of military aid, there was no ambiguity. What the French wanted was a British agreement to leave on the Continent permanently some

[16] *The New York Times,* Mar. 4, 1953.

[17] See p. 159.

[18] For its terms, see *Europe Today and Tomorrow,* No. 38 (May 1954), pp. 17 ff.

four British divisions already stationed in Germany in addition to some supporting air power. France wanted Britain to agree to leave these forces on the Continent and not retain over them the discretion to recall them at will. If Britain could be persuaded to promise such assistance, France felt that British forces would then always be available to equalize the French position *vis-à-vis* Germany in the Community in case France, as was expected, should have to withdraw forces in Europe for service overseas. Just how "permanent" the wished-for pledge was to be was not altogether clear. It was certain, however, that the French wanted to extend any British obligation beyond the twenty-year term formally set for the North Atlantic Treaty and embrace the fifty-year life span contemplated for the EDC Treaty.

Though rebuffed in February, 1953, the French persisted in their attempt to persuade Britain to take this responsibility toward EDC throughout the remainder of the Mayer administration and its successors, the governments of prime ministers Laniel and Mendès-France. But the French importunities did not produce a more positive British attitude. On the contrary, if they had any effect, it was one tending to discredit EDC with the British and to strengthen that element in Britain that had never been really friendly to the idea. Although the government of Prime Minister Churchill continued a formally "correct" attitude toward EDC, condemnation of the proposed military arrangement became much more open and forthright in private British quarters. Increasingly apprehensive of the competitive dangers involved in building up a federation or supranational power bloc on the Continent and thereby violating Britain's historic balance-of-power policy toward that area, private spokesmen of note, many of whom had been leaders in the European integration movement, began to make it clear that they had no love for EDC or any other Continental supranational arrangement. Their attitude, moreover, was probably more representative of the true British opinion than the formal policy of the government. At any rate, it echoed Britain's traditional policy.

Probably the most articulate in this respect was the Conservative, Sir Robert Boothby. "This EDC business," said Sir Robert late in 1953, "has already resulted in a fearful deterioration of Franco-German relations, which were incomparably better two years ago than they are today, due very largely to French fears and exasperation with their own performance, which has been stupid over this 'supranational' stuff, and also the pressure put upon them." He added that the effort to go farther with what he had called "this 'supranational' stuff" and seek adoption of the proposed European Political Community along with EDC would simply aggravate the division of the Continent "and would lead to an intensive struggle for markets between the Continental Community and Great Britain, and thus constitute a potential economic threat to this country."[19] Sir Robert's was the authentic voice of Britain—at least of the Britain at about the time Viscount Grey of Fallodon was serving as her foreign minister. It was also a voice that hardly reassured the French parliament on EDC.

As respects America, the French government's effort to secure assistance in its struggle with parliament yielded results scarcely more valuable than the efforts it had directed toward the British. Among other concessions, the French sought at least some form of monetary aid to allow them to equip native forces in their war in Indo-China and thus relax the drain on French resources and manpower. Such relaxation, it was urged, was essential if France were to fulfill commitments to EDC and NATO. France also sought stronger assurances of the indefinite retention of American manpower on the Continent than had already been given.[20]

American response to these overtures was not too encouraging. On April 16, 1953, some time after the visit to Washington by Prime Minister Mayer, President Eisenhower offered some reassurance to the French by stating that it would be American policy to keep the military force then stationed in Europe on that continent as long as any threat to peace might exist. Such a statement might have been interpreted as an American proposal to keep troops stationed in Europe for a considerable period, but it contained no formal assurance not previously given.

But if the French received little actual new assistance, they were nevertheless made aware of how strongly America favored EDC and with what disappointment America would view EDC's defeat

[19] *Europe Today and Tomorrow,* No. 33 (Dec. 1953), p. 6. See also another not dissimilar view in *European Review,* No. 33 (July 1953), pp. 1 ff.

[20] *The New York Times,* Mar. 23, 1953.

in the French parliament. On the occasion of the December, 1953, meeting of the North Atlantic Council in Paris, Secretary of State Dulles had declared that if EDC were not ratified and, as a consequence, France and Germany remained separated, he doubted whether "Continental Europe could be made a place of safety." He had then added the famous statement that such a situation "would compel an agonizing reappraisal of basic United States policy."[21] Admittedly extreme and decidedly ambiguous, such a statement was a scarcely disguised form of American pressure on France to ratify. Though less explicit, it was on a par with the pressure that the American Congress simultaneously tried to exert when it gave President Eisenhower discretionary power to withhold a billion dollars in proposed military aid to NATO unless EDC were ratified. So much of American policy and prestige had been invested in the success of EDC that French procrastination was beginning to irritate and to call forth rather extreme statements that subsequently might prove embarrassing. It was questionable, moreover, whether these actions were really helping French leadership to win over any faltering EDC supporters in the French chamber. The likelihood is that they created resentment over what was called "American interference," a condition hardly calculated to help French friends of the treaty.

Still another so-called "pre-condition" to EDC ratification, announced by Prime Minister Mayer early in 1953, was the satisfactory settlement of the Saar issue between France and Germany. In 1947, this rich industrial area had been temporarily united in a customs union with France and that country had been made responsible for the territory's defense and foreign relations. After the re-establishment of the semblance of an independent regime in Germany, that country made it clear that she reserved all rights in the Saar, and the territory's inchoate status became a principal point of friction between France and the German Federal Republic.

To solve this problem and overcome at least this obstacle to Franco-German *rapprochement* over EDC and the pending European Political Community, the Consultative Assembly at Strasbourg, under the leadership of an imaginative Dutch representa-

[21] *The New York Times,* Aug. 23, 1954.

tive, Marinus van der Goes van Naters, undertook to draft a plan that would have "Europeanized" the Saar territory. This plan, which assumed rather concrete form early in 1954, would have given the Saar the status of a European territory as soon as the Six had ratified the European Political Community. Meanwhile a temporary "European commissioner" was to have been appointed who would have been responsible for the territory's foreign affairs and defense and who would have operated under the jurisdiction of the Council of Europe's Committee of Ministers. At the same time France's existing privileged economic position would have been modified gradually and eventually there would have been no discrimination against Germany's interests in the territory. The whole scheme was to have been submitted to a referendum in the Saar to determine the attitude of the territory's inhabitants. During March, 1954, the German and French governments agreed in principle to this plan as one that might provide a solution for the issue. Thus, in 1954, at least one of M. Mayer's pre-conditions to ratification of EDC was on the way to solution.[22] A promise of settlement of the Saar issue did not, however, greatly facilitate favorable parliamentary disposition of EDC in France so long as the questions of the protocols and British-American assistance remained without satisfactory answers.

In February, 1953, after the Mayer cabinet had given rather clear indication of the concessions France would require before giving consideration to ratification of EDC, the American secretary of state, Mr. Dulles, made a visit to various European capitals to appraise the situation for the then relatively new Eisenhower administration. Upon his return to Washington he declared that there was still "a good chance" that EDC "will be brought into being."[23] Although Mr. Dulles continued to be optimistic during subsequent months, and although the American government never seems to have lost its hopes for EDC, the prospect of French parliamentary ratification of the treaty gradually deteriorated. The delay in submitting the treaty to the French Assembly, occasioned by the desire of the French government to secure various concessions from

[22] See *The New York Times,* Mar. 10, 1954. See also M. van der Goes van Naters, "L'Histoire de la Saare en Documents," in *European Yearbook,* II (1956), pp. 139 ff.

[23] *The New York Times,* Feb. 13, 1953.

its proposed EDC allies and others, continued into the spring of 1954. By that time the prospect of a conference between the West and Moscow at Geneva, scheduled for the end of April, provided added reasons for delay. Hopeful of securing a benevolent attitude from the Soviets at Geneva in an effort to settle the war with Ho Chi Minh, the Communist rebel leader in Indo-China, the French feared to irritate Moscow by proceeding with a treaty that they knew was anathema to Molotov and his cohorts. In consequence, further delay became the order of the day.

Shortly after the conclusion of the Geneva talks, the Laniel government in France gave way to that of Pierre Mendès-France. In a program announced before taking office the new premier had indicated that the EDC issue in the French parliament would be disposed of after a serious effort had been made to liquidate the Indo-China War. True to this timetable, Mendès-France submitted the treaty to a special study group of his cabinet. After some three weeks, this committee formulated certain proposed new amendments. The French prime minister thereupon declared that these amendments, substantially an expansion of the earlier protocols, would have to be accepted by the five other proposed associates of EDC if the treaty were to be made acceptable to the National Assembly. Without the amendments the treaty, he insisted, would be doomed.

But at a meeting with representatives of the other five EDC associates at Brussels on August 18, they made it clear that acceptance of the proposed French amendments would do what the protocols had threatened to do, namely, destroy the supranational character of the treaty altogether and produce what amounted to a merely conventional alliance, a result they were not prepared to accept. Moreover, acceptance of the amendments by the representatives of the other five would, they insisted, entail resubmission of the treaty to those four parliaments that had already ratified the EDC Treaty in its original form. This also was impractical, as had been the case earlier when the less ambitious French protocols had been suggested. Although willing to make minor concessions, the other five associates in EDC presented a united front to Mendès-France against accepting his "new" protocols.

The French prime minister's demands for revision were assailed at the same time in his own parliament by M. Robert Schuman. Speaking for sizable elements in his own party, the MRP, and for others, the former foreign minister insisted that the Mendès-France proposals would change substantially "virtually all the essential clauses of the Treaty" and "empty the Treaty of its content." [24] The Socialist, André Philip, also an early friend of EDC, offered similar criticisms.[25] A last-minute appeal to Mendès-France from President Eisenhower to maintain the supranational nature of the treaty and Prime Minister Churchill's pointed message to Chancellor Adenauer stating that Britain still supported the EDC plan had no effect upon the French leader's attitude nor upon the negotiations. Four days after they began, the Brussels talks ended in total failure.[26]

Little more than a week later the EDC Treaty, already marked for the scrap heap, was formally interred. Following the procedure he had outlined for his government, Mendès-France submitted the original draft of the treaty to the Assembly. He submitted it without comment, but he also made it clear that as it stood it did not have his endorsement and he was only too articulate about his belief that the treaty would fail to secure a majority. He also took pains to make it clear that the fate of his government was not to be tied in any way with the fate of the treaty. The actual defeat of the treaty came on a mere procedural motion, the substance of which was to postpone debate until later without naming a day for its resumption. That motion was carried by a vote of 319 to 264.[27] Those figures reflected fairly accurately the strength of both the treaty's proponents and the opposition in the chamber. Those opposed were not only the Communists and those who followed Marshal Juin and General de Gaulle. Opponents included also more than half of the Socialists and more than half of the Radicals, the prime minister's own party. Mendès-France himself, and six of his party associates, true to the premier's declaration of something less than benevolent neutrality, abstained from voting. Other groups in the Assembly were equally split.

[24] *The New York Times,* Aug. 19, 20, 1954.

[25] *Ibid.,* Aug. 20, 1954.

[26] *Ibid.,* Aug. 22, 1954.

[27] *The New York Times,* Aug. 31, 1954. For a precise description of the parliamentary maneuver that defeated EDC see *Council of Europe News,* No. 9 (Sept. 1954), p. 2.

Thus, to the consternation of some who to the very end did not believe that France would destroy the treaty, to the secret satisfaction of many others, and to the jubilation of still others, the intended arch of the whole postwar supranational structure in Europe was destroyed. The long and arduous struggle for the treaty had an inglorious end since the treaty had fallen on the issue of sustaining a mere procedural motion. As former Premier Reynaud pointed out, the treaty was defeated on a vote that actually was a vote not to debate it. "For the first time in the history of the French parliament," said Reynaud, "a treaty has been rejected without a word in its defense being spoken by its author or its signer." [28] He might have added that the treaty had been lost because a French parliament had proven incapable of action, because Britain had been too lukewarm and America probably too emphatic and certainly too obvious in her support of the treaty, and because the Soviets and the Communists outside of Russia had fought a good fight in behalf of their cause. EDC also went down to defeat because the project had dragged along for such a considerable period that the motivation that had originally propelled the Six toward this supranational alliance had weakened with the mere passage of time and the marginal ally, France, never enthusiastic about the project, had finally succumbed to her fears instead of allowing wisdom to guide her.

With EDC the allied project of a formal federation, embraced in the Political Community concept, was now also thrown upon the scrap heap. This ill-fated project never enjoyed even the half-life that had been vouchsafed to EDC. The treaty for the latter had at least been signed by the representatives of the Six, and four of their parliaments had ratified it. The Political Community project, on the other hand, never got beyond the stage of a mere draft treaty. Though endorsed enthusiastically enough at Strasbourg by the Ad Hoc Assembly when submitted to that body in 1953, and though properly regarded as one of the great intellectual achievements in the positive effort to give form to the idea of European unity, the Political Community project now had no chance of being realized. The draft treaty for that community, of which so much

[28] *The New York Times,* Aug. 31, 1954.

had been expected, was subsequently shunted about from one meeting of the foreign ministers to another and eventually it suffered the inglorious fate of simply being ignored. If EDC may be said to have enjoyed a half-life, its companion project must be said to have been just another abortion, and the attempt to give federal organs to at least a part of Europe had failed once more.

11 European Union—the Latest Phase

IT WOULD BE QUITE UNREALISTIC to regard the defeat of the European army project as anything other than a major setback for the whole movement toward European integration in our time. In that project, and the companion conception of a Political Community, experts had come to grips with the challenge of translating the broad ideal of unity into the hard reality. They had developed instruments that promised political viability and that appeared to meet the challenge of administrative utility. Through these plans for federal integration of the six states of "Little Europe," the inhabitants of that area were promised a real opportunity of surmounting anachronistic cultural and economic barriers imposed by traditional political boundaries, and of attaining thereby a far broader scope for economic enterprise and political development. Through these plans of unity, the Western world was also promised so intimate an integration of the national systems of France and Germany that, once achieved, it would have been unthinkable that these states would pursue separate diplomatic systems or that they would organize separate military structures that would sustain national diplomatic rivalry.

For a brief moment in time, moreover, public opinion in Western Europe had been brought closer to the acceptance of a transnational structure than ever before in modern history. Certainly it had come closer to acceptance of such a structure than the most optimistic political leader had thought possible only a few years earlier. Then, in one sudden and devastating action, the whole fair complex of thought, institutional devices, and favorable opinion had been brought low. Contemporary history will record few more reactionary events than the action of the French National Assembly in failing to ratify EDC on August 17, 1954.

It is quite possible, however, to overestimate the long-term significance of this rejection of EDC and its companion concept, the Political Community. Although these two projects may have died, and with their demise the most advanced institutional effort yet made to effect transnational integration of Western Europe may also have succumbed, it is difficult to kill the ideal of union itself. This is particularly true now that the ideal has, for a time, been in the main stream of political development. The fact is that, since World War II, European union, that is, an idea of union that transcends the concept of a mere concert of nations, or of an alliance or association, or even of a loose confederation, has ceased to be merely a scholar's dream. Such being the case, it has proven quite impossible to relegate this particular concept to the academic backwater.

To be sure, immediately after the August, 1954, defeat of EDC by the French National Assembly, supranational solutions for Europe did appear to have suffered a decisive rejection and the cause of federally united Europe appeared moribund. But that condition did not persist. Indeed, scarcely a fortnight elapsed before it became apparent, even to the enemies of integration, that they had won too great a victory on August 17th—that they could not possibly tolerate the apparent alternative to EDC, namely, a purely national solution of the defense issue. The world had traveled too far and the technology of weapons had progressed too radically to permit of a return to a pre-World War II or a pre-EDC conception of European organization in this sector. If Western Europe was not to have EDC, then some compromise falling between the solution EDC proposed and a purely national solution would have to be developed.

Actually the dominant motif in the discussions in the European chancellories and in Washington after the French Assembly had acted was one of consternation. Though having professedly anticipated the action of France, every other proposed member of the now defunct EDC found it difficult to accept that action. They asserted that an effective defense structure for Western Europe was impossible unless EDC were revived or an essentially identical plan were substituted. German, Belgian, and Dutch leaders were outspoken in their condemnation of the French action. The suggestion was even made that the remaining five nations, parties to the original EDC agreement, all but one of whom had already secured parliamentary ratification of that agreement, proceed with that project without France. The prevailing mood was well expressed by Dr. Adenauer, who said that the policy of European union formulated in some kind of European community "must be saved at all costs."

It is hardly surprising, therefore, that echoes of the French debate had scarcely been dissipated in the Palais Bourbon before diplomats, with British diplomats in the van, came forward with the substitute for EDC to be known as Western European Union. Officially this substitute was the product of a nine-power conference held in London in October, 1954, following EDC's defeat. This conference proceeded to develop what it hoped might be a substitute for EDC. It sought to do this by making appropriate amendments to the Brussels Treaty of 1948, an instrument that had created a joint command for certain forces of Britain, France, and the Benelux, and that thus had been a prelude to NATO. Britain and the Six now suggested that this structure be enlarged by the admission of the contemplated German forces and also those of Italy, and that the whole structure be known henceforth as Western European Union. Somewhat unenthusiastically this suggestion was accepted by spokesmen for the seven nations involved. Appropriate documents were subsequently signed at Paris, October 20-24, 1954, and the agreements came into force in May, 1955, following parliamentary ratification by the seven states.

These WEU agreements did not provide for a federal or supranational solution. To be sure, they anticipated a joint command under NATO, but, unlike EDC, they did not contemplate either the limited fusion of national forces that justified the appellation, "European army," or federal organs to exercise budgetary and administrative authority over common defense resources. Under Western European Union, national armies were to be perpetuated without modification and even the German army was to be restored, this being probably the most important of all departures from the original plan. Each of the seven states was to make a stipulated contribution to the NATO forces and place them under command of SACEUR, that is, the NATO commander, and Germany was to contribute her proposed twelve divisions in this manner.

But, though conventional in most respects, this proposed association under the amended Brussels Treaty did at least preserve the principle of integrated action in the security area. Like EDC, the Brussels Treaty pledged a fifty-year association of the signatory powers. Specific contingents of national forces were placed at the disposition of the NATO command; a common policy on the part of the signatories was anticipated both as respects the kind and quantity of weapons; and decisions on weapons were to be taken by a majority vote of the members of WEU's agencies, thus avoiding the possibility of a national veto so characteristic of international bodies. Finally, when the amended Brussels Treaty was signed, it was anticipated that the Saar territory would become a sort of ward of WEU and provisions were incorporated in the treaty for that purpose. This plan, however, subsequently became inoperable as a result of a referendum in the territory that went overwhelmingly against making the Saar "European." Nevertheless, the intention of the architects of WEU had been to give that body direct governmental responsibility for an area that might in time have become a sort of "European" territorial center.

Especially noteworthy in the development of WEU were the actions of Britain. She had refused association with EDC because of its essentially federal nature, but when EDC failed it was Britain that initiated WEU and became a charter member. Such a change of attitude was rationalized by the British because WEU, in contrast to the essentially federal EDC, was allegedly a mere "intergovernmental" agency. Be that as it may, Britain went much farther than merely joining WEU. Apparently, as a condition of establishing WEU, Britain had to pay a price that required a sacrifice of sovereign authority almost as great as might have been demanded by EDC membership. This was the price implicit in the pledge to her Continental allies to maintain four divisions and her Second Tactical Air Force across the Channel at all times. Britain promised not to withdraw these forces against the wishes of the majority of her associates in WEU. The only qualification affecting this pledge was the requirement that if Britain sought to withdraw against the will of her associates, they would consult the NATO commander and consider his views before coming to their final decision. Britain also reserved the right to withdraw in case of an acute overseas emergency.[1] Britain had to make this military pledge in order to bring the French to accept German participation in WEU. Had Britain made the pledge earlier, when EDC was before the French Assembly, and when the French were pressing Britain for precisely this type of guarantee, it is possible that EDC would have enjoyed a different fate at the hands of the French.[2]

Thus, though WEU may not have borne a textbook resemblance to the EDC supranational plan for merging Western Europe's defense forces, the kind of conventional alliance involved in WEU comes fairly close to the supranational system implicit in EDC, and the WEU alliance probably demands a greater sacrifice of national sovereignty over armed forces than any European nation has previously been prepared to make in peacetime. In any case, it is quite clear that, though Western Europe has had to forego application of a supranational solution for its security problem, such as was contemplated by EDC, it has nonetheless pushed the conventional concept of national association or alliance as closely as possible to the supranational concept in the solution that was finally adopted. Certainly both as respects its provisions and the history of its adoption, WEU makes it clear that the movement toward more effective union in Western Europe is far from dead.

But the vitality of the integration movement in Western Europe, discernible in the substitution of the WEU compromise for EDC, was even more dramatically reaffirmed in the action now taken by the French economist, M. Jean Monnet. Almost simultaneously with the acceptance of WEU, the "father" of European supranationalism undertook to reconstitute private initiative in favor of federal integration. Taking a page from the record of Churchill's action in 1948 in organizing the European Movement,[3] Monnet, on Novem-

[1] In 1957, because of her shift from conventional to atomic armament, Britain began negotiating with the trans-Channel nations to secure assent to her decision to reduce her forces on the Continent.

[2] See Art. 6, Protocol II, "On Forces of Western European Union," in Appendix I to Brussels Treaty of Mar. 17, 1948, as amended Oct. 23, 1954.

[3] See p. 22.

ber 11, 1954, resigned his presidency of the High Authority of the Schuman Community in order, as he put it, "to take part with complete freedom of action and speech in the construction of European unity." [4] Ten months later, on October 14, 1955, Monnet announced the formation of his Action Committee for a United Europe.

In succession to Coudenhove's Pan-Europe Movement and his European Parliamentary Union and to Churchill's European Movement, Monnet's was the third major private grouping of pro-European forces since World War II. Its successful organization was in itself emphatic evidence of the persistence of the appeal of the European ideal. But the real significance of this new private movement was to be measured by the character of the adherents whose support was gained by the French leader. Most of the thirty-three founding members of M. Monnet's Action Committee were outstanding representatives of the moderate political parties of the six states of "Little Europe," including Socialists, Clericals, and Liberals, and all of the non-Communist trade unions in these same states. In joining M. Monnet's committee, these leaders pledged their best efforts to secure the official support of their respective organizations for the committee's European policies.

Even more significant than the range of representation in the new Action Committee was the success M. Monnet enjoyed in healing the schism in French socialism that had been produced by the bitter debate over EDC. Equally significant was the pledge of support he received from Herr Ollenhauer and his German Social Democrats. These had been persistent foes of EDC and traditionally had been only lukewarm toward all forms of Western unity of a suprasovereign nature. No aspect of M. Monnet's successful initiative in reviving the European Movement was more heartening to all friends of that ideal than this broad range of support that he secured among the states of "Little Europe" and the success that attended his efforts to overcome previous schisms.

The standard to which the Committee rallied, moreover, was uncompromising in its advocacy of supranationalism. M. Monnet minced no words in rejecting the ambiguous sort of integration exhibited in WEU. To achieve the Committee's objectives, said this

[4] *Bulletin from the European Community for Coal and Steel,* No. 11 (Dec. 1955), p. 3.

leader of Europe, "it is necessary to put aside all specious solutions. Mere cooperation between governments will not suffice." "It is indispensable," continued M. Monnet, "for states to delegate certain of their powers to European federal institutions responsible to all the participating countries taken as a whole."[5] Only in the case of Britain was he willing to compromise on this issue of the modification of sovereignty. Mindful of Britain's past objections to supranationalism and apparently mindful also of the special importance attached to her benevolent support of any Continental grouping, he defined for Britain a position of "close association" with any federal arrangement that might be developed by the Six.

Elsewhere in the call to the founding members of the new Action Committee, Monnet made it clear that the basic purpose was "to achieve a United States of Europe by concrete accomplishments." To that end, representatives on the Committee explicitly agreed to support plans by which sovereign states would "delegate certain of their powers to . . . European federal institutions."[6]

Monnet's efforts to revive public interest in the supranational concept of unity among the states of "Little Europe" bore fruit almost immediately at the governmental level. Six months before he officially announced the formation of his committee, a conference of the foreign ministers of the Six had been held at Messina, Italy, and, on June 2, 1955, that conference had adopted a resolution calling for intensive study of a possible pooling of efforts to exploit atomic energy and for the development of a customs union and common market among the Six. The conference had declared that a united Europe was "indispensable." Monnet's committee now undertook the task of developing precise plans for the projects suggested at Messina and of organizing favorable public and parliamentary opinion among the states involved.

Plans for an atomic energy community and for a similar agency to develop a common market were subsequently officially elaborated by an intergovernmental committee headed by that veteran "European," Paul-Henri Spaak, and official encouragement was given the work of this committee at meetings of the foreign ministers of the

[5] *Ibid.*, p. 2. See also *The New York Times*, Oct. 14, 1955.

[6] *Bulletin from the European Community for Coal and Steel*, No. 11 (Dec. 1955), p. 1.

Six held at Venice in May and at Brussels in June, 1956. At the Venice meeting, the intergovernmental committee's report on the two projects was formally accepted as a basis for further negotiation and the development of appropriate treaties. Moreover, in March, 1956, the two plans were extensively debated at a special meeting of the Common Assembly of the Schuman Community held in the Belgian Senate Chamber in Brussels. At the conclusion of that meeting, all but one of the 78 members of this body, which represents virtually all political groups in each of the six nations except Communists and other extremists, voted a resolution emphatically endorsing the preparation of a treaty to eliminate customs barriers among the Six and to introduce a common market.[7] Then on February 20, 1957 the prime ministers of the Six, meeting in Paris, came to an agreement on all pending issues affecting negotiations to prepare treaties for a European Atomic Energy Community and a European Market Community, the latter to be known officially as the European Economic Community.[8] Finally, on March 25, at a meeting in Rome, the representatives of the Six formally accepted and signed the two treaties and recommended them to their respective parliaments.[9]

As subsequently developed, the treaty for the proposed European Atomic Energy Community, unofficially known as "Euratom," will bring under one jurisdiction all civil exploitation of nuclear energy, including the purchase and production of nuclear ores and fuels within the Community area and overseas, and the guarantee of an adequate supply of fissionable materials to all authorized public and private users. In addition, the new authority will supervise the use of patents and discoveries relating to the exploitation of nuclear power, supervise and enforce a central system to protect the public against the hazards of radiation, encourage appropriate investment

[7] *Bulletin from the European Community for Coal and Steel*, No. 15 (May 1956), p. 7.

[8] *Ibid.*, No. 22 (Feb.-Mar. 1957), pp. 1 ff.

[9] For a summary of the treaties' provisions, see *The New York Times*, Mar. 26, 1957, p. 12. Complete texts in English translation, with annexes, have been published by the Information Service of the European Community for Coal and Steel, Washington 5, D. C. Their titles are as follows: "The Treaty Establishing the European Economic Community with Complete Annexes" and "The Treaty Establishing the European Atomic Energy Community."

in this field, create a common nuclear research center and organize schools for training specialists, and participate with public and private bodies in building certain joint atomic installations. The Community is authorized to enter into contracts with its member states, individuals, or companies to carry out parts of the program. To this end "nonexclusive licenses" may be issued for the exploitation of patents within the Community's jurisdiction. This discretion, if properly exercised, will make possible some degree of private enterprise in the development of this new source of power.

When Euratom was first proposed, its supporters urged the Six to forego military applications of atomic power. However, in deference primarily to certain segments of opinion in the French National Assembly that had become vocal when Prime Minister Mollet first sampled parliamentary opinion on this project,[10] it was agreed that the Community might allocate fissionable materials to the authorities of WEU, successor of the now defunct EDC, which was discussed earlier in this chapter. Subject to various requirements, WEU could then retransfer such materials to the governments of any of the Six for exploitation in a nuclear weapons program.[11] Essentially, the discretion thus given means that fissionable materials may be conveyed to France for nuclear arms since that country is the only one of the Six that has indicated interest in such a program and that is also in a position to take advantage of the discretion to use fissionable materials for such a purpose. Fissionable materials allocated to a military program will undoubtedly have to be derived from extractive sources within the proposed Community since it is unlikely that any foreign sources of such materials, for example American sources, will permit the application of materials exported to the Community to other than civilian purposes.

Supporters of the common market project consider this proposed second new community to be a logical extension of the Schuman Community. They point out, quite correctly, that a common market for all goods and services produced among the Six had been the ultimate objective of those who developed the Schuman Community,

[10] See *The New York Times,* July 12, 1956.

[11] Except for the German Federal Republic, which had agreed to forego such armament.

and now that success had crowned this more limited effort, it was desirable to proceed farther along the way toward this final goal.

As formulated in the treaty signed at Rome on March 25, 1957, the common market concept for "Little Europe" gives priority to the gradual elimination of national tariffs and other limitations now affecting trade among the Six in order that a customs union among them may eventually be established. Within a minimum transitional period of twelve years, tariffs among the Six will be gradually eliminated "if permitted by their general economic situation and the conditions of the sector [of industry] concerned." Taxes that have the effect of tariffs are likewise to be eliminated within the transitional period, although special concessions are made to France to permit her to extend certain important duties and aids to exports beyond the specified transition period. Quotas and other arbitrary quantitative restrictions on trade among the member states of the Community are also to be gradually eliminated and all state monopolies are to be so modified as to prevent discrimination against any citizen of the Six. The prime objective is to develop a uniform commercial policy among the Six toward the rest of the world. In such a uniform policy the most obvious and perhaps the most important aspect would be a common tariff. When this is attained, after a suitable interval, it is to represent a mathematical average of the tariff levels of the Six as of January, 1957.

Originally it was expected that agriculture would be the last economic activity to be brought under common control. However, the treaty calls for an agricultural organization, common to the Six, that will act on behalf of their agricultural economies in stabilizing prices, establishing minimum prices, subsidizing production, and stockpiling commodities. Hence, although the aim in this sector may be uniform legislation and administrative regulations, agriculture is not likely to become the beneficiary of any more liberal policies than have governed it since 1930.

After establishing a customs union and common agricultural machinery, and after harmonizing social legislation and public welfare policies and overcoming artificial national limitations on Community-wide transport—an agenda that admittedly will tax the economic wisdom, administrative ingenuity, and capacity for equity of all the states and of all the vested interests in those states, and that will certainly require the transitional period of twelve years that has been suggested—the Community organs are to move forward toward more affirmative action. Such action contemplates the development of a common commercial policy toward the rest of the world, promotion within the Community of the free movement of capital and labor, the application of resources to production without consideration of national or regional advantage, and the distribution of goods and services within the Community unhampered by any arbitrary restrictions. Some of these objectives admittedly will encounter many obstacles. The free movement of persons from one Community state to another, for example, can come into being only gradually. Moreover, in the interest of public order, security, and public health, apparently each Community state will retain the right to make discriminatory regulations affecting residents of other Community states.

To secure some coordination among member states on general economic policies, and maintain stability in the various national currencies, price levels, and the volume of employment, it is proposed to establish an advisory monetary committee that will assist the Community organs in developing economic policy. Apparently the Community will represent all of the Six and negotiate on their behalf in matters affecting the Community's common tariff policy toward other states.

From the experience under the Schuman Plan, the drafters of this Common Market Treaty have derived the idea of a special social fund that is to provide some protection for workers who may suffer job displacement because of economic changes, and particularly because of the abolition of special tariffs. The fund is to be used to retrain displaced workers and to assist in their re-employment. At the same time, each of the Six, acting through its own legislature and under the direction of appropriate Community organs, has agreed to bring about uniformity, or an approach thereto, in matters affecting social welfare, conditions of labor, and other conditions affecting employment.

Still another developmental institution that suggests experience derived from the Schuman Plan is the proposed European Investment Bank. Its objective will be the promotion of a common investment policy. From its own resources and funds borrowed on the capital market, this bank is to provide both its own loans and guarantees to advances from private lenders that are designed to promote economic development in the Community. The billion-dollar capital of the bank, which will consist chiefly of national currencies of the six states, is to be subscribed by each of the six governments. The Federal Republic and France will each contribute $300 million to the bank's capital.

A special feature of the Common Market Community project, which delayed negotiations for a time and which threatened on one or two occasions to bring these negotiations at least to a temporary halt, is the plan to incorporate to some extent the overseas territories of certain of the Six. These are the African and some of the other colonies and territories of France, including certain trusteeship areas; Belgium's African territories, Italy's Trust Territory of Somaliland, and the Dutch colony of New Guinea. Such areas are to be "associated" with the common market.

To give meaning to the concept of "association," tariffs are to be gradually reduced, trade is to be "expanded," and a special investment fund is to be created to promote public works in the overseas territories. Somewhat over a half billion dollars has been subscribed by the Six for this purpose, the largest subscription having come from France and the German Federal Republic. The bulk of the total is to go into the French territories. The net effect of this "association" will be to broaden market opportunities in colonial territories on the part of each of the Six, including producers in such states as the German Federal Republic that have no colonies. It will also mean that these six states will enjoy economic privileges in this colonial area that will be denied to outsiders, a situation to which Britain especially objects.

In devising the structure of these two new agencies and authorizing their powers, various leaders, especially M. Spaak, fearful of strengthening the hands of the Rightist elements in the French and other parliaments opposed to federal institutions, sought to avoid identifying the supranational aspects of the communities. As respects the common market, M. Spaak declared in March, 1956, that he was not interested in reviving the controversy over supranationalism that had generated so much heat during the period when the French National Assembly had been considering the ratification of the EDC Treaty. He stated that he wished the experts to create workable institutions for both Euratom and the European Market Communities; thereafter the jurists might decide whether or not these institutions were supranational.[12]

Little doubt exists, however, that both of these proposed creations are to be classed as supranational bodies, although of the two the Euratom Community is probably the more advanced neo-federal body. Both treaties are of indefinite duration. Within the sphere of competence allotted to the two communities, any action taken is irreversible and not subject to national veto. Moreover, decisions that are taken by the Community authorities are directly applicable to the concerns of individuals and private corporations and are enforceable against them. Disputes concerning the use and interpretation of power by Community organs are decided finally by the Community judicial authority in the same manner as in the coal and steel pool. Each of these aspects of the Community's operation constitutes a criterion of an essentially federal institution.

Operating authority in each community is to be exercised by a commission to consist of nine members, in the case of the European Market Community, and of five members in the case of the Euratom Community.[13] These bodies are intended to have powers similar to those vested in the High Authority of the Schuman Community; however, within the area of jurisdiction assigned to the two communities, the Commission has less power of decision on matters of policy than has the High Authority within the area of authority assigned the Schuman project. Both Commissions, and especially that of the European Market Community, are subject in greater measure to the directions of the Community Council of Ministers, which is the direct representative of the sovereign authority of each member state, each of the latter having one representative. The Council of Ministers often requires a unanimous vote in coming to a decision, behaving in such cases like an international assembly of any confederation. But decisions on some matters, regarded as

[12] *Bulletin from the European Community for Coal and Steel,* No. 15 (May 1956), p. 8.

[13] The institutions of the two proposed new communities are described in Arts. 138-188, The Treaty Establishing the European Economic Community, and in Arts. 107-170, The Treaty Establishing the European Atomic Energy Community (Euratom).

less vital to national interests than others, and proposals originating in the Commission, may be decided by a majority vote of the Council. In this case, each of the three larger states, Italy, France, and Germany, is to have four votes on the Council; Belgium and Holland each two votes; and Luxembourg, one vote. Any twelve votes constitute a valid majority except when the Council of Ministers is considering proposals from the common market Commission; in that case there is the further requirement that the majority must include the votes of at least four states.

In the atomic energy pool, as already suggested, the five-man Commission has more discretion than its counterpart in the common market agency. This is largely because of the technical nature of the Community's jurisdiction and the relative absence of vested interests. Nevertheless, here too the Council of Ministers remains the dominant political organ, having authority to decide all issues of policy except such as may properly be appealed to the Community court. The Council of Ministers is composed of the same representatives as in the Market Community and votes in substantially the same manner.

An Economic and Social Committee, common to the two communities, has advisory powers similar to the body of the same name in the Schuman Community, and though somewhat larger than the Schuman committee, it is composed of substantially similar elements and, in time, is likely to be merged with the older body. The court for the two new communities is the same court that already has been functioning in the older supranational agency.

Provision has also been made for a common Parliamentary Assembly to meet in annual sessions for the purpose of exerting parliamentary control. To enforce the Assembly's supremacy in the Community structure, the treaties give power to vote censure of either of the two commissions by a two-thirds vote. When such a vote is carried against either commission, its members must resign and new members, enjoying the Assembly's confidence, are appointed.

The Assembly of the two new communities is to consist of some 142 representatives, 36 being allotted to each of the three larger states, France, the German Federal Republic, and Italy. Initially these representatives are to be elected by the parliaments of each of the Six, but the treaties provide that one of the first acts of the Assembly after it is constituted shall be the drafting of a law providing for the popular election of its representatives.

It will be recalled that when the European Political Community was proposed in 1953, it was anticipated that its assembly would supplant all existing assemblies of supranational bodies and become in fact a federal European parliament. This ideal of a single popular and representative forum for European institutions has not been abandoned. On the contrary, as soon as the institutional question arose as respects these proposed new communities, leaders of the European Movement insisted that there could be no "fourth" assembly, that is, no assembly in addition to those of the Council of Europe, the Schuman pool, and WEU. On February 2, 1957, the bureaus of the three existing assemblies meeting in Brussels, apparently inspired chiefly by M. Spaak, adopted appropriate recommendations that were then sent to the foreign ministers of the Six. With all members concurring, the bureaus urged that there be no "fourth" assembly. They suggested instead that the Schuman Assembly be enlarged to serve both the older community and the two new ones, or that a new assembly be created for the two proposed communities and the existing Schuman Assembly be merged with this new popular body. In any case, the objective was one popular assembly for all supranational communities in "Little Europe," a goal that, as the bureau members observed, was being postponed indefinitely by the proliferation of such bodies. There was even some discussion, apparently not discouraged by Britain and other nonmembers of "Little Europe," about the desirability of establishing a single assembly in lieu of all existing European parliamentary or pseudo-parliamentary bodies, including the Consultative Assembly of the Council of Europe.[14] It seems clear that if and when the two new communities are actually organized a single parliament will be set up for them and the Schuman pool.

What fate lay in store for these two most recent supranational proposals for "Little Europe" was a question that had no clear answer at the time signatures were appended in Rome in March, 1957. As usual, M. Spaak, who with M. Monnet shares much of the

[14] *Council of Europe News*, Vol. 7, No. 3 (Mar. 1957), pp. 1-2.

honor of having initiated the treaties, was optimistic. Following the signing ceremony the Belgian statesman confidently predicted ratification before the end of 1957. Reasons existed to support the belief that public and parliamentary opinion was more favorably inclined toward these projects than toward EDC in 1954. Thanks to the efforts of M. Monnet's Action Committee, the cause of this new venture in supranationalism had been well presented to the European public, and it could be rather confidently predicted that the support of most of the center and moderate parties of the states involved, including this time that of the German Social Democrats, would be forthcoming when the treaties were formally presented for ratification in the respective national parliaments.

At the time the treaties were signed it was freely conceded that their real testing ground would be France's National Assembly. Even if the parliaments of the remaining states of the Six were disposed to support the documents, their fate, so it was said, was likely to be settled in this mercurial forum even as that of EDC had been settled there. In that assembly the two new treaties had their enemies, or at least their untrustworthy friends. Remnants of the Gaullist Right, the forty-odd Poujadists, certain Radical followers of M. Pierre Mendès-France and, of course, the Communists, constituted a fairly sizable opposition to eventual ratification. Moreover, the French Assembly, often plagued by unstable cabinets and preoccupied with North African matters and the issues of tax reform, monetary inflation, and other fiscal measures, had plenty of excuses for sidetracking the treaties if excuses were wanted, and, by refusing to act either favorably or unfavorably, it could mete out to them the same fate of a lingering death by attrition that it had meted out to the EDC Treaty.

Of the two proposals, that for the European Atomic Energy Community appeared in March, 1957, to have the better chance of eventual ratification. As early as July, 1956, Prime Minister Mollet had succeeded in persuading a majority in the French Assembly to endorse this proposal in principle.[15] Moreover, from the time the energy plan was first proposed by M. Monnet's Action Committee,

[15] The vote was 342 to 183; see *The New York Times,* July 12, 1956. M. Mollet secured similar endorsement from the assembly for the common market plan, 322 to 207, on Jan. 22, 1957, *ibid.,* Jan. 23, 1957.

it had had firmer support than the common market plan in all of the six nations. The reasons for this condition are quite clear. Euratom is not only more limited than the Market Community project as to subject matter, but the single subject with which it deals, namely, nuclear power development, is not afflicted with vested national and private interests as are many aspects of the market project. Moreover, the power deficit in Western Europe is considerable. It has been estimated that even with a reasonable increase in sources of conventional power, "Little Europe" would be importing almost 40 per cent of its energy requirements by 1975. The Suez crisis of 1956 had also dramatized the fact that dependence upon Middle Eastern oil for part of Western Europe's energy requirements was fraught with grave political uncertainty. Hence, any alleviation of the energy shortage such as is promised by nuclear exploitation is likely to be welcomed, particularly since the cost of such nuclear power is not much greater than the cost of energy from more conventional sources.[16] Economists in Western Europe had also reminded political leaders that the expenditure required to harness the energy of the atom is so huge that none of the Six in "Little Europe" is alone capable of providing the necessary financing. The limitations of unadulterated nationalism had never been more strikingly demonstrated.

Washington's policy had also brightened the outlook for the proposed Atomic Energy Community and had given it greater appeal than the common market plan. Shortly after M. Monnet's Action Committee suggested this project, a committee of three experts on nuclear fuels went to Washington to confer with the President, the State Department, and the United States Atomic Energy Commission. Their purpose was to determine what help the United States government might offer. In February, 1957, President Eisenhower announced that the United States would allocate some 20,000 kilograms of U-235 for sale or lease outside the United States, the uranium to be exploited for civilian power requirements. As a result of this announcement the proponents of the new Community were able to conclude that the availability of

[16] This is true of Western Europe. In the United States conventional energy costs relatively less than nuclear energy.

fuel for reactors would not be a "limiting factor."[17] Moreover, Washington officials clearly indicated that the United States government would give the most sympathetic consideration to any request for assisting the new Community financially and technically. The various economic and related obstacles that this promise of cooperation and aid from the United States was expected to overcome greatly encouraged the European sponsors of Euratom to move rapidly with this project and assisted them in strengthening the will of the vacillating supporters and overcoming the opponents of the treaty among their own constituents.

As for the common market, although the prospects for its acceptance seemed less hopeful than for Euratom when the treaties were signed, those prospects also improved subsequently. The improvement resulted from the fact that the treaty conferees surmounted successfully some of the obstacles that had originally threatened to prevent the consummation of any treaty. Among the obstacles thus surmounted were objections on the part of some of the Six to the proposed association of overseas territories with the European market and the fears of agricultural producers in some of the proposed member states that they would be exposed to too competitive a price structure. Britain's simultaneous expression of interest in being associated, at least in a limited way, with a free trade area on the Continent also provided a fillip to the hopes of the supporters of the proposed new community. These were among the developments that produced guarded optimism about the Market Treaty's prospects shortly after its signing despite awareness of the potential opposition of all sorts of vested economic interests, particularly of the protected interests of the relatively weak, and hence vulnerable, economies of certain states among the Six.

As the weeks succeeded one another after the ceremonies at Rome in March, it became apparent that the future of both treaties was even brighter than the most optimistic had dared to hope. A little more than three months after the delegates at Rome had appended their signatures to the documents, the French National Assembly, under the leadership of the Maurice Bourges-Manoury gov-

[17] For text of the Joint Communiqué of the United States government and the Euratom Committee of Three, see *Bulletin from the European Community for Coal and Steel*, No. 22 (Feb.-Mar. 1957), pp. 6-7.

ernment, ratified the two treaties by substantial majorities. For the Economic Community plan the vote was 341-234; for the Euratom pact the vote was 335-243. As anticipated, the opposition consisted of some nineteen Mendès-France Radicals, the Communists, the Poujadists, and a scattering of Gaullists and Right-wing Independents. Thus the legislative hurdle that had seemed at the outset to be the most serious was the first to be overcome and it was overcome quite comfortably.[18] A short time afterward, on July 24, all thc formalities of parliamentary ratification in France were fulfilled when the Council of the Republic voted approval of the two treaties by a vote of 222-70.[19]

Four days before official action had been taken on the two treaties in Paris, the Bundestag of the German Federal Republic also ratified with a sizable majority, and the Bundesrat followed on July 19. Italy, the third major power in "Little Europe," also spoke affirmatively through its Chamber of Deputies, having ratified the treaties on July 30 by a vote of 311-144, with some fifty-four Nenni Socialists abstaining. Shortly thereafter, the Italian Senate completed ratification, and the three Benelux nations took similar action within a matter of weeks. Belgium's Senate acted finally on the two treaties for the nation's parliament on November 28, 1957, providing an overwhelming affirmative majority of 134 to 2. Luxembourg's unicameral parliament indicated its adhesion to the two treaties two days earlier by a vote of 46 to 3. The definitive step to bring the Netherlands formally into the two new communities was taken by that nation's upper chamber on December 4. This was also the final action required to complete the process of ratification among the Six. During December, 1957, the acts of ratification were deposited at Rome, and following the so-called "summit conference" of NATO at Paris in mid-December, heads of government of the Six met to appoint the 30-odd officials required to provide political leadership and administrative direction for the two new communities. At the same time, the leaders of the Six deliberated on the choice of an administrative center for the two new communities.

[18] For accounts of the ratification, see *The New York Times,* July 10, 1957; also *Bulletin from the European Community for Coal and Steel,* No. 24 (June-July 1957), p. 1.

[19] *Council of Europe News,* Vol. 7, No. 8 (Aug. 1957), p. 4.

The site so chosen may well become a kind of "District of Columbia" for Europe and serve as Europe's "capital." Keen competition existed among various cities for this honor, these cities including, among others, Strasbourg, Milan, Brussels, and Luxembourg.[20]

Thus by the end of autumn 1957, when this volume went to press, it seemed reasonably certain that the optimistic timetable for inaugurating the new communities, which had been suggested by M. Spaak in March of 1957, would be observed. Even the less optimistic observers were concluding that the institution of the new supranational machinery might take place by January, 1958, and certainly not later than the spring of that year; that the common market for nuclear materials could become operative by January, 1959; and that, in the proposed new Economic Community, the first reduction of tariffs among the six participating nations, amounting to the scheduled 10 per cent, could also take place by January, 1959.

Such developments coming so soon after the defeat of EDC are truly an extraordinary manifestation of the strength of the supranational concept in Western Europe. From the ashes of the defeat suffered in the French parliament in August, 1954, a defeat that appeared at the time to have burned out the last vestige of enthusiasm for a Europe united along federal lines, the ideal of such a Europe rose again in 1957, Phoenixlike, to command reaffirmation from Europe's leadership. Hence, for the third time since 1950, the six nations of "Little Europe" were launched on a program for achieving an essentially federal plan of union in certain important areas of public jurisdiction. Moreover, all other Western European nations, whether or not they were represented at Strasbourg, were observing this renewed effort with great interest. Many of them, fearful of being left in the lurch in the sweeping reorganization of economic life provided by the two new communities, though still unwilling to join the Six, were beginning to give serious consideration to some means of association short of outright membership that might give them a means of influencing the course of events.

[20] See various issues of *The New York Times*, including those for July 25 and 31, Nov. 25, and Dec. 5 and 15, 1957.

12 Supranationalism's Chief Asset—The Schuman Community After Six Years

As SUGGESTED in the preceding chapter, a consideration that played no insignificant role in the revival of the supranational integrative movement in Western Europe after the defeat of EDC was the apparent success of the Schuman Community.[1] This creation has been exercising all of its treaty prerogatives only since August 1, 1954. Nevertheless, it has already justified the more sanguine expectations of its creators, MM. Schuman and Monnet. Indeed its record during the past five years has leaned so heavily toward the credit side of the ledger that it has been no small factor in reviving the hopes of the friends of supranationalism. As we have noted in the preceding chapter, the Schuman record has become the principal argument for extending the supranational common market beyond the primary products of coal and steel to embrace the entire production of the Six.

The success story of the Schuman Community is all the more dramatic because it has been achieved under circumstances that were distinctly unfavorable. As suggested earlier in this volume,[2] the Schuman Community was to have been merely the first of several similar authorities to be set up within the territorial area of the Six. Orphaned by the demise of EDC and the proposed Political Community, the Schuman Community became quite isolated. It lacked both the institutional matrix in which it was intended

[1] See Chapter 7 for a discussion of its inception and structure.
[2] See p. 72.

to function and to thrive and the encouragement of an interested public opinion. So unpromising had the future of this creation become in 1954 that many observers, among whom were several who had been the Schuman Community's strong champions, freely predicted that it would soon wither away. Faith in its future persisted only among the half dozen who had been directly responsible for its establishment or who were members of its governing body, the High Authority. Even they evinced no great enthusiasm for the future of this creation after the French National Assembly had finished with EDC, and they could hardly have anticipated so favorable an issue for their handiwork as has developed during the post-EDC period.

It will be the purpose of this chapter to trace the history of the Schuman Community since its official inauguration in Luxembourg on August 10, 1952, and to comment on various aspects of its achievement in fulfilling its objectives in the economic area. In doing so, we shall try to relate that achievement to the evolution of the broader political objective of federal integration of Western Europe.

The proposed common market for coal, iron ore, and scrap became effective for the Community on February 10, 1953; that for steel became effective on May 1, 1953; that for special steels, on August 1, 1954. Hence, except for certain transitional limitations on the Community's discretion that were scheduled to expire August 10, 1957, five years after the Community's inauguration, the discretionary authority conferred by the treaty has been in effect since 1953.

Appraisals of the record since that date have been numerous, and although scarcely definitive, they have been rather penetrating, and nearly always favorable. As might be expected, much discussion has revolved about the question of the Community's relative success in achieving its central purpose, that is, a common market for coal and steel that is also a free market. The answer to that question, in turn, has depended in the first instance upon the degree of success that has attended the Community's efforts to eliminate cartelism.

As suggested earlier,[3] adequate power for dealing with cartelism

[3] See Chapter 7.

is provided in the Schuman Treaty. Under its terms, any policy or decision of a group of industries to affect prices, restrict production or capital development, or allocate markets is automatically void. Cartel inquiries by the High Authority are facilitated by its power to compel information, a private firm being liable to a fine of as much as 1 per cent of its annual turnover if it proves refractory. Cartels that persist despite orders to dissolve may be fined as much as 10 per cent of the value of annual turnover. Nor may any industrial concentration or merger be effected without the High Authority's prior permission. This permission may be withheld if it appears to the High Authority that the proposed concentration or merger may lessen competition or influence prices in a manner prejudicial to the consumer. If a merger or concentration should come into existence that the High Authority believes is a cartel, the High Authority may call for its immediate dissolution, segregate the assets involved, and resort to daily fines to secure compliance with its order.[4]

During the period of transition to a common market, the High Authority occasionally encountered criticism of its cartel policy. In 1953, for example, it announced a decision to maintain price ceilings on coal in the Ruhr and certain French areas, a decision that led the government of the Netherlands to lodge a complaint with the Community Court. The Netherlands' complaint was subsequently withdrawn after the High Authority announced that it would speed up efforts to end monopoly practices among sellers and buyers of coal in the Ruhr, Belgium, and elsewhere. These efforts of the High Authority must have proven fairly satisfactory because, at a subsequent meeting of the Community's Common Assembly, its members saw fit to praise the High Authority's action.

A related criticism was directed at the High Authority's agreement, made in January, 1954, to allow certain sellers discretion to revise established prices upward or downward within certain percentage limits and to keep their action secret. Although the High Authority's action in allowing such discretionary pricing was intended to be quite temporary, it was vigorously assailed by the French and Italian governments and by certain private firms. A

[4] Schuman Treaty, Arts. 60-61.

complaint was again lodged with the Community Court and that tribunal proceeded to annul the High Authority's action. The Court's decree was memorable because it established a precedent for action against a supranational authority on the plea of at least two sovereign states.

Pressure to maintain private arrangements "regulating" distribution has obviously been considerable. Spokesmen of both French and German industry have complained that the High Authority's policy is too open and too free. They have accused the High Authority of lack of wisdom in interfering with private arrangements to provide market equilibrium especially in periods of relatively high demand such as followed the outbreak of the Korean War. They have also asserted that the High Authority ignores experts in industry and in industrial associations although presumably such experts know more about the needs of the industry than the members of the governing body of the Community. Sympathetic spokesmen of national interests, usually a euphemism for marginal producers who fear a competitive market, have also insisted that the Luxembourg organization has ignored them. Even the German Socialists, which is a party supposed to represent primarily the interests of the German worker, have occasionally protested the High Authority's efforts to modify the production and distribution policies that the Ruhr industrialists were currently observing.

There can be no doubt that the High Authority has resisted successfully such pressures of vested interests to place the Community behind private restrictive practices. Its policy during this transitional period of its existence has been that of pursuing a middle course, cushioning the weak against too strong an impact from the policy of a common market, but keeping constantly in view the ultimate objective of a free market, which means a competitive market.

In its attempt to assure a common market that is also free, equal success has attended the High Authority's policy of overcoming the effect of market restrictions and discriminations of a public nature, that is, those resulting from national policy and public regulation. Here, of course, abolition of tariff walls among the Six has been only one of the objectives. All sorts of discriminatory practices and special situations have had to be coped with. Marginal producers obviously have an interest in preserving their artificially secured position in the market, and they are likely to do what they can to persuade the Community High Authority to perpetuate their status or to change it only very gradually. Provisions in the treaty, moreover, imply a responsibility for the Community of exercising a protective policy for marginal industry, in the interests of both producer and workmen, especially during a period of transition to a Community market. Thus, for the five-year transitional period after the inauguration of the Community, the High Authority was authorized to levy a tax on the more efficient coal producers and use the proceeds to bolster the market position of the weaker producers. This policy of protection could be carried out by the Community in conjunction with the governments involved. The treaty also contained special transitional provisions for assisting French and Belgian mines where productivity is notoriously low. Both the High Authority and the governments involved may subsidize and otherwise "compensate" these mines for a limited period while their prices are brought into line with those of more efficient producers. Ultimately it is anticipated that, through modernization and other kinds of rationalization, the weaker Belgian and French mines may be assimilated to the general market structure of the Community.

Obstacles encountered by the Benelux states in working out their projected customs and subsequent economic unions indicate how notoriously easy it is to yield to the temptation of perpetuating indefinitely certain protective measures and how difficult it is to overcome the entrenchment of entrepreneur and workmen in a protected market situation. Actually, the only safeguard against such perpetuation is the conviction of those in charge of policy for the Community that restrictionism and the maintenance of the *status quo,* however understandable from the short-run economic point of view and from the point of view of the immediate human factor involved, cannot be allowed to persist if the real purpose of the Community is to be achieved.

That such a conviction has obtained in the High Authority seems apparent. Despite certain concessions that have been made to maintain a protected situation, the record in general is one that convinces even the skeptical that the management of the High Authority means to do what it started out to do, namely, to make the Western European market both a common market and a free market. The High Authority has been sympathetic to special situations that have been protected in the past, but it has sought diligently to scale down the area of restriction and the scope of public protection and absorb all markets to a common level. At the end of 1954, rebates given to purchasers of German coal had been practically eliminated, and French treasury subsidies to French coal producers had been halved. Considerable progress had been made in bringing about an approach to equilibrium between the market position of Belgian and other Community coal producers. When special steels came under the jurisdiction of the High Authority in 1954, a customs rate of 10 per cent was authorized for the five-year transitional period for such steels produced in Italy, but the High Authority has reserved the right to review this rate each year and progressively reduce it.

In addition to the Community's industrial policies that are directly designed to prevent restrictionism, there are others, less important and somewhat tangential in their impact, that also reveal the Community's intention to pursue an open, as opposed to a closed, market policy. One of these is the prospective issuance of a so-called "European labor card." This is intended to permit freedom of movement and employment within the Community for various categories of skilled or semiskilled workers, whatever their country of origin among the Six. About one-sixth of the available total labor force may be affected. Still another step has been the effort to overcome frontier limitations on the movement by rail within the Community of the products falling within the common market. This has been done by abolishing national differentials in rates and special frontier charges and by establishing instead Community "through rates" for such products. As a result of the High Authority's initiative during the summer of 1954, and the action of the Community's Council of Ministers in January, 1955, it is estimated that the policy of Community-wide rates on coal, iron ore, scrap, and steel will have come into being by 1958.[5]

That the common market introduced by the Community has been reasonably effective in maximizing output and trade is evidenced by the growing volume of trade in Community products among the six

[5] *The New York Times,* Jan. 24, 1955; also *Bulletin from the European Community for Coal and Steel,* No. 15 (May 1956), pp. 8-10.

Schuman states. In the three-year period following the inauguration of the Community, trade in steel increased 151 per cent; scrap, 357 per cent; iron ore, 37 per cent; and coal, 40 per cent. This of course was a period generally favorable to industrial expansion, and the same results might have been accomplished if the purely national market structure had persisted. Nevertheless, when the scale of expansion of trade in Community products is compared with that of other products, there appears to have been a much greater expansion of the former, a fact that can probably be safely attributed to the common market. Thus in the period under consideration, trade in products subject to the Community market increased some 93 per cent whereas trade in other products increased only 59 per cent.[6] The Community, moreover, appears to make greater economic sense as a producing and trading area than the former national units. In the case of steel, as M. Monnet recently pointed out, the common market seems to have been decisive in cushioning effects of both market contraction and expansion. For the first time in recent history, said M. Monnet, the market in Western Europe had acquired such proportions that it appeared to be immune to the influence of American activity in this basic product. At any rate, after 1952, a discernible reduction in American activity had no appreciable effect on the Community states, and subsequent economic revival in them preceded American recovery by several months.[7]

Equally serious efforts have been undertaken to pursue the third principal objective of the Community, namely, the policy of expanding production and increasing productive efficiency, thereby attaining the higher plateau of production and of income for investors and workmen upon which Monnet and European converts to American methods have placed so much emphasis. In this area, one of the more promising developments was the Community's success in persuading the Export-Import Bank of the United States to grant a development loan. This occurred in April, 1954. The loan, amounting to $100 million and carrying extremely favorable interest rates, was authorized during the visit of M. Monnet, then president of the High Authority, to the United States. In issuing the loan,

[6] *Bulletin from the European Community for Coal and Steel,* No. 16 (June 1956), p. 8.

[7] *Ibid.,* p. 8.

the United States government re-emphasized its desire to encourage private American capital sources to offer the Community favorable terms. Although private sources in America have been slow to underwrite loans to the Community, private Swiss banks did grant a loan to the High Authority in June, 1956. This loan of 50 million francs was for an eighteen-year period at an interest rate of 4¼ per cent.

Vigorous and effective exploitation of the resources provided by these loans have characterized the Community's investment policy. The proceeds have been re-lent at relatively low interest rates to firms within the Community to carry forward plant expansion and modernization. Firms in Western Germany received the largest amount. The High Authority's loans within the Community are administered by the Bank for International Settlements at Basel, Switzerland, an institution that has become the Community's chief banking and fiscal agency.[8] One of the secondary results of the American loan to the Community has been an increase of the flow of private capital directly to firms within the Community. Moreover, the low cost of the American loan and the ability of the High Authority to re-lend at a favorable rate has brought down the cost of private borrowing. It is estimated that between $3 and $3.3 billions were invested in coal and steel enterprises between 1953 and 1955, and that an annual rate of $1 billion could be maintained for some time thereafter.[9]

Development and modernization loans to private firms in the Community are covered not only by the security offered by the actual borrowers but sometimes also by some sort of supplementary guarantee provided by the state in which the borrowing firm is located or by some other public body or industrial association. In addition, the lender has the security provided by the High Authority's own loan-guarantee fund. This is a fund accumulated from an annual levy of as much as 1 per cent of the value of total production that the Schuman Treaty permits the High Authority to

[8] Details of the Bank's activity in this connection are provided in its *Twenty-sixth Annual Report* (Basel, June 11, 1956), pp. 224-225. The Bank's report indicates that the High Authority has obtained further loans in Belgium, Germany, Luxembourg, and the Saar.

[9] *Bulletin from the European Community for Coal and Steel,* No. 16 (June 1956), p. 3.

assess upon producing firms within the Community area. The proceeds of this fund are used not merely to guarantee private lenders against loss but also to pay the administrative expenses of the various Community agencies. Because of the expansion of production within the Community in recent years, this levy has proven to be so productive that the rate actually assessed in January, 1956, was reduced to less than one-half of 1 per cent and the High Authority agreed that the total proceeds of this fund should never exceed $100 million.[10]

Additional evidence that the High Authority is committed against maintenance of a static economy is to be discovered in its various projects designed to compensate in part for the human and social cost of its industrial modernization program. In a two-year period prior to June, 1956, major projects of this sort have cost the High Authority some $16 million. The funds have gone into workers' houses and into efforts to retrain workers who have become surplus because of industrial mergers or technological displacement. The specific projects financed by the High Authority have resulted from efforts to merge certain steel firms in France into four companies of a size that could compete more effectively in the Community-wide market; to eliminate marginal mines in Belgium and South France and assist in the migration of miners in France to the more productive Lorraine region; to mechanize coal mines in Sardinia; and to modernize and merge certain Italian steel plants. Usually the High Authority's outlay for such projects has been matched by the national governments involved. It is thus quite apparent that the social and labor clauses of the Schuman Treaty are not a dead letter. They are being invoked on a broad scale in order that the High Authority and the economy of the Community may assume some of the noneconomic costs of the dynamic economic policy that is currently being pursued.[11]

Less tangible but nonetheless significant evidence of the progress of the Community is afforded by the excellent administrative record of its various institutions. The nine-man High Authority has been blessed with the outstanding leadership first of Jean Monnet and,

[10] *Ibid.*

[11] *Bulletin from the European Community for Coal and Steel,* No. 1 (Oct. 1954), pp. 7-8; No. 15 (May 1956), p. 12; and No. 16 (June 1956), p. 3.

after his resignation, of the former French prime minister, René Mayer. Among the governments of the West, the prestige of these two individuals, and their dedication to the concept of supranational integration, has been of immense value to the High Authority during the Community's formative years.

Each of the Community's auxiliary agencies has also established an enviable record of achievement within its particular sphere of action. Members of the ministerial council, although occasionally animated by a somewhat narrow nationalistic point of view, have provided indispensable liaison between the High Authority and the national governments in those cases where national and Community policy must be reconciled if action at either level is not to prove abortive. The seven-judge Community Court, organized under the presidency of the Italian jurist, Massimo Pilotti, has several times advanced to a decision cases involving both private firms and national governments, and it has entered judgment that in the nature of the case must be final.[12] Late in 1956, it had five cases on its docket. The Schuman Court is fast evolving a series of precedents that will provide a unique body of federal law, procedural and substantive, within the limited jurisdictional orbit comprehended by the Schuman Treaty. Even the least significant Community agency, the purely advisory fifty-one member Consultative Committee, has become an important instrument for making known the views of economic constituencies within the Community, and is apparently consulted regularly by the High Authority.

Of all the auxiliary organs of the Community, the most notable record of growth and accomplishment has been enjoyed by the Schuman Common Assembly. This first parliament of a supranational European body is invested with no legislative authority. Its only formal prerogative of importance is that of supervision and control. To that end it is invested with power to oust the High Authority by a two-thirds vote of its membership. But the procedure of European parliaments and the traditions of democratic assemblies generally have provided more than one important precedent for this body's activity, and the usages that it is gradually building up are transforming it into a significant voice of the Com-

[12] See p. 150.

munity. Seven Assembly standing committees existed in 1957, each responsible for a broad area of jurisdiction. The meetings of these committees, held fairly regularly, are usually attended by at least one member of the High Authority who takes the lead in explaining policy and answering such criticisms as may be voiced by the committee members. Increasingly, moreover, groups in the Assembly avoid voting as national party blocs. Instead, similar ideological party groups from each of the six states form a solid Community-wide party bloc and cast votes without reference to national loyalties. According to the Schuman Treaty, the Assembly is scheduled to meet once each year, but this regular session is supplemented by various special sessions.

Of late this assembly has become the most important public body in Western Europe engaged in promoting the supranational ideal. Mention was made earlier of its use as the constituent agency for drafting the abortive treaty for a Political Community.[13] More recently, as was also noted,[14] it met in special session in the Belgian Senate Chamber to consider the report of the intergovernmental committee, which was planning the treaties for Euratom and the proposed common market signed at Rome, March 25, 1957. At the conclusion of the session, it gave almost unanimous endorsement to these proposals.[15] Its membership continues to be selected from the parliaments of the respective countries and most of these serve also in the Consultative Assembly in Strasbourg, but the demand for popular election of the members becomes more insistent year by year.[16]

The Community's advancing prestige and acknowledgment of the significance of the role it is discharging in Western European politico-economic organization are reflected in the scope of its external relations. Several countries, among them the United States, Sweden, Norway, and Austria, have recognized its status as an

[13] Chapter 9.

[14] See p. 134.

[15] For further description of this important debate see *Council of Europe News*, No. 6 (June 1956), p. 7.

[16] An interesting description of the Assembly and a summary of a recent report by a committee headed by the French deputy, Alain Polner, recommending new prerogatives for that body is contained in *Bulletin from the European Community for Coal and Steel*, No. 16 (June 1956), pp. 1 ff.

international entity and have accredited missions to it that enjoy ministerial or ambassadorial rank. A permanent mission also represents the Community at meetings of the OEEC. In its relations with GATT (General Agreement on Tariffs and Trade), the Community is regarded as a single contracting party representing the interests of all its associated states for issues arising out of the Community's jurisdiction. At a recent conference of GATT in Geneva, the High Authority, acting on the basis of special powers conferred by the Community's Council of Ministers to negotiate on behalf of three Community members, France, Germany, and Italy, secured certain reductions in import duties on steel from the United States and Austria. The first treaty with a sovereign state, signed by the High Authority on behalf of the Community as an international entity, was one concluded with Switzerland on May 8, 1956. In it, Switzerland and the Community agree to consult in advance of any action either may take that might affect the market position of the other.[17]

Probably the most important association that the Community has established is that with the United Kingdom. It will be recalled that from the very beginning of the European Movement Britain adopted an ambiguous policy toward the question of supranational integration and then rejected the concept altogether. At the same time, she has often reiterated her desire for some form of intergovernmental arrangement to handle common problems that would not derogate from her sovereignty. This latter was the institutional policy she announced toward the original proposal to pool the market for coal and steel, and although the Continental leaders proceeded without her to set up their supranational arrangement, they were fairly confident that after their arrangement had been set in operation Britain, in deference to her own national interests in this field, might well be persuaded to agree to some form of association with the supranational Community. Indeed, during the months the Schuman Plan was being ratified by the parliaments of the six nations, André Philip, the French Socialist leader who was one of the chief protagonists of the Schuman Community, indicated his conviction that as soon as the High Authority set up shop it would open negotiations with the British government "with a view to

[17] *Bulletin from the European Community for Coal and Steel,* No. 16 (June 1956), p. 5.

bringing about general coordination with British industries."[18] Moreover, on August 11, 1952, only one day after the Community had formally become a going concern in Luxembourg, the British government itself issued a declaration that it desired to establish "a close and lasting association" with the new Community.

Hence world opinion was not too surprised when an "Agreement of Association" between the United Kingdom and the various states of the Schuman Community was signed at London on December 21, 1954. The agreement set up a joint council of eight, to be known as the "Council of Association," to develop common policies on matters affecting investment, efforts to check deflationary or inflationary trends, cartel and fair-trade matters, and the elimination of tariffs and other restrictions between the Community and the United Kingdom. Under the agreement, either side may decline to "associate" on any matter of policy.[19]

Spokesmen of the Community, particularly MM. Monnet and Mayer, eager to find institutional concepts to expand integration on the Continent, regard this "association" as a possible formula for other alignments between Britain and supranational agencies. It may thus provide a solution for the problem posed by Britain's steadfast insistence on mere intergovernmental arrangements while her trans-Channel neighbors demand something that is institutionally more unitary and more durable. Said M. Mayer recently: "The signatory nations to the Schuman Treaty participate fully in the federal institutions of the Community while the United Kingdom through a Treaty of Association with the Coal and Steel Community cooperates with its federal institutions. This formula, I believe, may give us the best of both worlds."[20]

In arriving at any final appraisal of the Schuman Community, it must be recalled that many public prerogatives, the exercise of which strongly influences the status of the common market for coal and steel, remain with the six national governments. National powers of taxation and social legislation remain undiminished. So

[18] *The Schuman Plan,* previously cited, p. 45.

[19] *Bulletin from the European Community for Coal and Steel,* No. 4 (Jan. 1955), pp. 1 ff.

[20] *Bulletin from the European Community for Coal and Steel,* No. 14 (Apr. 1956), p. 3.

do regulatory powers affecting fiscal and monetary policy. The exertion of any of these prerogatives will obviously influence the entire national economy and may readily modify, for good or ill, such actions as the High Authority may have taken in the limited domain committed to its supervision. Moreover, all authority over production, distribution, and investment, affecting all goods and services except those committed to the Community, remains with the national governments. As an astute American writer has observed, the integration achieved through the Community is an example of "sector integration," a form of integration that is "profoundly illogical" since "each industrial sector of the national economy is tied intimately to other sectors through a network of markets, through common wage policies, and through a common social and political environment." [21]

This dichotomy in the regulatory authority over areas of the economy can easily lead to contrary economic policies by the various agencies, national and Community. In time of stress, because of inflationary pressures or a serious recession, a national government might well apply defensive measures without too much regard for the policy of its neighbor states or the Community. In the long run, however favorable the present outlook may be, this dichotomy in authority and policy could affect the common Schuman market adversely and even threaten to destroy it. Undoubtedly a spirit of accommodation will normally prevail among the associated governments and the Community, and such a spirit will go far to maintain the required uniformity of policy. Nevertheless, professional economists and fiscal experts properly maintain that the only remedy for this underlying weakness in the Luxembourg arrangement is to expand the concept of economic integration so as to include the entire economy in the Community area. These potential inadequacies of the Schuman Community thus provide support for those political leaders who are intent upon advancing the idea of broader unification of the economy of the Six.

The exploitation of both the successes and the weaknesses of the Schuman arrangement as an argument for a supranationally con-

[21] F. R. Root, "The European Coal and Steel Community," Part II, in *Studies in Business and Economics,* University of Maryland, Vol. 10, No. 1 (June 1956), p. 11.

trolled common market embracing all production among the Six has other than merely an economic objective. As suggested at the time this plan was broached, and as frequently reiterated in these pages, that objective is political. True to their views, often expressed throughout the vicissitudes of the European Movement since 1947, even those most intimately associated with the creation and administration of the Schuman Community consider its record significant primarily from the point of view of the contribution that such a record will make to sustain progress toward European federal unity. This is the view of the Community's principal creator and first president of its High Authority, M. Monnet. As we have already noted, his resignation at the high point of a successful career as the Community's chief administrative officer was motivated by his desire to lead the effort to revive supranationalism on a broad scale.[22] In that effort he has exploited the record of the Community to the best advantage. Such has also been the objective of Paul-Henri Spaak, ardent supporter of European causes. It has likewise been one of the principal aims of the Common Assembly. Both have used the record of the Schuman Community and their institutional prerogatives to advance the political cause of federation. How this was done has already been related.[23]

All this, of course, should occasion no surprise, for, as we have frequently noted, the larger political objectives of the Schuman Community were clearly stated when it was first broached. The Community's political, as distinct from its economic, purpose is stated in the very preamble of the Schuman Treaty, the contracting parties having declared that they were "resolved to substitute for historic rivalries a fusion of their essential interests," and "to establish, by creating an economic community, the foundation of a broad and independent community among peoples long divided by bloody conflicts; and to lay the bases of institutions capable of giving direction to their future common destiny."[24]

M. Schuman was also quite definite about the long-term political purpose of his plan. On the very day he outlined it to the Strasbourg

[22] See p. 132.
[23] See pp. 99, 107, 133-134.
[24] Preamble, Schuman Treaty.

Assembly in 1950, he declared that his primary purpose was to use the Community to unify France and Germany and reconcile them politically. The Community, he said, was to be a decisive step toward such a reconciliation, and the reconciliation in turn would make possible the economic and political unification of Europe. "Europe," he said, "cannot be united in a day, nor in a single framework; it will be formed by concrete measures capable of forging real bonds of solidarity and friendship among her peoples." [25] André Philip was even more explicit as to the way in which the Coal and Steel Community would lead to a federal Europe. "We will make a start," he said, "and after the first Schuman Plan Authority has been set up, others will follow. Thus gradually, one after another, by the functional method, there will be set up various European Ministries, which will be responsible towards what will become a European Parliament." [26]

Such expectations as these were frustrated in 1954 with the defeat of EDC and the shelving of the Political Community. But with the revival of interest in supranational solutions in 1956, the Schuman Community became an even more significant steppingstone toward federation than it was when it was first proposed; for by 1956, as this chapter has tried to show, it had become more than an idea. By that time it had a record of solid achievement and offered empirical evidence of the value of supranational authority—evidence that it will be difficult to refute. Moreover, its logical shortcomings are themselves an argument favoring extension of the supranational concept.

Thus the once orphaned Schuman Community, which many observers thought would gradually wither away after it was set adrift in 1954, has become a principal ally of the supranationalists. Its record since 1952, including both its achievements and its shortcomings, has demonstrated the wisdom of supplementing Europe's existing national political structure with a broad supranational structure, one that approaches federalism. Only thus, it would appear, can Europe proceed with confidence toward the solution of many of the politico-economic problems of an age that has dis-

[25] See A. Philip, *The Schuman Plan,* cited earlier, pp. 7-8.
[26] *The First Five Years,* p. 64.

covered technology and identified matter with energy. Meanwhile, the record of the Schuman Community provides the principal argument for proceeding immediately toward the development of a market that embraces the entire territory of "Little Europe" and supranational regulation of the exploitation of nuclear energy for peaceful purposes.

13 Toward a Twentieth-Century Conception of European Union

LITTLE MORE THAN A DECADE has elapsed since Sir Winston Churchill delivered at Zürich his seminal plea for a united Europe. In that relatively brief period, he and Coudenhove-Kalergi, the pioneers among the proponents of this idea in the twentieth century, have seen it exert a profound influence upon the mind and action of Europe, an influence that, for scope and intensity, has rarely been equaled by that of other great ideas in history. Indeed history has rarely vouchsafed the man of ideas and the propagandist such an extensive and immediate impact upon human actions and institutions as has been afforded these two progenitors of the European Movement. Supported by some of the Continent's first minds, this movement has laid the foundations of a veritable revolution in political concepts, one that bids fair to develop, in time, symbols, institutions, and loyalties for a community whose significance transcends that of the traditional national state in the European area, and that promises to spark, in the not-too-distant future, a thoroughgoing reorganization of the politico-economic structure of Europe or at least of a substantial section of that continent.

Inspiration and nurture for this intellectual revolution concerning the future politico-economic form of Europe have been provided in part by the practical experiments in transnational and supranational institutions elaborated in Western Europe since the end of World War II. These have afforded concrete demonstrations that a politico-economic community broader in scope than the traditional national state can be successfully created. They have also afforded positive technical evidence that such communities may provide solutions for current socio-economic problems—solutions that are quite beyond the power and capacity of the existing nation-state. Despite the failures that have been encountered in the case of some of the efforts, failures that in the case of EDC and allied projects were particularly grave and that it may take many years to repair, there can be no doubt that what has already been accomplished in developing centripetal European institutions has permanently changed the political face of that continent and significantly altered its economy.

Earlier we commented at length upon the contribution that the Schuman Community has made in advancing the cause of European integration. That contribution, as we noted, has taken the form of educating Europe on the advantages and disadvantages of the only truly European supranational experiment of modern times. The Luxembourg project has demonstrated not only what can be done in the limited area confided to its authority but has also revealed glimpses of a more prosperous future for European capital and labor if the project's limited authority were widened to include the proposed common market and an economic policy that was European in scope rather than the result of parochial national aspirations and policies.

Equally important in advancing supranational concepts has been the contribution made by the Common Assembly and related Schuman institutions in providing an official forum for such leaders as Monnet, Mayer, Spaak, and others when they took up the publicity cudgels for such concepts. The Schuman Community institutions provided indispensable assistance in Monnet's creation of his Action Committee in 1955.[1] As was noted in the preceding chapters, the Community's operations have also enabled Monnet and his colleagues to use this experiment in their efforts to illustrate the true meaning of supranational institutions for the European public and hence to habituate many Europeans to the operation of such institutions. Last but not least, both the High Authority and Common Assembly of the Schuman Community have also served as models of

[1] See p. 132.

political and administrative agencies, truly supranational in outlook and composition.

What can be said of the contribution to the European Movement made by the Schuman Community for Coal and Steel may also be said, albeit with somewhat less emphasis, about the contribution of the abortive supranational experiments such as EDC and the European Political Community. Although these did not go beyond the stage of a constitutional draft and hence never achieved administrative reality, they required their protagonists to think through workable plans. In so doing, they advanced greatly the conceptualization of supranational organs and advanced also the understanding of the institutional forms and of the measure of authority that would be required if a federal Europe, or an approximation thereto, should one day become a reality. This accommodation of the mind and the imagination of man to the concept of supranational government in Europe has continued in more recent years through the discussion generated by the treaties for Euratom and the common market. Now that these treaties have been ratified, federation ceases to be an academic concept both as respects the daily life of some 160 million Europeans and as respects their ideas of state and government.

Of especial importance among the institutional experiments that have advanced the concept of European union since World War II is the Council of Europe at Strasbourg. Advocates of supranationalism and federation have looked askance at this apparatus—as we have had frequent occasion to note in these pages. As pointed out in an earlier chapter,[2] the supranationalists originally regarded the Council of Europe as a mere way station on the road to true federation, and they were defeated in their efforts in 1950 to transform it into something akin to their objective. Their failure to achieve their goal and the tendency since 1949 to regard the Council of Europe as the embodiment of the British idea of mere intergovernmental arrangements has caused many advocates of supranational European unity to dismiss Strasbourg as a relatively unimportant "talk-shop."

Such a view, however, is unfair and shortsighted. It does less than

[2] See p. 47.

justice to the Council of Europe's intrinsic importance in advancing the administrative form of European unity. Nor does such a view do justice to the great service that the Strasbourg apparatus has rendered since its creation in advancing the cause of a more perfect union than that embodied in the Council's own Statute. The fact is that history is likely to accord Strasbourg far more credit for advancing "Europe" than contemporaries are wont to give it.

Let us consider briefly the service that the Council of Europe has rendered in its ten-year (1958) existence to the cause of "more perfect union" in Europe. Not the least important part of this service has been that of providing a concrete symbol of unity. At no time before 1949 had protagonists of the European idea had so tangible an expression of their hopes as that embodied in this instrument. In the House of Europe at Strasbourg, and in the various diplomatic and administrative agencies housed in that structure, there came into existence a physical expression of the European idea that, merely because it was official and tangible, has exerted more influence upon many minds in the decade since 1949 than all the slogans for unity and the most persuasive reasoning about the potential benefits of integration.

But Strasbourg's main contribution toward advancing "Europe" has been that of serving as one of the principal official European forums for the cause of union. It provided a center where the leading personalities of the Continent could expound their plans for integration to their colleagues from all over Europe and where such plans could be advanced toward institutional reality. In the hall of Strasbourg's Consultative Assembly, leaders of the European idea such as Churchill, Spaak, de Gasperi, Schuman, Adenauer, and many others of equal stature have often taken the initiative in proposing bold new courses of action, and they have inspired debate on such proposals among their intellectual compatriots from all of Western Europe. The Council of Europe's committees, especially the Committee on General Affairs of the Consultative Assembly, have often been cast in the role of constituent bodies to draft plans of fundamental importance in advancing the basic unity of the Continent in political, economic, and social matters or to appraise or amend such plans.

As a consequence, Strasbourg has become the inspiration for

much of Europe's thinking about "Europe" and has played a major role in translating ideas into action. It was in its Consultative Assembly that such supranational concepts as the Schuman Plan, EDC, and the Political Community were first formulated officially. There, too, to a considerable extent, they were elaborated; there they were regularly debated; and there important amendments were suggested. In the chambers of the House of Europe was originated also the documentation in support of the various plans for greater integration of the Continent. Finally, in these same chambers were initiated and developed the various proposals to advance the moral level of European and international law, an advance typified by the creation of the European Bill of Rights.

In May, 1956, Dr. Walter Hallstein, secretary of state for foreign affairs in the government of West Germany, spoke for all the parties in the German Bundestag in praising the constructive service that the Council of Europe has rendered throughout its existence to the cause of united Europe. In a letter to the secretary general of the Council, Dr. Hallstein said that the debate in the Bundestag "had brought out how far progress achieved in European collaboration up to the present time and over numerous fields of international activity has been due to the systematic and persistent effort of the Council of Europe and to governmental and parliamentary representatives to the organization as well as to the Secretary General and his staff." [3] Dr. Hallstein concluded his letter with the observation that long and detailed debate in the German Bundestag confirmed "how useful has been the work so far accomplished by the members of the Council of Europe." [4] In a similar vein, Mr. J. W. Beyen, then foreign minister of the Netherlands, and like Hallstein a "strong" European, speaking in the seventh session of the Consultative Assembly in July, 1955, declared that the Council of Europe was *"the centre and framework of all efforts being made towards the unification and integration of Europe"* [italics in the original].[5]

M. Guy Mollet, the French Socialist leader who, at the time, was president of the Consultative Assembly and who in 1956 was prime

[3] *Council of Europe News,* Vol. 6, No. 6 (June 1956), p. 4.

[4] *Ibid.,* p. 5.

[5] *Council of Europe News,* Vol. 5, No. 8 (Aug. 1955), p. 7.

minister of France, has been even more laudatory in his appraisal of the contribution of the Council of Europe to the European idea and to such integration of the Continent as has already been achieved. Speaking before the American Committee on United Europe on September 6, 1955, M. Mollet referred to the semiannual sessions at Strasbourg as a "great European forum in which the problems of European unification and of international security are studied and debated by parliamentary and government leaders." [6]

These statements of some of the foremost Europeans about the significance of the Strasbourg enterprise are no exaggeration. As M. Mollet said in the same address from which we have just quoted, the Council of Europe has initiated and drafted some of the most important European legislation of our time, including the European Convention on Human Rights, to which allusion has been made earlier, a European Fund for assisting refugees, and several other major conventions to promote social and cultural intercourse. In his address, M. Mollet also supported the observations previously made that the Council of Europe could claim much of the credit for having launched the idea of EDC, an idea that, though it proved to be abortive, nonetheless helped to promote the reintegration of Germany with the West. Mollet also claimed for the Council the creation of a "European climate" without which the Schuman pool "might never have seen the light of day." [7] The former French prime minister would doubtless have been equally emphatic in attributing much of the success achieved in advancing the cause of Euratom and the common market to the "European climate" provided by Strasbourg. Even a cursory survey of the debates in the Consultative Assembly in 1956 and 1957 would confirm the justice of such an observation.

Occasionally the enthusiasm of the "strong" Europeans for the cause they support has not only obscured Strasbourg's contribution to their maximum program but has also caused many to forget that the majority of Western European countries interested in integration are not yet ready to go beyond a minimum program, and that these are presently satisfied with the degree of union

[6] "The New Drive for European Union" (New York: American Committee on United Europe, 1955), p. 6.

[7] *Ibid.*, p. 7.

implicit in the Council of Europe. If "Little Europe" is the Europe of the Six, Strasbourg is the Europe of the Fifteen, which includes the Six. Officially, at least, Britain, the Scandinavian states, and other European nations "peripheral" to the Six presently do not care to proceed any farther along the integration ladder, and though association in the Council of Europe may leave much to be desired on the part of those who wish to move forward toward confederation and federation, the stern fact is that such progress is not immediately possible. Hence, although the federalists or supranationalists may dismiss the Council of Europe as a mere "intergovernmental" agency, it is nevertheless a viable instrument of association—one that fulfills the needs and aspirations of many states at this stage in the evolution of the European Movement.

Thus, whatever its structural and functional weaknesses, and however disappointed the "strong" Europeans because of its constitutional deficiencies, the record of the Council of Europe suggests that it has made an important contribution to the cause of European union. Even the Council's severest critics in 1949 and 1950 were willing to admit, a decade later, that it had strengthened immensely the moral community of Europe and provided much of the ideological and cultural background for eventual constitutional unity.

Affirmation of the validity of that observation was provided during the first part of the eighth session of the Consultative Assembly in April, 1956. At that time the Assembly's Committee on General Affairs, under the leadership of the Italian Christian Democrat, Signor Lodovico Benvenuti, long an ardent supporter of the maximum objectives of the European Movement, formulated a far-reaching statement of general European policy. Intended primarily as a statement of European policy toward Asia and the Far East, it nevertheless provides an excellent summary of the basic aims of the contemporary movement toward unity in Europe.

The statement insists that no European country can work out its own salvation: that "even the largest would be weakened—and the smallest swallowed up" if they negotiated separately with the USSR. The authors of the statement labor the point that the military defense of Europe is more than an American interest, that, indeed, it is primarily a European interest, and it exhorts Europeans to make the sacrifice necessary for their own defense. The statement suggests, further, that solidarity cannot tolerate inaction, and that "European integration must therefore continue, hand in hand, with closer cooperation between the members of the Western community." The statement adds that a "reborn Europe linked to the Atlantic Community by free trade and the unrestricted exchange of services and the movement of capital and manpower *would be the main bulwark of the Western world*" [italics in the original].[8] Some of these objectives, especially the last quoted, are advanced enough to satisfy even the most radical exponent of federation for Europe. They suggest that sizable elements of the Council of Europe have never been far behind the more progressive ideas of the "strong" Europeans, even though they may not have wished to proceed immediately beyond the constitutional structure provided by the Pact of Westminster in 1949.

Experimentation with intergovernmental and supranational institutions in Europe since World War II has undoubtedly done much to habituate some Europeans to politico-economic institutions that transcend the jurisdiction of the national state. Undoubtedly, too, this experimentation has raised appreciably the level of understanding of the aims and possible advantages of such institutions. But the contribution of these experiments has been but a part of the broader impact made upon the European mind by the European Movement since World War II. We shall turn now to a more systematic statement of the present-day conceptions of this movement and to an appraisal of the influence that such conceptions are likely to have upon the political and economic future of Europe.

The main achievement of the Movement since 1945, whether expressed in private statements, in official or semiofficial declarations, or in actual administrative experiments like the Schuman or proposed Euratom and Economic Communities, has been to relate the attainment of certain basic social objectives to the reorganization of Europe, or at least of Western Europe, as a unified political entity or as a political entity in which the existing national states have appreciably modified their sovereignty. In doing this, the Movement has made reasonably clear the administrative inadequacy

[8] *Council of Europe News*, Vol. 6, No. 5 (May 1956), p. 5.

and relative parochialism of the existing national state structure. Affirmatively it has identified rather concretely and in some detail the nature of those social objectives in the attainment of which a greater degree of political integration of the Continent can assist materially. The result of this process has been to give new vigor and vitality to a venerable tradition of Continental unity.

Let us turn now to an analysis and appraisal of this modernized version of European union for the development of which, since the Second World War, the European Movement has been largely responsible. In this process of modernization it may be said that the Movement has reconceptualized and brought up to date the historic ideal of European unity, dating back to Roman times, and given it a degree of intellectual rigor and political acceptance that it has never previously possessed. It is the revitalization of this historic conception of European union that constitutes the Movement's really important achievement since the end of World War II. Compared to that achievement, the institutional changes that have sought to realize unity administratively, however important intrinsically, are relatively insignificant.

The objectives of the European Movement, as formulated in the writings of Coudenhove-Kalergi, Churchill, and Briand before the Second World War, were occasionally vague and sometimes appeared to defy both logic and the dictates of experience. But whatever the limitations of their statements, these founders of the twentieth-century Movement did not compromise with objectives of a short-term or temporary nature. Their objectives, on the contrary, were long range and as comprehensive as may be imagined. They declared their fundamental aims to be the rationalization of Europe's economy, greater self-sufficiency for that Continent both economically and militarily, the permanent abolition of the military rivalry among the states of the Continent, especially between France and Germany, whose common boundary had provided the military cockpit for the previous century, and the somewhat vague but nonetheless indispensable objective of advancing the cultural values that were European instead of purely national. Also involved among the objectives voiced before World War II was the hope that if that portion of Europe that was free and democratic could be united [9] it would serve as a counterweight to the Soviet. The purpose here, however, was more than merely military and strategic; what was sought was a better focus upon the ideals of free Europe in order to give Stalin and Communism more effective competition in the existing struggle for men's minds. The military and diplomatic aspects of the competition with Communism were secondary.

In voicing these longer-range aims, the advocates of unity before World War II were perhaps most specific about their economic objectives. Indeed few post-World War II exponents of European integration formulated such objectives of unity more succinctly and more persuasively than did several authorities during the period when M. Briand was preparing his proposal for a greater degree of European integration before the League of Nations. Objectives in this direction were especially well formulated in papers delivered at the Congress of the Federal Committee of European Cooperation at Madrid, Spain, in May, 1929. In his discussion of the subject, Professor Truchy, of the Faculty of Law of Paris, advocated an "organization of European production in mass and by various categories, the application in that great factory which is Europe of the principle of *division of labour* [italics supplied], as it is applied in all modern industrial enterprises, as a result of an evolution which has been perceptible since the beginning of the present century." [10]

Another French delegate to this Congress, M. Yves le Trocquer, at the time his nation's minister of public works, reiterated this purpose of making possible the rationalization of production and distribution in the European continent, and he was even more explicit than his colleague. He pointed directly to federal America, declaring that the "finest example of the scientific organization of labour that has ever been given is furnished by the United States." [11] M. le Trocquer then drew the inevitable moral, namely, the need in Europe of a federation like the American on whose agenda the elimination of intra-European customs barriers would be given first place, or at least a position of high priority. The European

[9] This idea was apparently construed liberally, for Coudenhove speaks of having invited Mussolini to join his Pan-Europe. See his *Crusade for Pan-Europe*, previously cited, pp. 170 ff.

[10] Herriot, *The United States of Europe*, previously cited, p. 80.

[11] Quoted in Herriot, *op. cit.*, p. 81.

"productivity teams" from the Schuman Community that visited the United States under the auspices of the Marshall Plan and strongly advocated an American type of federal union to assist Europe's economy had antecedent observers, who had come to the same conclusion a generation earlier without the same opportunity to collect empirical data.

In the revival of the European Movement after World War II, both these economic and other primary objectives of the prewar phase of the Movement were restated. Few if any essentially long-range objectives were added. Rather, as noted in earlier chapters, the postwar period of the Movement was noteworthy for its extension and elaboration of the objectives that had been stated at an earlier period, and for developing political and administrative procedures to realize these objectives and for testing such procedures in the crucible of experience.

At the same time the exigencies of the postwar world in Europe and the desire to restore a modicum of order and security to the war-ravaged Continent had an effect upon the Movement that was not entirely healthy. During the years immediately following VE day, European statesmen were wont to exploit the immediate contributions to European stability that might inhere in the unity movement. Thus Churchill himself, although one of the more articulate exponents of the basic aims of the Movement before 1940 and the man who provided the political impetus for reviving it after Yalta, became understandably concerned with the problem of Europe's survival and the immediate problems of reconstruction, and he sought, therefore, to exploit the Movement's potential contribution to that immediate problem. He was especially impressed with what the united Europe idea might contribute to the immediate security of the West and particularly of Western Europe against the Soviet Union's threats during the so-called "Cold War." Hence, in his Iron Curtain speech at Fulton, Missouri, he laid the basis for identifying the European unity movement as a military instrument to assist in the immediate task of countering postwar Russia. He hoped thereby to establish quickly a power balance in an area where, at least temporarily, only a vacuum yawned.

Unquestionably Churchill's preoccupation with the immediate objective of exploiting European unity to counter postwar Russia caused him to place great emphasis on the military and security aspects of the Movement at the expense of other objectives. Despite the obvious liabilities of such exploitation, Churchill returned frequently to his short-range view. He reiterated it especially at the outbreak of the Korean War in 1950 when, as a representative of Britain at Strasbourg, he offered his ambiguous recommendation for the formation of what he called a "European army" to assist in protecting the West against the overt military threat of international Communism.

To this essentially short-run conception of the strategic utility of European unification the United States also became strongly attached. Although otherwise an advocate of an altruistic and benevolent policy toward the broad objectives of European union, Washington was sorely tempted by the promise of an immediate contribution to America's national interest implicit in Churchill's kind of short-range exploitation of that concept. Here, it appeared, was an opportunity for Europe to provide a *quid pro quo* for America's contributions to the Continent, both economic and military. And Washington not surprisingly yielded to the temptation to support such a program.

The European Defense Community project was born in part of this purpose to provide quick security, and that purpose was never eradicated from the mind of the public. EDC had other aims than merely that of making more effective the West's existing effort through NATO to counter the Soviet threat and to assist America and Britain in discharging the responsibilities they had assumed on the Continent for that purpose. The possibility that, in time, EDC would succeed in overcoming Franco-German rivalry and division in the West and, by removing that rivalry, provide the opportunity for effective unification, was alone sufficient to place that concept in the category of acceptable long-range objectives of the European Movement. Had this ultimate objective of EDC been accomplished, moreover, EDC might have served as an enduring counter to Soviet expansionism instead of merely supplementing a "crash" policy to contain the Soviet.

But the immediate military objectives of EDC were never supplanted or even supplemented in the public mind by its potential long-range contributions. Far too large a sector of European opinion continued to regard EDC as an immediate military weapon against Russia. As such, EDC, and integration generally, were supported, albeit with reluctance, as long as the current situation required support, but as soon as the Soviet icicle had seemingly melted and "neutralism" had gained an increasing number of converts in Western Europe, the short-run military interpretation of European integration, now symbolized by EDC, became something of a liability to the entire Movement and contributed not a little to EDC's defeat. Had Washington, especially, been a little less vocal about the short-term aim of bringing the ten or twelve German divisions to the immediate defense of Europe against the Soviet menace, and had it been a little more vocal about such longer-range aims of EDC as the conciliation of France and Germany and the desire to make the Rhine a perpetually peaceful border, the EDC instrument might have experienced a more desirable fate. At any rate, even if, as is likely, EDC had gone down to defeat, the cause of European unity might not have suffered to the same degree from popular suspicion, engendered by the EDC debate, that unity in Europe was just another device for power mobilization and that the principal objective was military.

National security and the resolution of military and diplomatic rivalry among the states of Western Europe, combined with steps to provide a better balance against the long-range threat of the Soviet Union, thus remain among the principal aims of the contemporary European Movement. They are aims that, taken together, look toward permanent strategic and diplomatic gains rather than temporary military advantages. They are aims that, even if we allow for the steps taken under WEU, are little nearer realization than before EDC was proposed and defeated.

At the same time it should be pointed out that this general security objective has stimulated much pertinent discussion among supporters of the European Movement since World War II and especially since the demise of EDC, and this has given this objective a substance and a precision that were formerly lacking. Basically the contemporary strategic aim of the spokesmen of the European Movement is to use union as a means of creating a "third force" or a "third super power." It is hoped that through such a creation it will become possible to establish a better balance, both in a strategic and political sense, between the combined nations of Western Europe, on the one hand, and those "giant" political units, the United States and the Soviet Union, on the other. In other words, the long-range strategic objective of the Movement—if such it may be called—has become more comprehensive than it was before World War II. The elimination of rivalry between nations of the Western European area, especially between France and Germany, is still sought; so too is the equilibration of the strength of the West with that of international Communism. But the more comprehensive and more affirmative aim voiced by the more enthusiastic spokesmen of the European Movement, particularly since the defeat of EDC in 1954, is to create a third great power. This they propose to do by amalgamating the nations of Western Europe, or most of them, in a federal or confederal structure, and thereby cumulate their diplomatic influence and their military potential. By so doing, they hope to restore what they consider to be the proper role of European nations, and particularly of Western European nations, in the world's councils.

This "third force" or "third power" idea is predicated on the assumption that this is indeed the age of super powers and that the continuation of Western European nations as purely sovereign entities must inevitably entail their relative and absolute decline. The rise of such potential super powers as India and China, and the rapid advance to the status of a world power of such former British dominions as Canada and Australia, merely underscore the desirability of resorting to such an integrative instrument as federalism, or something like federalism, to insure to the combined nations of Western Europe what is conceived to be their appropriate influence in world affairs in the second half of the twentieth century.

Many ancillary motives fortify the favorable attitude that West European spokesmen exhibit for this revised strategic objective of the contemporary European Movement. There is, as already suggested, Western Europe's continuing fear of the Soviet Union and the desire to counter that power with something more than a mere military alliance. There is also growing fear of the United States and perhaps some jealousy of the stature and influence of that federation in the contemporary world. More specifically, there is the fear that America's contemporary leadership may lead the world astray.

It is a fear that impresses few Americans but it allegedly influences Europeans. Europe, in their opinion, must become a power in order to provide some checkrein for American policy.

During the postwar years of attrition of the European states' position in regional and world affairs, leaders of various Western European governments have been particularly vocal in promoting this "third-force" concept. One of the more articulate has been that tried and true champion of European union, Germany's Chancellor Adenauer. In September, 1956, after what appeared to have been a unilateral decision by America to reduce her military commitments on the European continent and to shift from conventional to atomic armament, and after some not too friendly American comments on Germany's allegedly limited contribution to NATO and her failure to expedite that contribution, Adenauer took advanced ground on the necessity of cumulating Western Europe's power through the institutional device of a confederation. His aim, he said, was to equilibrate Western Europe with Russia and the United States. The German chancellor's precise suggestion was that Western Europe begin again at the point that had been reached by the unity movement at the time the French National Assembly vetoed EDC in 1954 and adopted EDC's pallid substitute, WEU. With the aid of Britain, the Six, said Adenauer, should transform WEU into a confederation of seven nations that could then develop a common foreign policy and common defense arrangements, the will of the confederation to be determined by a majority vote of the recommended seven members. The chancellor added the highly pessimistic observation that "if the European peoples continue to make their policies on the basis of the past, Europe will go down and become only a historical memory." [12]

Even as the German chancellor was speaking, his views were being given added significance by the crisis then developing over Egypt's nationalization of the Suez Canal. Indeed, it would be difficult to imagine a more persuasive argument for combining Western European nations into a single power than the outcome of the Franco-British intervention in Egypt in 1956. A venture that, a generation ago, either one of these powers could have managed

[12] See *The New York Times,* Nov. 19, 1956.

successfully was now quite beyond even their joint strength in an era in which America, one of the two so-called "giant" powers of the time, pitted her diplomatic influence against them and the other, the Soviet Union, made only thinly disguised threats against them of intervention with hydrogen bombs and intercontinental missiles. Unilateral or bilateral efforts of France and Britain to protect their respective national interests in the Suez Canal area had to be abandoned in the midst of a successful effort to implement such a policy militarily because even their partnership in the venture could not command sufficient resources, either moral or physical, to withstand the opposition of the two giant powers. The result was perhaps the most ignominious diplomatic defeat that either Britain or France has suffered in a hundred years—one that strongly documented the thesis that the resources of all of Western Europe would have to be mobilized under a single direction if that area or any nation in that area was to avoid a secondary role in world affairs in the future. For all but the Colonel Blimps, the die-hard chauvinists, and the professional patriots, the Suez affair and its aftermath offered the most convincing demonstration yet experienced that the national state system of Western Europe was inadequate to protect Western Europe's interests. After Suez the idea of uniting Europe into a "third force" came of age.

Closely related to the broad strategic objective of the contemporary European Movement is the belief, rarely voiced by most Europeans but decidedly present in their thinking, that the day of empire is past and that substitutes will have to be found for empires, colonies, and colonial systems if the metropolitan state is to compensate itself for their loss. That substitute may well be the assigning of colonial responsibility to an association of European states, as in the proposed economic community among the Six, in the hope that an association might succeed in maintaining control where the individual state has failed. In the Economic Community Treaty, as we have seen, France has already persuaded her associates among the Six to assume responsibility with herself for maintaining a flow of capital to her colonial possessions and to those of other states in the Community. At the same time steps have been taken in that treaty to establish the framework of a customs union between these colonial territories and the metropolitan territory of the Six.[13] Indeed an even more comprehensive plan of union has been proposed for Western Europe and African colonial territories—a plan that approaches the status of an economic union. This, it has been suggested, might be called Eurafrica!

That a union of Europe's colonial powers might assist them in overcoming the current challenge to their authority is a view that apparently receives support from various quarters. Such a view, for example, was voiced with considerable frankness by political leaders from most of Western Europe who attended the meetings of the Liberal International at Stresa, Italy, on September 13, 1956. In their resolutions, they asserted that if Europe had been united, President Nasser of Egypt would never have succeeded in nationalizing the Suez Canal, and the Franco-British difficulties with Egypt, the British difficulties with Cyprus then looming large on the international horizon, and the current French troubles in North Africa would, in their opinion, have been quickly resolved.[14] Asian-African nationalism, said the spokesman of the International, was a great new force in the world today, challenging especially to European colonial powers, and it could be met effectively only if the metropolitan European nations united. Unification, it was held, would contribute to the solution of the colonial question either by making Europe more independent of colonial raw materials and markets, or by establishing a multipower, and hence a more effective, metropolitan European political control over colonial territories, or, perhaps, by achieving both of these conditions.

It would appear that the concept of European unity is not necessarily always a response to the challenge of the new and progressive but may also be a recipe for maintaining vested interests and for maintaining a kind of modified anachronism. Certainly some of the proposals to exploit the concept of European unity as a means for preserving Europe's colonial advantages come close to those advanced three and one-half centuries ago by the Duke of Sully in recommending his "Grand Design" to Henry IV of France, or even to the ideas of Pierre du Bois who, in his *De recuperatione terrae*

[13] See Arts. 131-136, Treaty Establishing the European Economic Community.

[14] For these views, see *The New York Times,* Sept. 14, 1956.

sanctae (*On the Reconquest of the Holy Land*), written in 1306, three centuries before Sully, sought European union under the aegis of Philip the Fair of France in order the more expeditiously to conquer the Holy Land and African peoples along the Mediterranean littoral.

Let us turn now to the more purely economic aims of the European Movement. As already suggested in this chapter, these aims were particularly well stated by those spokesmen of the European Movement whose activity antedated the Movement's revival in 1947. Unlike the Movement's strategic objectives, these long-range economic aims suffered less from the immediate postwar political considerations. The temptation to distort them was certainly present. Heroic emergency measures were obviously required in 1945 to rescue individual European nations from the effects of the destruction wrought by World War II and to restore a functioning national economy even on a minimum basis. Every affected nation, vanquished and victorious alike, wished to overcome the war's direct destruction of capital plant, bolster its internal and external credit position, protect its currency against precipitous inflation, shift from military to civilian production, and direct production in such a way as to promote employment and re-establish a balance of payments in its international account.

Fortunately for the European Movement, the pressure from such essentially transient objectives was mitigated greatly by the Marshall Plan and the various supplementary plans for economic aid and the administrative instrumentalities that arose in the wake of General Marshall's address at the Harvard Commencement in 1947. As a result of America's economic support and the policies and actions of such European administrative agencies and planning bodies as OEEC and EPU, Europe's immediate economic needs were largely satisfied. Thus the movement toward unity in the economic realm, although certainly not immune to the impact of problems created by the requirements of economic restoration, had an opportunity to concentrate upon the broader and more fundamental objectives set for it in the thirties by the Pan-European leaders. Clearly the enduring contribution of the Marshall Plan in unifying Europe was not its direct encouragement of the unity movement—although that was not inconsiderable—but the fact that it left the historic European Movement for union free to concentrate upon its proper long-range objectives in the economic area.

These objectives, as noted earlier,[15] included, among others, the rationalization of European trade and production, the establishment of a more efficient division of labor, and the setting up of transnational political and administrative structures that would make it possible for industry, trade, and agriculture not merely to recover a past prosperity but to expand, grow more efficient, and support the needs of a growing population and that population's inevitable demand for a constantly rising standard of living. It was the relative freedom to concentrate upon objectives such as these, permitted by the Marshall Plan, that led to the very considerable institutional advances toward unifying Western Europe in an economic sense. It explains in part the creation and relative success of the Schuman Plan. It also explains the momentum that has led to the plans, seriously advanced after 1956, for a European common market among the Six and for supranational efforts to exploit nuclear energy.

Like the followers of Coudenhove-Kalergi and Briand before World War II and the experts of that period who sought to rationalize Europe's economy, the leaders of "Little Europe" in 1958 are convinced that intergovernmental arrangements such as the British have been wont to advocate will not suffice to achieve that goal. The proposed supranational nuclear energy and economic unions among the Six, superimposed upon the Schuman pool and joined, perhaps, to a free-trade zone consisting of the remaining Strasbourg nations, will represent a considerable advance. But for "Little Europe" at least such arrangements are still short of the goal presently entertained by its more influential spokesmen. They continue to look askance at the kind of segmented supranational control over economic life typified by the Schuman Plan or by the currently discussed common market. Such control may constitute a step in the right direction and, as such, will be loyally supported by the leaders of the Movement. But the more advanced "Europeans" are quite aware of the weaknesses of what we have called the "segmented" type of economic regulation. Nor does the "syndicated" community

[15] See pp. 172-174.

approach to supranationalism seem to them any less a temporary expedient in 1958 than it did in 1950, when the idea first took form. For such "Europeans," the final goal remains political federation and comprehensive supranational control of the economy.

That this continues to be the maximum institutional goal among the advanced "Europeans" of "Little Europe" and hence a part of their credo as supporters of the European Movement was recently made almost vehemently clear by Jean Monnet. In organizing his Action Committee for promoting unity in Europe and reviving the common market concept during 1955, Monnet gave what is likely to become a classic exposition of the relation of economic advance and centralized supranational authority on a continental scale. Many people, said Monnet, feel that because Europe had rather quickly revived after World War II, "cooperation between nations is enough." But this, he insisted, "shows a profound misunderstanding of the situation." The rate of economic advance, as distinct from mere recovery from the war, has not been sufficient in Western Europe. Indeed the crucial fact is that the rate of economic progress in Western Europe has actually been lagging behind the rate in the Soviet Union or in the United States. The explanation, said Monnet, ". . . is not that they [Russians or Americans] are more inventive or hard-working than the Europeans. It is that, despite the difference of their regimes, *they are both developing their economies on a continental scale* [italics supplied]. By contrast, the resources and the markets of the European countries are separate from one another and small." [16]

André Philip, the French Socialist leader, has been even more emphatic on this point. By 1953, said Philip, the United States had gone from $160 billion of output registered in 1929 to $270 billion. Europe, on the other hand, had reached a level of output in 1953 just barely above that attained in 1929. Among the various reasons for this "stagnation" in Europe, insisted Philip, the most important was the lack of profitable incentive in producing for small markets of 30 or 50 or even of 80 million people. The French Socialist concluded his remarks by stating that Europe's traditional exports were being threatened. New exports were possible, he said, "but only on

[16] As quoted from Monnet in *The New York Times,* Dec. 6, 1955.

the lines of a new type of industry which cannot function within the ancient framework of the national state."[17]

Reaffirmation of these views of MM. Monnet and Philip is included in the report of the nineteen-member Schuman Community Trade Union Delegation that visited America at the end of 1954 and to which reference was made earlier in this chapter. The visit took place under the auspices of the then Foreign Operations Administration of the United States. In its formal report the committee observed that a "Common Market *subject to common institutions* [italics supplied] is necessary for the effective economic and social potentialities offered by a large market."[18] These representatives of trade unionists appeared to be quite as "American" as Jean Monnet himself and quite as enthusiastic about the results secured from the American capitalistic system and the American federal structure. As one commentator on their report observed, "What the Community trade union team appears to seek is a general common market with a central authority having power over general economic policy."[19] It seems that America's federal system and the common market that that system has nurtured has deeply affected the thinking on both sides of the economic bargaining table in Western Europe, that is, of both labor and management.

It thus becomes clear that economic integration provides the major long-range aim of European union. For those in the postwar European Movement who advocate a maximum program, this economic objective has priority over all other objectives—assuming, of course, that it can be isolated from others. What is not so certain is the validity of the assumption that the economy of Europe or of any significant territorial portion thereof, such as the region of the Six, can be rationalized, given the abolition of customs barriers and the establishment of a common supranational regulatory authority. Certainly if such rationalization is to be achieved, extraordinary sacrifices will have to be made in some areas. The vested advantages of particular economic groups, such as the agricultural

[17] *Europe Today and Tomorrow* (May 1953), pp. 4 and 5. Apparently M. Philip did not "correct" for any inflationary influences.

[18] Quoted in *Bulletin from the European Community for Coal and Steel,* No. 17 (July-Aug. 1956), p. 8.

[19] *Ibid.,* p. 8.

producers, deriving from established economic and social policies of national governments, will have to be modified, and the comparative advantages enjoyed by some areas over others will have to be foregone, at least in part, to raise the economic and social levels of less favored regions.

The political authority in such a proposed union will, moreover, have to summon more courage and political integrity than is currently being displayed in the proposed member states if such authority is to deny the temptation to yield to one of the greatest of contemporary political evils, namely, that of resorting to political power in the attempt to achieve almost any social or economic goal. Yielding to that temptation instead of being content to allow the interplay of spontaneous private forces in the economic sphere can have the effect of simply aggravating or compounding the evil of contemporary neomercantilism, which is another way of saying that if these six or more states in Europe merge their authority over economic affairs, they may well have a more difficult task in resisting the contemporary propensity to nationalize industry and in trying to safeguard the spontaneity and rational efficiency of private enterprise than if they continue on their separate national courses. On this score there are American critics of the whole idea of European integration—leaders like Clarence Randall—who think that the whole European Movement is one directed toward extending the sterile institutions of economic nationalization and supergovernmental distribution cartels. Such suspicions do not come lightly to a man of the stature of this American.

To be successful, moreover, rationalization of the economy will also require an area large enough, and diversified enough, to insure that industry is adequately complemented by agricultural and extractive economies. Whether "Little Europe" can eventually meet such requirements is not too clear. The likelihood is that if it is to achieve the degree of diversification within a protected common market that will insure a high level of economic equilibrium, it will have to rely, to a considerable extent, upon ancillary arrangements with other European states, or pursue a policy of trade expansion with the rest of the world, or possibly integrate its economy with that of the colonies of several of "Little Europe's" member states. The latter plan, it will be recalled, is contemplated in the

European common market treaty. Only thus will a market restricted to "Little Europe," and presumably insulated to some extent against the rest of the world by tariffs and other regulations, be likely to possess sufficient absorptive capacity to justify the assembly line, the concepts of automatic production, and the high levels of investment that will achieve the goals sought by the integrationists. Leaders such as Monnet, Spaak, and Philip doubtless understand these requirements. Certainly they have evinced no doubt that they can be met. Even so, the plans for "Little Europe's" economic integration suggest a paucity of expert study of problems such as the foregoing and relatively little effort to bring them to the attention of the rank and file.

Finally the question remains whether, even in the case of "Little Europe," Monnet and his colleagues will succeed in the foreseeable future in erecting the kind of comprehensive supranational authority in the economic field that they know will be required if they are to succeed in their aims. They are certainly aware of the fact that the "sector" approach, typical of the Schuman project and typical of all the single-purpose communities of the postwar period, including the latest plans for a common market, will hardly permit of the formulation of policies that can effectively rationalize the economy and reap the social and material benefits inherent in an extensive common market. Political power will be required not only to control production and distribution but also to establish a common fiscal policy—or at least one planned for the entire territory embraced in the market—uniform social welfare legislation, and a common tax system. In short the supranational agency set up to govern a unified economy in Europe or a part of Europe will have to comprehend all segments of a modern state's jurisdiction over the economic structure.

It seems unlikely, even in "Little Europe," that all these conditions for success in the economic field can be satisfied. On the other hand, the relatively great success already achieved in the economic area by the European Movement sustains the fainthearted and engenders faith in the optimist that all the pitfalls we have identified can be avoided. The success already achieved in the economic field suggests that, whatever the obstacles and whatever the immediate outlook, the future goals can and will be attained. Hence enthusiasm for this objective of a more rational economy, promised by integration and the economic and social gains that integration appears to offer, remains high. Attainment of such an economy through appropriately unified institutions in Europe continues to be the paramount and the most popular objective of the contemporary European Movement.

Economic rationalization, avoidance of intracontinental political rivalry, security of free Europe against the Communist threat, compensation for the loss of colonial power, and equilibration of the states of Western Europe with America and other so-called giant powers—these are the maximum goals that inspire the European integrationist in 1958. They are the principal objectives of the modernized conception of united Europe that the European Movement has taken from the advocates of unity before 1940 and adapted to its needs and aspirations since the close of the second global conflict. They are the principal "planks" in the contemporary "platform" of the European integrationist. Supplemented by the actual experiments in "structuring" Europe that have been taking place since 1949, this "platform" offers a program for advancing the unification of Europe's political and economic institutions that is intellectually respectable and that, in the main, is feasible in a practical sense. It remains to be determined in a concluding chapter to what extent such a modernized conception of European union has the support of those for whom it is intended, that is, of the Europeans.

14 The European Movement and the Future of Europe

HOWEVER CLEARLY DEFINED the objectives of the contemporary conception of European integration may be, the conception has little chance of being realized in practice unless it eventually becomes anchored emotionally and intellectually in the outlook and behavior of the ordinary European man and woman. Few candid observers are likely to believe that the broad rank and file of Europeans has up to the present time been greatly impressed by the European Movement. The average farmer, workman, and even the middle-class professional and businessman remain largely unaffected by the Movement, patriotism remaining for them essentially, and understandably, national in its context.

It is quite possible, as André Philip suggests, to overemphasize the importance of grass-roots opinion and its relation to the European Movement. Especially is it possible to do this at the precise stage that the Movement has now reached. Speaking at the Second Hague Congress of the European Movement in October, 1953, the French Socialist leader reminded his hearers that public opinion is not generated in a vacuum and cannot be expected to lead. Taking note of the fact that some of the Congress had suggested that institutional advances toward federation should be slowed until opinion was ripe, he observed that such persons displayed "a curious conception of education which required opinion to be formed in the abstract rather than by means of concrete achievement." He added that "it was by means of action and achievement that man's education was effected." [1]

Journalists and sociologists generally would probably agree with this "elitist" conception of the generation of opinion and with the implication as to "opinion's" role in advancing ideas and institutions. At the same time, it is unlikely that either Philip or any of his colleagues would deny that, however opinion may be formed and whatever its role in advancing novelty, there is a necessity of maintaining a satisfactory correlation between the state of opinion and overt steps taken to advance a program of change. No one had a better illustration of the truth of such a generalization than M. Philip himself when some ten months after his comments at The Hague, the French National Assembly defeated EDC despite the leadership that M. Philip and most of his Socialist colleagues had given that proposed step toward federal Europe.

Since that event and possibly as a result, at least to some degree, of the revelation that it offered as to the state of Europe's opinion about "Europe," public understanding of the issues involved in the European program has probably improved somewhat and been brought more nearly abreast of developments in the European Movement. Certainly great advances have been made in popularizing the European concept since those days immediately after World War II when interest in that theme was largely confined to the level of the political leader and the intellectual.

Professional poll takers and other observers have been especially impressed by the extent of the favor shown the cause of unity by youth groups in France and Germany, especially by youth in university circles.[2] Efforts to interest the public have, moreover, not been limited to appeals to young people. In recent months especially, the Schuman pool authorities have actually sought to interpret the material advantages that might be derived from that experiment for the average coal and steel worker, and they have not failed to draw the moral of even greater gains should a common market be developed and other forms of economic integration be

[1] *Europe Today and Tomorrow* (Nov. 1953), p. 10.

[2] See Robert C. Doty, "Young Intellectuals," *The New York Times*, Dec. 5 and 6, 1952; see also description of a plebiscite in Delft, Holland, *ibid.*, Dec. 18, 1953.

brought about. The Council of Europe has also sought in various ways to generate popular interest and enthusiasm in the European cause. This it has sought to do by various kinds of public relations activity, the award of special prizes and honors, and the promotion of university courses and seminars. In December, 1955, the Council agreed on a major symbol of "Europe," accepting after long delay and much discussion the design of a "European" flag.[3]

Probably the most important evidence of the penetration of European ideas into the public consciousness is reflected in the attitude toward "Europe" taken by political parties, particularly in Britain and the Six, and by related or auxiliary organizations. Until 1956, at least, both Labour and Conservatism in Britain zealously reflected the national attitude of opposition to any but minimum institutions for the European idea. With one or two notable exceptions, not a single leading British politician of either major party gave endorsement to anything but a traditional conception of intergovernmental organization for Europe. As we have noted in earlier chapters, Sir Winston Churchill gave the utmost moral stimulus to the idea in the early days of the postwar revival of the Movement, that is, in 1945 and 1946, but his official actions subsequently, whatever the implications of his more sonorous periods, have never sanctioned an advance beyond the minimum institutional concepts of official British policy.

On the Continent, however, and especially in France, Germany, Italy, and the Low Countries, the attitude of the political parties and their leadership has been quite different. Except for the extreme Right, the Communists, and such fellow-traveling Socialist groups as Pietro Nenni's faction in Italy, all partisan elements in these states have professed adherence to the cause of united Europe in some form, and most of them, unlike the British parties, are not averse—at least in principle—to supporting a federal or quasi-federal organization.

In France, large segments of partisan groups immediately to the right of Center have been strong supporters of both the Schuman Plan and the European army. The former, for example, was supported by all but three of the 74 Radical deputies in the National

[3] The flag consists of an ultramarine blue field upon which is superimposed a circle of twelve five-pointed gold stars.

Assembly and by all of the UDSR.[4] The first vote in the Assembly on the European army plan also aligned the great majority of both these moderate Rightist groups on the side of that project although, admittedly, opposition elements in them grew in size as the army project moved through its various parliamentary tests until it met defeat in August, 1954.[5] Only the Gaullists and various similar conservative groupings of peasants and dissident Republicans maintained unqualified resistance to supranational European ideas. In general it may be said that the moderate Rightist parties representing professional elements, small proprietors, and the more dynamic commercial and industrial elements in French society have generally been supporters of more than token schemes for European unity. Agrarian elements and those on the Right, whose vested interests are closely identified with the preservation of a purely national structure, have been inclined to look askance at such schemes.

The inclination to support the cause of European union observable in the moderate Right in France has had its parallel among the remaining states of "Little Europe." In each of them "Republican" and traditional "Liberal" parties usually have contributed articulate leadership to the cause of "Europe" and strong parliamentary support to supranational solutions. Thus French Rightist European leaders like Paul Reynaud, René Mayer, Antoine Pinay, and Edouard Bonnefous have had their counterparts in Roger Motz, the Belgian Liberal; J. W. Beyen, one-time foreign minister of the Netherlands; and the late Count Carlo Sforza, Italy's foreign minister after World War II and the symbol of her resistance to Mussolini. The policies of these men and of the groups they have led have all supplied an implicit testimonial of the appeal of European union to partisans of the moderate Right.

Toward the other end of the political spectrum are the Socialists of the Six whose support of federal or quasi-federal ideas has been vigorous. The list of names of Socialist leaders who since World War II have been in the forefront of the movement to give supranational institutions to Europe reads like the *Who's Who* of federal Europe's principal political protagonists. At the top of that list is

[4] Democratic and Social Union of the Resistance.

[5] For tabulation of votes, see Philip Williams, *Politics in Post-War France* (New York: Longmans, 1954), p. 439.

Paul-Henri Spaak, the Belgian Socialist, a man who, with one or two other personages of the period, has earned the title of "Mr. Europe." At least a dozen other West European Socialist leaders have acquired more than national prominence because of their contribution to the European Movement. Among them are Georges Bohy, Henri Rolin, and Fernand Dehousse of Belgium, and M. van der Goes van Naters and F. J. Goedhart of the Netherlands. Outstanding among the Socialist proponents of strong European solutions in France is the former prime minister, M. Guy Mollet—who wears the European mantle of his deceased Socialist colleague, Léon Blum—and André Philip. The Italian Right-wing Socialist leaders Giuseppe Saragat and Matteo Matteotti have also been supporters of the Movement in recent years.

Even the German Social Democrats, bitter foes of EDC and only indifferent supporters of any European organization more ambitious in structure and purpose than the Council of Europe, have let it be known that their opposition is not inveterate. Off and on, they have officially professed their willingness to consider "European solutions" sympathetically, provided Germany is first unified. How sincere this profession may be is open to question. Conditional assertions of that kind demand little in the way of action when, as in this case, the condition is virtually impossible of realization in the immediate future. But there can be no doubt of the fact of the German Social Democrats' recent acceptance of some sort of suprasovereign association of Western Europe for industrial exploitation of nuclear energy. Agreement by their leader, Erich Ollenhauer, and his immediate associates among the German Socialists to support such a plan represents a major gain in the long effort to consolidate moderate Marxian and Labor opinion in support of supranational institutions for Western Europe including Germany.

Thus committed to the cause of "Europe," the Socialists are partners in supporting that cause with that other major political aggregation in all of the Six—the Clerical Center. Occasionally the charge has been ventured that united Europe is primarily a Clerical ideal and that it is kept alive chiefly by the Clerical parties and the Vatican. Such a charge obviously cannot pass muster in view of the support of the Movement that is derived from all "constitutional" party groups from the Marxian Socialists to the far Right of the spectrum. The charge doubtless has its roots in certain traditional conceptions of European unity supported by the Roman Church, but it clearly finds no support in the Church's present-day premise for its support of European unity. Nor can the charge be squared with the predominantly secular—especially economic—motivation that enlists the vast majority of the contemporary supporters of European institutions.

But if the Clerical Center has no monopoly of the European Movement there can be no doubt that its leaders and its party rank and file in all of the Six provide the Movement's most solid, most persistent, and most loyal support. Through such leaders as Robert Schuman, Konrad Adenauer, and the late Alcide de Gasperi, the Clerical Center, consisting of the Mouvement Républicain Populaire in France, the Christian Democratic Union in the German Federal Republic, and the Christian Democrats in Italy, and equivalent groups in the Benelux, have provided the European Movement with a hard core of public and parliamentary support that since the end of World War II has rarely, if ever, wavered in advancing the movement from one plateau of achievement to another.

The Clerical groups in the various countries have provided their chiefs with able colleagues who have exhibited a dedication to the European cause that often rivaled that of the leaders. The French MRP especially has given the European cause many chieftains besides Schuman. Outstanding have been such individuals as François de Menthon, Robert Bichet, Paul-Henri Teitgen, and the former prime minister, Georges Bidault. De Gasperi's successors in the European cause in Italy have been the former premiers Giuseppe Pella and Amintore Fanfani, and Lodovico Benvenuti. Dr. Walter Hallstein and Kurt-Georg Kiesinger have provided Dr. Adenauer with able assistance in his European policy, and in the Low Countries, Paul Struye, Henri Heyman, and Mlle. Marga Klompe have ably represented their parties' constituents in promoting the European idea at Strasbourg and elsewhere. There can be little doubt that without the championship of the Clerical parties among the Six, the European Movement would not have been advanced as far as it has in the past ten years.

One of the more recent indications of the extent of the support for the Movement coming from the organized parties and other groups was that afforded by the formation of Jean Monnet's Action Committee to which we have alluded earlier.[6] Besides representatives of all the Christian Democratic or Clerical parties of the Six, M. Monnet's committee embraces the leadership of every one of the Socialist parties of "Little Europe," including Herr Ollenhauer of the German Social Democrats and Signor Matteo Matteotti of the Right-wing Italian Social Democratic party. The committee roster also carries the names of a variety of moderate Liberal and Independent groups, including the German Free Democrats, the German party, the Belgian Liberal party, the Dutch Protestants, the French Radical party, the French UDSR, and the Italian Republican party. All the major labor unions except those under Communist domination are also included in the committee. Clearly no group favoring "Europe" has ever had a broader base, at least among the Six; the committee convincingly refutes any suggestion that the European Movement is limited to a single political constituency or belief.[7]

Thus, although European grass-roots opinion may still be largely national in its focus, there can be no question that the conception of integration, in its various forms, is rapidly acquiring a broad and representative base in parts of Europe. The European Movement is obviously an issue of domestic politics. In appraising the impact of the Movement on public opinion in European countries great significance is to be attached to the fact that the issues posed by European integration and greater political union are issues on which the leadership of mass political parties take a stand. The stand they take, moreover, is usually a forward one. Apparently their support of unification in its various forms is good politics; such support has voter appeal.

It is this apparently growing appeal of the concept of unification to the broad masses that suggests the degree of progress that proponents of the ideal have made since the days of Coudenhove-Kalergi's Pan-European Union, or even since Churchill provided the catalyst for the formation of the postwar united European Move-

[6] See p. 132.

[7] For the composition of M. Monnet's Action Committee, see article entitled "The New Monnet Plan" in *Bulletin from the European Community for Coal and Steel,* No. 11 (Dec. 1955), p. 2.

ment. Despite the defeats that have been suffered, particularly the damaging one of EDC's rejection and the death of the Political Community in 1954, the resurgence of nationalism of an uncompromising kind in certain states, and the continued rejection of the Movement in many quarters as a fool's dream and quixoticism of the worst sort, the cause of "Europe" continues to make conquests.

In appraising the contemporary significance of the European Movement it is desirable to supplement our consideration of popular opinion with a comment on the official positions taken toward the Movement by the affected states. At this level it is possible to avoid the enthusiasms and ideological loyalties of special groups, which sometimes distort popular opinion, and deal instead with the views of those charged with the responsibility of preserving national interests. Here too, however, the significant fact is the relatively important role that the concept of integration has begun to play in determining the direction and substance of the foreign policies of the major Western powers.

In the course of this volume it has become reasonably clear that the so-called Six of "Little Europe," that is, France, West Germany, Italy, and the Benelux nations, are far in advance of other Western European states in their willingness to accept centripetal European institutions. They appear willing to support some of the most advanced plans for unity—plans that go beyond confederal and approach federal institutions. The recent adoption of the two treaties providing for a common policy in exploiting nuclear energy for civilian purposes and for a far-reaching customs and economic union constitutes a major step by the Six toward a real federation. Now that these two treaties have been ratified by their respective parliaments, the six states are likely to become virtually a single entity within a decade or two in regulating all issues affecting their internal economic concerns and their commercial policies toward other states. Having taken such a step, moreover, it is unlikely that unity among them will be long delayed as respects other facets of public jurisdiction.

For this trend toward federalism, France as a nation has traditionally shown the least enthusiasm among the Six, and history since World War II suggests that, despite the support given the federal movement by such leaders as Monnet, Mayer, Schuman, and other individual Frenchmen, and despite the favor she has shown for the two new community treaties, France may still stop this trend and even reverse it. For this there are various reasons of which the most important is the instability of the French parliamentary system. The notorious difficulty experienced by French prime ministers in securing parliamentary majorities for affirmative courses of action, a difficulty that reflects the deep and bitter divisions of French political life and of France's social structure, is only too well known. There are, moreover, many constituencies in French society, besides those represented by the parliamentary Right wing of Poujadists and Gaullists and by the parliamentary Left composed of Communists, who see national danger in too close an association of France with the other five nations. France's economy, though relatively balanced and stable, is a weak economy. Both her agriculture and her industry are vulnerable if they must compete with those of Germany and other proposed partners among the Six. Hence, even if she accepts membership in the new communities, France may well "drag her feet" when, during the next decade, she faces decisions on the question of whether to make serious adjustments in her economy—many of them demanding real sacrifices—that implementation of the common market will require. Moreover, whenever the occasion comes for France to cast the die either for or against a greater degree of unity in Western Europe, she has a tendency to reveal her true attitude toward a German partnership. That attitude is one of fear and indecision. Such was her attitude when she was called upon to decide finally on EDC and it is likely to be repeated whenever the issue of integration presents itself. Fearful of German demographical superiority and German scientific and technological prowess, French leaders feel they must proceed with caution lest they concede too much discretion to supranational bodies in which Germany might exercise a hegemony dangerous to French interests. Such fears are fairly certain to create more than one crisis in the effort to integrate France's economy in that of a quasi-federation during the next decade as provided in the new community treaties.

On the other hand, the French have strong parliamentary forces dedicated to European union. They are also realists: leading Frenchmen are perfectly well aware that their nation cannot hope to stand out indefinitely against the integrative trend in Europe. If, therefore, France can solve some of her more pressing domestic problems and set her parliamentary house in order, and if her partners in the new-born European economic union will exercise restraint and offer those compromises that France considers essential for the protection of her agriculture and other particularly vulnerable interests, France may yet prove to be a staunch "European" nation, willing to move forward with others toward the goal of unity that some of her more far-seeing statesmen and intellectual leaders have envisioned for the Continent. It should be added that a prime political condition of France's continued membership in the Six and her support of supranational plans is assurance that such action will not weaken her entente with Britain, which has perdured for more than half a century, nor damage her tie to NATO. France must continue to have the promise of British diplomatic and military support and the support of the NATO alliance to guard against the possibility that in the community of the Six she might one day have to face a disgruntled German partner—one, moreover, who might have become stronger than in 1958 because of Germany's reunification.

If France continues to move forward toward a greater degree of supranational unity in Western Europe, there is little doubt that a similar inspiration will govern Italian policy. To be sure, Italy, like France, began to have difficulty after 1954 in maintaining governments with sufficiently long-range authority to develop major policies and assure their continuance. In 1958 the dominant Christian Democrats and their occasional minor allies such as the Republicans and Liberals were having trouble in maintaining their control of Italian policy against the revisionist demands of the left Socialists, Communists, Monarchists, and neo-Fascists, who are all "anti-European." Despite these threats from Left and Right it seems likely that the party of de Gasperi, Pella, and Zoli will continue to dominate the Italian scene, and as long as it does, advanced conceptions of European unity are likely to continue being considered in harmony with the nation's fundamental interests.

Italian leadership has been quite forthright in its support of plans for economic integration and, as we have seen, promptly secured the ratification of Euratom and the common market treaty in the two houses of Italy's parliament early in the fall of 1957. Although some parts of the nation's economy will require temporary protection against too severe competition, abrogation of customs and similar barriers to a broader market would ultimately favor Italian commercial interests. A broad economic union will offer a means for ridding Italy of her excess employable population and give her specialty manufactures access to some of the richest markets in the world. Moreover, having lost her colonial empire in World War II, Italy is not averse to seizing upon the possible compensation that may inhere in the pooling of the remaining colonial empires of Western Europe and acquiring access to these markets on the same terms as the remaining members of the Six. On balance, therefore, Italy appears to have more to gain than to lose in integrating many of her interests with equivalent ones of her neighbors, and this seems to be the conclusion of those who are currently responsible for Italian policy.

What now of the German Federal Republic? Officially it has supported with virtually no reservations all proposals for greater unity in Western Europe that have been advanced since 1948. Chancellor Adenauer, himself an old and tried friend of union as we have often noted, has usually been far ahead of most of his own partisans and of many in his governing coalition in providing the intellectual foundations for the European idea. For him, progress toward European union, and German support of such a goal, has been not merely an expression of his own convictions as to the future of Germany and of Europe but tactically sound procedure for assuring Germany's return to her former status as a great and respected European power.

Others than the octogenarian chancellor may be governing Germany in the near future, and it is quite possible that they will not muster his enthusiasm for the European cause. The German Social Democrats have never been more than lukewarm toward the whole idea and their tolerance of such concepts as Euratom by no means guarantees they may not become somewhat less than partial toward European ideas if they should capture the government or become the dominant force in it. There are also industrialists and even labor union leaders in West Germany who see no particular value in the current plans for the economic integration of the Six in view of the immense strides that the German Federal Republic has taken in the economic realm since Hitler. By 1958 Germany has become the dominant creditor nation in Western Europe, and the values of a common market or any form of supranational regulation of her economy are not nearly so appealing as they were shortly after World War II. In the case of Germany there is, in addition, the constant threat that the Soviet Union will use the demand for a German veto on integration as the price for a more promising attitude toward the great issue of reuniting the two halves of Germany and restoring divided Berlin as the capital of a united German state. This is an objective for which even Adenauer might compromise his loyalty to the European cause. The immediate prospect, of course, is continued German support of the integration plans of the Six. German leaders are well aware that if those plans are consummated the Federal Republic will become the dominant member of the "Little European" union. Such being the prospect, there appears to be little reason for most German leaders to refuse participation if the other five states are willing to move forward.

Britain remains the leading Western European state outside the community of the Six. Her attitude toward integration continues to be something of an enigma, as we have had occasion to note on more than one page of this book. Although British spokesmen have not always been unambiguous about their nation's policy on "Europe," her Foreign Office has frequently reiterated quite explicitly her unwillingness to proceed beyond the concept of Europe expressed in the Council at Strasbourg. British leaders have been especially emphatic about their rejection of any European institution that savors of supranationalism or federation.

Nevertheless, despite this policy of keeping the supranational institutional ideas of the Six at arm's length, there is evidence that Britain is experiencing at least a slight change of heart on this matter. The process began in the autumn of 1954 when, EDC having been cast on the scrap heap, the British took the lead in developing the Western European Union plan as a substitute. As suggested earlier, this project is a distinct advance on a conventional military alliance, even though it is not the supranational project typified by EDC. When, moreover, the Schuman Community was formed, Britain found it to her advantage to establish the fairly intimate relationship of an "associate." It was a case of success in attaining a situation that is the ideal of the political art, namely, of enjoying most of the privileges of a project without assuming any of the responsibilities.

This flirting with the fringes of supranationalism presaged similar activity on Britain's part subsequently and a growing conviction on the part of certain echelons in the British government that Britain's whole policy toward the unity plans of the Six ought to be re-examined. Actual steps toward a reappraisal came in the summer of 1956 when leaders of the Six announced their hopes of negotiating the common market treaty. That announcement brought rather prompt action from Britain. Apparently fearful of an economic union restricted to the Six, the Macmillan government countered with a proposal for a free-trade zone among as many Western European nations as might join. In this zone there were to be no tariffs among the participating nations, but each would be free to develop its own commercial policy and tariffs against outsiders. It was expected that the Six would join this zone as a unit, and while eliminating tariffs against other states in the area, would continue with their own special supranational economic union. Britain stipulated that special reservations would have to be made in favor of her agricultural producers and that her system of imperial preferences could not be affected by the proposed arrangements.

What had happened was that when the economic community among the Six was launched, Britain at first sought to dissuade the proposed participants from going forward with their proposal. Then a strong movement developed within Britain, among both of the major parties, to put Britain into the proposed economic union and make a seven-power arrangement. It was this movement, especially vigorous among some of the career civil servants and university people, that called the turn for the Macmillan government and stimulated it to make the suggestion for a free-trade zone in Western Europe to supplement the more intimate plans of the Six.

What has happened to Britain is not too difficult to understand. Economic recovery on the Continent since the Second World War has made that market much more desirable than it was some years ago. Imperial preference and Britain's obligations to the Commonwealth, although still important, are relatively less so than they were, and their maintenance at the cost of a European system seems less desirable than was the case when the Council of Europe was formed in 1949. Moreover, the British intellectuals, industrialists, and diplomatists who feel a responsibility for the nation's future are of the opinion that quasi-federalism and supranational unity are likely to go farther among Britain's European neighbors than Britain had thought possible. As a result, a new politico-economic structure may well be in the making across the Channel and entirely new directions may be given to policy in that area. If Britain is to become a part of that new structure and affect the development of new policies, especially in the economic field, she will have to join that movement, or at least become intimately involved in it. To delay may mean that the door will be closed and British influence may decline. Such apparently is the thinking about "Europe" that since 1956 has brought Britain closer to the supranational ideas of the Six than at any time since the European Movement was revived in 1946.

Some months after the free-trade zone proposal had been made, apparently still in response to the "new wind" blowing in British councils, the British foreign minister, Selwyn Lloyd, proposed the coordination under some central authority of the many "European" organizations. The proposal would have brought such disparate agencies as the Council of Europe, the Schuman pool, the proposed new supranational communities of the Six, Western European Union, OEEC, and even NATO under some common coordinating authority, although apparently they would have continued essentially autonomous in the discharge of their respective functions. A related proposal would have encouraged the consolidation into one body of all the various European parliamentary bodies.[8] Just how a miscellany of this sort might operate with advantage under common direction is not clear. It is a proposal not untypical of the British, especially on this broad subject of European union. Undoubtedly it mystified some of Britain's more logically minded Continental friends. They, however, doubtless welcomed the gesture

[8] See *The New York Times*, Jan. 31, 1957.

as an earnest of Britain's revived interest in more effective Continental unity.

The leaders of the Six have in fact been quick to reciprocate this more cordial British attitude toward a stronger integration policy. As pointed out earlier, when Monnet first set out to lead the Six toward the common market project, he was careful to insist upon a surrender of sovereignty for all potential members save Britain. For her alone he was willing to compromise on that issue, suggesting that in any economic community of a supranational nature Britain might, if she wished, become attached as an "associate"—the quasi-membership for which a precedent had been established in her relations with the Schuman pool. The fact is, of course, that the Continental supporters of supranational communities want British support on almost any terms. She is needed to umpire between France and Germany. She is needed also if peripheral Europe, that is, those countries that are members of the Council of Europe and not among the Six, is ever to be persuaded to accept a European structure providing for more intimate association among the members than that afforded by the Strasbourg machinery.

The recent evidence of Britain's willingness to move somewhat beyond Strasbourg in her conception of "Europe" does not mean that she is likely to move too fast in that direction. Her statements of policy regarding "Europe" are doubtless sincere, but she can scarcely intend to abandon her traditional official position that the intergovernmental apparatus of the Council of Europe is her maximum concession to the demands of the integrationists. Nor will any apparatus juridically in advance of Strasbourg be likely to appeal soon to any of the remaining states, in addition to the Six and Britain, that are members of the Council of Europe.

That body is, moreover, destined to continue to be the maximum conception of "Europe" for those other European nations, not now members of Strasbourg, that might one day wish to become more closely identified with the European Movement. This is especially the case with the states still captives of the USSR. For Poland and other states in thrall to the Soviet, the lesson of their history is that the isolation of unqualified and unmodified national sovereignty is a luxury that they cannot afford if they wish to remain independent. If the threat to them does not come from the West, it comes from the East. Hence the hope of the captive states, should the Soviet writ ever be repealed, is to enter some sort of European union, and the formula for union that is likely to appeal at the outset is that offered by Strasbourg. That identification with some sort of European union, such as the Strasbourg apparatus, is the hope of free spokesmen of the captive states was made abundantly clear in the declarations of policy adopted by the Congress of the Free Representatives of Central and Eastern European Countries that met in London on March 29, 1957. Of the various recommendations the congress adopted, the first two demanded withdrawal of Soviet troops and the establishment of a democratic constitution. The third recommendation demanded "the integration of our liberated countries into a united Europe, within which they would maintain close cooperation based on their common interests." [9]

Thus for the indefinite future the aspirations and needs of the various European states are likely to require both a minimum and a maximum institutional expression for the European Movement. On the one hand there will be those whose policy permits them to move rather rapidly toward the more radical program, that is, toward institutions that are supranational or quasi-federal in character. On the other hand, the larger number of European states will find satisfaction in the minimum institutions of Strasbourg, institutions that are intergovernmental in nature and that juridically may be denominated quasi-confederal. In other words, there will continue to be what is popularly denominated the Europe of the Six or "Little Europe" and the Europe of the Fifteen, which includes the Six and which we may call "Greater Europe."

The former, though identified as "Little Europe," is in reality a grouping that has all the earmarks of a super power. It has 162 million inhabitants, about 450,000 square miles of territory, and a labor force of some 69 million. Technically it is one of the most advanced areas of the world and it will provide a real testing ground for free-market concepts and liberal trade policies promised by the supranational institutions that it appears it will shortly adopt.

Greater Europe supports a limited interpretation of the concept of "Europe"; most of the states in that grouping wish to identify

[9] *Polish Affairs,* No. 5 (fifth year, May 1957), p. 15.

their solidarity not juridically but diplomatically, and proceed slowly, a step at a time, toward the greater goal envisaged by the European prophets. But the Europe of the Fifteen can also provide converts for the ideas of the Europe of the Six, and, as we have indicated, it appears that already serious progress in that direction has been made in the case of Britain. In time, as a result of this development, it may become possible to identify the beginning of a third "European" group falling between the Six and the Fifteen, in which Britain would take the lead.

That progress from the limited concept of "Greater Europe" to the more intimate association of "Little Europe" is expected and desired has been made clear by the architects of the latter. "Little Europe" is emphatically not a "closed" but an "open" movement, into which all other European nations are cordially welcomed and in which it is confidently anticipated they will one day participate. This policy has been restated again and again since the day in 1950 when the syndicated supranational approach toward federation was first envisaged by the proponents of the Schuman Plan. The latest reiteration took place at Rome in March, 1957, when the Six signed the treaties for Euratom and the common market. Christian Pineau, the French foreign minister, was especially insistent on reminding Europe and the world that the Six were seeking nothing limited or monopolistic, but were merely taking the initiative with the hope that all of Europe would follow. "It is our duty," said M. Pineau, "to proclaim once again our desire to associate with other countries, notably Great Britain, without which the Europe we want to build would be incomplete." He added that the acceptance of the common market arrangements would in no way "have as its effect the creation of an isolated little Europe, as certain people charge, but will be the framework of the greater Europe which is our ultimate aim."

On the same occasion, Germany's Chancellor Adenauer, intent as always on reminding the world that the Six are merely pioneering for the rest of Europe, underscored M. Pineau's assurance that the Six were merely leading the way and would welcome the support of all European states. "Membership is open to all the European states," declared the German leader. "If a state believes it is not in a position to participate in full, we have provided for close collaboration in other ways, notably through the creation of the free-trade area."[10]

The growing role of the European idea may also be discerned in the attitude exhibited toward it by the two contemporary super powers that flank Europe on the West and the East, that is, the United States and the Union of Soviet Socialist Republics. As respects the latter that, for at least a part of its territory, can claim to be European, the policy toward "Europe" has been one of uncompromising opposition. It is a policy that has colored the Soviet's relations with every major Western European state and that has been reflected in the opposition to European ideas on the part of the domestic Communist parties in the West, notably in France and Italy. Even before World War II had ended and the European idea was beginning to gain converts among members of the resistance movements in Hitler-occupied Europe, local Communists, faithfully following the Moscow line, were already strongly condemning European ideas and stressing the view that the cause of national restoration would suffer if complicated by such ideas. Often the Russian Foreign Office has tried to play off one Western European power against another, using to good advantage the proverbial French fear of the Germans. As for the Germans, the Russian recipe has been the threat to withhold any prospect of their reunification if West Germany persisted in following the European line.

Although Soviet Russia has not succeeded in stopping the trend toward unity, she has occasionally experienced some sizable successes in delaying the trend. Her most notable success in thwarting the "European" trend came in the summer of 1954, when EDC was defeated in the French National Assembly. The Communist legions in France, and the Soviet's own policy of relaxing the Cold War, a relaxation that continued throughout the months prior to EDC's defeat and that eventually led to the Summit Conference at Geneva in 1955, contributed not a little to the fate that overtook EDC.

Following the announcement in 1956 of a resumption of efforts toward supranational institutions among the Six, the Soviet Union revived its familiar tactics for blocking advance. Its diplomats and

[10] Quoted in *Bulletin from the European Community for Coal and Steel,* No. 23 (Apr.-May 1957), pp. 2 ff.

journalists have directed more than one unflattering barb toward Monnet, Spaak, and other champions of the revived effort. Euratom, despite its obvious restriction to peacetime exploitation of nuclear energy, is branded as a tool of NATO and a device to promote military blocs. Apparently Moscow is well aware of the fact that EDC was vulnerable precisely because it came to be regarded as purely a military instrument and is trying to identify Euratom with EDC. In her efforts to block the proposed Atomic Energy Community, Russia has even gone so far as to provide an alternative proposal. This was a proposal to establish an all-European atomic energy organization that would include the Soviet Union and that would collect and coordinate information and exchange data among members. It was a proposal that has not gotten far beyond the diplomatic pouch.

What Russia fears in the European Movement is precisely what the Western European leadership hopes the Movement will bring about, namely, a new power bloc that, in an economic and strategic sense, can overcome the vacuum left in Western Europe after World War II and can effectively checkmate the drive to the West that Russia began after Hitler was overcome. Also involved in Russia's motivation is the not unreasonable fear on her part that any European unification movement that embraces Germany may well mean the aggrandizement of Germany and subsequently a resumption of the historic German threat to the peoples of the Slav lands. Whatever the motives of her opposition, there can be no doubt that Russia regards the European Movement as one of the major developments of the present era and she is determined to marshal all her force to oppose and deter it.

A complete contrast to the Russian view of the Movement is afforded by America's view. Where the Russians oppose the Americans have consistently upheld the Movement. Indeed, as this volume has tried to indicate, America, since the days she was host to Coudenhove-Kalergi, has been a stalwart supporter of this ideal. Americans might be said to have believed in European union before Europe did, and sometimes America's championship of the cause has been somewhat embarrassing to the Europeans.

This support makes no exceptions of any part of the European program. However fearful some American industrialists may be of the competition of a Europe without internal tariff walls, official America supports a unified European economy. She also supports attempts at political integration and sympathizes with the desire of some Europeans to make Europe a kind of third super power to provide a balance between America and the Soviet Union. We have already noted the strong support that President Eisenhower gave to the proposed European Community to harness atomic power for peaceful purposes.[11] An equally strong endorsement has been given to the common market plan, the United States having declared that it "welcomed" the proposal.[12] On May 26, 1956, at an address at Baylor University, President Eisenhower restated the faith that the United States has always had in the beneficial effects of European unity, which has animated its benevolent attitude toward that concept since the revival of the European Movement after the war. "With unification," said the President, "a new sun of hope, security, and confidence would shine for Europe and for the free world." [13]

The President identified the potential benefits of unity with the whole free world. But America has also been more specific and perhaps somewhat more articulate about the relation of her own national interests to the European Movement. Allusion to these objectives has been made rather frequently on these pages. In sum they suggest that America has endorsed unity in Europe because unity would contribute toward the better realization of the larger aims of the Marshall Plan and its successors, strengthen the North Atlantic Alliance, and build a massive and enduring obstacle to Russian expansionism. There has also been the belief that unity might mitigate, and perhaps end, the rivalries that have plunged European states into war in the past. The net effect would be to reduce the economic and military commitment that America has had to make in Europe, especially since the beginning of World War II, and give greater effectiveness to whatever commitment America did make. One fact appears to emerge from the history of America's attitude toward European union, namely, that this concept has been a major aim of American foreign policy since

[11] See communiqué on atom pool in *The New York Times,* Feb. 9, 1957.
[12] *Ibid.,* Jan. 16, 1957.
[13] For address, see *Department of State Bulletin,* June 4, 1956, p. 917.

1947 and there is no reason to doubt its continued hold upon the American public and government.

The revival in 1958 of the march toward further institutionalization of the ideal of integration, interrupted by the defeat of EDC and abortive death of the Political Community in 1954, is a testimonial to the vitality of the European concept. Despite the obstacles likely to be encountered, there is hope that Euratom and the new Economic Community, once they are actively established, will become viable supranational institutions among the Six, and that their operation will begin a new chapter in the history of European institutions. But neither these new communities nor other institutional symbols and apparatus constitute the really significant development that has occurred during the years since World War II. That development, as we have attempted to point out in this chapter, is the extent of the conquest that the idea of integration appears to be making of the European mind, especially in the years since EDC was defeated. It is the growing appeal that the Movement has developed for the masses of the public. It is the growing clarity with which European leaders formulate the contemporary objectives of the European ideal and the increasingly favorable public reaction to those objectives. It is these considerations that persuade observers that the European Movement is today a development of the highest importance to the world.

United Europe is thus no longer an idealist's dream but a practical goal of politics. It is one of the profoundly revolutionary ideals that is currently influencing opinion and institutional developments in one of the most important regions of the world. In time the European Movement could bring about a renaissance of Europe's world position, a position currently being eclipsed as a result of relative economic decline, the dynamics of contemporary world politics, the growing role of the so-called non-European super powers, and the impact of the colonial revolution.

In Europe, at least, the finger of time may well write finis to the isolated state system that comes down from the eighteenth century. It has become increasingly clear to the leadership of Western Europe that such a system cannot provide the degree of integration that will insure the social and material values that contemporary political organization is expected to achieve and foster. Indeed, it has become apparent that the national states themselves cannot survive or the cultural values of national groups be safeguarded unless some broader form of political integration than that provided by nationalism eventually emerges. The decade since the end of World War II has underscored this conclusion and brought conviction to more than one outstanding European statesman and moral leader. The ancient framework of the national state system may and doubtless will persist indefinitely without much overt change, but its internal decay, brought about by its failure to secure the moral and material aspirations of the rank and file, will become increasingly apparent as time moves on. What will supplant that system, moreover, is clear. The European Movement has supplied or will supply the alternative in Europe. The future of political organization in Western Europe lies with the concept of regional and continental integration fostered by that Movement.

What the future holds for the European Movement has never been expressed more appropriately than in the inscription that appears on the cornerstone of the building in Luxembourg that houses a European secondary school. This school was established for the children of officials of the Schuman Community stationed in that city—officials who come from each of the six states that make up the Community. The cornerstone was laid with appropriate ceremonies on July 5, 1956, with Joseph Bech, prime minister of the Grand Duchy, and M. René Mayer, president of the Community's High Authority, in attendance. In the English translation the Latin text of the cornerstone inscription reads as follows:

> The young pupils educated in contact with each other, freed from their earliest years from the prejudices which divide one nation from another, and introduced to the value and beauty of different cultures, will have a growing sense of their common solidarity. Retaining their pride in, and love for, their own countries, they will become Europeans in spirit, ready to complete and consolidate the work that their fathers have undertaken for the advance of a united and prosperous Europe.[14]

[14] Translation provided by the editors of the *Bulletin from the European Community for Coal and Steel,* No. 17 (July 1956), p. 12.

APPENDICES

Draft Constitution of
THE UNITED STATES OF EUROPE

PREAMBLE

The states of Europe, animated by a desire to safeguard their common cultural heritage, to avert the scourge of internecine war, to rid themselves of the intolerable burden of armaments, to assure social security and an ever-rising standard of living, to guarantee the personal, national and religious freedom of all Europeans, and to make a positive contribution to a more orderly world, have agreed upon these ARTICLES OF ASSOCIATION AND UNION.

SECTION I—THE STATES AND THE UNION

Article 1. The organization established by the following ARTICLES shall be known as the United States of Europe, hereinafter referred to as the UNION.

Article 2. The UNION is an association of sovereign states which have decided to establish and maintain common institutions in the interest of their security, prosperity, and liberty.

Article 3. Member states retain their sovereign rights unimpaired except in so far as these rights are limited by these ARTICLES.

Article 4. The UNION shall have its own flag and seat of government.

Article 5. Accession to the UNION shall be a voluntary act. Member states shall be those which ratify these ARTICLES by the processes hereinafter formulated.

Article 6. The existence of the UNION does not preclude the organization of groups of member states for purposes not inconsistent with those of the UNION. The consent of the UNION shall always be required for such group organizations.

Article 7. The UNION shall guarantee the reserved sovereign rights and boundaries of each member state and is authorized to take appropriate measures to secure this guarantee.

SECTION II—INTERNAL CONSTITUTIONAL STANDARDS OF MEMBER STATES

Article 8. The constitution of each member state shall have the character of fundamental law enforceable in an appropriate state court.

Article 9. The constitution of a member state shall provide for at least one house of its parliament elected by free, equal, and secret ballot by the adult inhabitants of one or both sexes who are citizens.

Article 10. The constitution of each member state shall secure to its parliament the power to pass all laws and to vote taxes, appropriations and other measures relating to finance and property.

Article 11. The constitution of every member state shall make the privileges and prerogatives of its parliament inalienable and shall guarantee in explicit terms that these privileges and prerogatives may not be transferred to any other authority except for the duration of an emergency as described in Article 32.

Article 12. The constitution of every member state shall assure the rights of the opposition in its parliament.

Article 13. The constitution of every member state shall guarantee local or regional autonomy to linguistic minority groups forming a regional majority within a clearly defined territory of the state, provided such groups desire an autonomous status within the member state. The desire for autonomy shall be determined by a plebiscite held under the authority of the UNION.

SECTION III–INTERSTATE RELATIONS

Article 14. Every member state shall give full faith and credit to the public acts, records, and judicial proceedings of every other member state when these relate to the private rights of persons.

Article 15. Except where a political offense is charged, every member state shall render up a fugitive from justice to the executive authority of the member state from which he fled.

Article 16. The UNION may enact model legislation on any subject outside of its immediate competence and recommend the adoption of such legislation to the appropriate organs of the governments of the member states.

Article 17. Citizens of member states may travel freely across the frontiers of any other member state for the purpose of temporary residence. For such a purpose no passport or visa shall be required. Persons with a criminal record and those likely to become public charges are subject to such regulations as the member state chooses to establish. The permanent migration of persons from one member state to another is subject to such regulations as the Congress of the UNION may establish.

Article 18. Every dispute arising between member states must be settled by peaceful means. If the dispute is of a juridical nature, it must be submitted for adjudication to the Supreme Court of the UNION. If the dispute is of a non-juridical nature, the Council of the UNION shall have power to bring about a final settlement by majority vote.

SECTION IV–THE RIGHTS OF THE INDIVIDUAL

Article 19. Every person is equal before the law; there shall be no discrimination among persons or classes of persons based on race, language, or religion.

Article 20. Every religion shall be respected and its adherents shall have the right to practice its form of worship provided they do not advocate seditious or treasonable practices or contravene regulations affecting public safety or morals.

Article 21. Liberty of the press, publication, speech, and of teaching are guaranteed. A member state shall not impose any censorship except in time of emergency as defined in Article 32.

Article 22. Neither any member state nor any governmental authority thereof shall ever attempt to exercise monopolistic control over any instrument or medium of opinion or propaganda. Where such instrument or medium is publicly owned or operated, full opportunity shall be afforded organized groups, other than those having official status, to use such publicly owned or operated instrument or medium on fair and reasonable terms for the purpose of expressing their opinion or propaganda.

Article 23. The people of a member state shall have the right peaceably to assemble for the purpose of petitioning the authorities for a redress of grievances. Any other peaceful method of petitioning for a similar purpose shall be authorized.

Article 24. Every form of organization, political, economic, and cultural shall be authorized. No organization shall be dissolved nor shall its property be confiscated unless it has been judicially ascertained that such organization secretly or openly advocates the overthrow of the established social and political order by violence or that it advocates disrespect for, or violation of, existing law.

Article 25. The right of private property is guaranteed subject to the member state's recognized powers of taxation, police regulation and expropriation for the general welfare with compensation.

Article 26. No person shall be denied the use of his native tongue whether or not it is recognized as an official language.

Article 27. No person shall be deprived of life, liberty, or property except in accordance with due process of law.

Article 28. No person may be seized or imprisoned unless apprehended in the commission of a crime or unless a warrant of arrest, specifically naming him and giving reasons for his apprehension, has issued from a proper judicial magistrate or tribunal.

Article 29. A person arrested and imprisoned for cause shall be given a speedy and impartial public trial; he shall have the right to obtain counsel, to be confronted by witnesses against him, and to the issuance of compulsory process to obtain witnesses in his behalf.

Article 30. No person shall be indefinitely confined or be restricted in his movements except as a punishment for a crime of which he shall have been duly convicted in a regular court of law.

Article 31. A private dwelling house shall be immune from search and the effects therein may not be seized except by authority of a warrant issued by a proper judicial magistrate or tribunal.

Article 32. Martial law and courts-martial shall not supersede civil courts and civil processes for non-military affairs, nor shall a state of siege be declared except in time of war or emergency duly proclaimed by the highest executive authority of the member state. To continue in effect, such executive proclamation must be ratified by the parliament of the member state within three months. Otherwise the proclamation shall lapse and no new proclamation, relating to the same emergency, may thereafter issue unless authorized by the parliament of the member state.

Article 33. Torture may not be used to extort a confession or for any other purpose. No cruel or unusual punishment shall ever be imposed; nor shall any person be placed twice in jeopardy of life or limb for the same alleged offense; nor shall the conviction of any person adversely affect the civil rights of any of his relatives or associates.

Article 34. No person shall ever be held as a hostage.

Article 35. The secrecy of postal, telephonic and telegraphic communication shall be inviolable. The authorities of a member state shall not interfere with such communication except in a period of emergency as defined in Article 32.

Article 36. The stipulation of these minimum rights and privileges in any member-state constitution shall not be construed to deny or disparage other rights which may likewise be stipulated in such constitution or which may be derived from the general law or public policy of such state.

Article 37. Every member state of the UNION agrees to incorporate a statement of the rights stipulated in this section (Articles 19-36) in its own constitution, to provide effective administrative and judicial process for their enforcement and to facilitate appeals from its own courts to the Supreme Court of the UNION whenever interested parties, whose rights as defined in this section (Articles 19-36) have allegedly been violated, invoke the procedure of appeal as described in Article 90.

SECTION V–SOCIAL RIGHTS

Article 38. Member states of the UNION agree that lasting peace depends, in part, upon an integrated and progressive policy aiming at freedom from want. They accordingly pledge themselves to provide within their own respective jurisdictions a comprehensive system of social assistance, such a system to take account of the magnitude and distribution of national income. This system shall include: compulsory insurance against accidents, illness, old age, and unemployment; medical assistance to expectant mothers and infants; social assistance to mental defectives and the incapacitated; and pensions for widows and orphans.

Article 39. Member states agree to assure universal and compulsory primary education and opportunity for secondary education for all children and adolescents and to provide higher and technical instruction for all students of outstanding qualifications at public expense if not otherwise provided.

Article 40. Member states agree that within their respective jurisdictions, they will enact legislation for the protection of labor. Such legislation shall guarantee the right of collective bargaining and arbitration of disputes between labor and management. It shall also fix the maximum hours of work and minimum wages for various employments and provide standards for sanitary conditions in factories and other places of employment.

Article 41. In the regulation of their respective internal economies, member states pledge themselves to seek to exploit fully their natural resources and protect the interests of consumers with a view to increasing their national income and raising the standard of living of their inhabitants.

Article 42. Member states agree to inaugurate an agrarian reform in the case of the latifundia which shall aim at establishing the rural population on privately owned holdings directly cultivated by the proprietor. Such a reform shall be supplemented by adequate agrarian credit facilities and the utilization of agricultural co-operatives.

Article 43. Member states agree to co-ordinate their efforts for the establishment of a European health service and for combating disease and epidemics.

Article 44. Should the Congress of the UNION adopt a single official language for intra-European intercourse, member states agree to provide instruction in the use of that language in addition to instruction in national languages.

Article 45. All social rights identified in this Section (Articles 38-44) shall also be made available in each member state to residents who are citizens of other member states.

SECTION VI–DEFENSE

Article 46. The UNION shall have power to take all measures to prevent its member states from menacing international peace and order and to protect the territory of the UNION against aggression.

Article 47. To protect and defend the UNION, a professional armed force shall be organized, trained, equipped and commanded under the UNION's sole responsibility.

Article 48. Member states are bound to assist the UNION in all matters pertaining to the organization, training, equipping and housing of the UNION's forces. This stipulation includes facilities for airfields, ports, bases, fortifications and other installations.

Article 49. No more than one tenth of the total strength of any branch of the armed forces of the UNION shall consist of nationals of any one member state.

Article 50. The UNION shall own, supervise or otherwise control the production of munitions and other war material or any type of production which can readily be converted into the production of munitions or war materials. It shall also control the traffic in munitions and armament.

Article 51. All officers of the armed forces of the UNION, including their commander-in-chief, shall be appointed and recalled by the UNION. During their term of service, the personnel of the armed forces of the UNION owe allegiance exclusively to the UNION.

Article 52. Member states may maintain armed forces for internal order and security on their respective territories under regulations established by the UNION.

Article 53. Member states possessing or controlling colonial territories may be authorized by the UNION to maintain colonial forces in those territories. Such forces can never be transferred to the Continent of Europe without the consent of the UNION.

SECTION VII–FOREIGN AFFAIRS

Article 54. The UNION shall have power to conduct foreign relations and to conclude treaties and agreements to further the purposes of these ARTICLES. Member states may conclude treaties with the approval of the UNION, and may exchange diplomatic and consular representatives among themselves and with foreign states.

Article 55. The UNION shall co-operate with other states or groups of states to establish a world organization for the maintenance of peace and security.

SECTION VIII–COLONIAL TERRITORIES

Article 56. Colonial territories shall remain under the direct jurisdiction and sovereign authority of the member state to which such territories are attached. This applies also to protectorates and mandates of member states.

Article 57. The nationals of every member state of the UNION shall have the same rights and privileges in the colonial territory of any member state as are enjoyed by the nationals of that member state.

Article 58. The governing member state is bound to act in its colonial territory as a trustee for the people of such territory. It shall promote the cultural and economic life of dependent peoples as rapidly as possible and shall introduce among such peoples a system of political education calculated to advance them most rapidly from a condition of political dependence to one of political responsibility and ultimate self-government.

SECTION IX–ECONOMIC POLICY

Article 59. The economic policy of the UNION shall aim at the unification of the European economy; within five years following the organization of the UNION, the Congress is authorized to establish a European customs union with intra-European free trade.

Article 60. Pending the establishment of a customs union, the member states agree not to establish unilateral tariffs, foreign exchange controls, import quotas, export premiums, transport differentials, blocked accounts, multiple currencies in one and the same state, or any other obstacles affecting the interstate trade of the UNION. Such controls shall only be established by agreement between member states affected.

Article 61. As one step toward a unified European economy, the UNION shall use its power of enacting model legislation to provide for the reduction and ultimate elimination of all internal trade barriers.

Article 62. By enacting model legislation, the UNION shall indicate the type of price and wage policies to be implemented by member states to encourage production and consumption.

Article 63. The UNION shall assure the unification of the European transport system within a period to be determined by the Congress.

Article 64. A central bank of Europe shall be established by a special statute of the Congress. It shall have the prerogative of issuing currency and shall serve as a clearing and rediscounting agency for the central banks of member states.

SECTION X–REVENUES OF THE UNION

Article 65. The Congress may levy upon member states for contributions to the treasury of the UNION, the contribution of each state to be in proportion to its ascertained national income. Collection shall be made by authorities of each member state.

Article 66. The revenue of the UNION shall also include all of the net proceeds of import duties levied by the member states upon their mutual trade and fifty per cent of the net proceeds of import duties levied upon goods coming from outside the UNION.

Article 67. Proceeds from the domain of the UNION, whether from exploitation or sale of immobile property or from operation of enterprises producing goods and rendering services, shall go to the treasury of the UNION.

SECTION XI–THE CONGRESS

Article 68. The deliberative organ of the UNION shall be a Congress consisting of a House of Representatives and a House of States.

Article 69. In the House of Representatives, the member states shall be represented according to the following formula:

a) states with more than 40 million inhabitants . . 10 representatives
b) states with less than 40 million but more than 20 million inhabitants . . . . 8 representatives
c) states with less than 20 million but more than 10 million inhabitants . . . . 6 representatives
d) states with less than 10 million but more than 5 million inhabitants . . . . 4 representatives
e) states with less than 5 million but more than 2½ million inhabitants . . . . 2 representatives
f) states with less than 2½ million inhabitants . . . 1 representative
g) any member state possessing colonial territory shall have one additional representative
h) for purposes of representation in the Congress of the UNION, San Marino shall be identified with Italy, Monaco with France, and Liechtenstein with Switzerland.

Article 70. The representatives of the member states in the House of Representatives shall be chosen by the popularly elective chamber of the parliament of the member state.

Article 71. The House of States shall consist of two delegates from each member state of the UNION with more than 2½ million inhabitants and of one delegate from each member state with less than 2½ million inhabitants. The principle of Article 69(h), governing the representation of San Marino, Monaco and Liechtenstein in the House of Representatives, applies also to their representation in the House of States.

Article 72. Delegates of member states to the House of States shall be chosen as each member state shall determine.

Article 73. When sitting separately, the two houses of Congress shall be co-ordinate in authority and their agreement shall be necessary to a decision.

Article 74. Each house shall be competent to determine the character of its internal organization and its rules of procedure subject to the following requirements:

a) pending the choice of a single official language by the Congress, English and French shall be the official languages
b) a member of either house may speak in his native tongue and be provided with the services of an interpreter
c) a record vote may be demanded on any principal question by any member and the vote be taken accordingly
d) an absolute majority of the members of each house shall constitute a quorum and decisions shall be taken by majority vote unless otherwise stipulated in these ARTICLES.

Article 75. The Congress shall meet on call of the president of the House of Representatives at least once each year. The President of the UNION may call it into special session.

Article 76. Except as otherwise expressly provided in these ARTICLES, the Congress shall have power to deal with all matters falling within the competence of the UNION. Except as otherwise expressly provided in these ARTICLES, the Congress shall have power to establish any department, office, agency, or other unit necessary to the operation of the government and administration of the UNION.

Article 77. The two houses of Congress shall constitute a single assembly when the following matters are considered:

a) the election of the Council or its individual members
b) the proposal of an amendment to these ARTICLES
c) the election of judges of the Supreme Court.

Article 78. When sitting as a single assembly, each member of the Congress shall have one vote; two thirds of the total membership of the combined houses shall constitute a quorum.

SECTION XII–THE COUNCIL

Article 79. The executive organ of the UNION shall be a Council of seven members elected for terms of four years by the two Houses of Congress meeting as a single assembly. Not more than one member of the Council shall come from the same member state.

At least three of its members must be citizens of states with a population of more than twenty millions.

Article 80. The Council shall be responsible to the Congress for all of its acts.

Article 81. Each year the Council shall elect, by majority vote, one of its members to be President of the UNION and another member to be Vice President of the UNION. They shall serve as chairman and vice chairman, respectively, of the Council. No incumbent President may be re-elected or be elected Vice President for the year following his presidency.

Article 82. The Council shall discharge the duties assigned to it by these ARTICLES or by Congress.

Article 83. Such administrative departments as Congress may erect shall be placed under the immediate supervision of a member of the Council. The Council shall indicate which department each member shall supervise.

Article 84. In case of an internal or external threat to the peace and safety of the UNION, the Council is authorized to use whatever measures the emergency may require, including the use of the armed forces of the UNION, to combat such threat. It shall immediately report the circumstances and the measures taken to the Congress.

SECTION XIII—THE SUPREME COURT

Article 85. The chief judicial organ of the UNION shall be a Supreme Court consisting of fifteen judges. They shall be elected by the Congress sitting as a single assembly by a two-thirds vote. The judges of the Court shall choose one of their number to serve as president of the Court.

Article 86. The Congress shall choose the judges of the Supreme Court from lists of nominees prepared by the Council consisting of all present members of the highest courts of the member states and of a maximum of 100 jurisconsults of recognized standing.

Article 87. The tenure of the judges shall be for life. A judge may be removed for mental incapacity or for the commission of an act which discredits him morally. Charges of removal shall be made by majority vote of the House of Representatives; a decision on the charges thus brought shall be rendered by a majority vote of the House of States.

Article 88. The Court, as a plenum, shall have original jurisdiction over (a) any dispute of a juridical nature arising out of the interpretation of these ARTICLES; (b) any dispute concerning the competence of any officer or agency of the UNION, including the Congress and the Council; and (c) any dispute of a juridical nature arising among member states of the UNION as defined in Article 18.

Article 89. In exercising its original jurisdiction, decisions of the Court shall be taken by an absolute majority.

Article 90. The Supreme Court shall have appellate jurisdiction over any case involving a claim that the requirements of section IV (Articles 19-36) have been violated. Appeals may be taken by the interested parties to the Supreme Court of the UNION directly from the highest court having jurisdiction in the member state where the violation is alleged to have been committed. On its own initiative, the Court may also call up for review and decision any case involving an alleged violation of the requirements of section IV (Articles 19-36).

Article 91. A panel of five members, designated by the president of the Court, shall be competent to hear and decide by majority vote any case appealed or called up for review under the provisions of Article 90. No judge who is a citizen of the member state where the dispute originates or who has national ties with the disputants may sit. In making its decision, the panel shall consult with the appropriate experts drawn from the secretariat of the Court or appointed by it who have special knowledge of the national area involved in the case.

Article 92. A special statute of Congress shall provide for the organization of the Supreme Court; the Court shall draw up its own rules of procedure.

SECTION XIV–ACCESSION TO THE UNION-TRANSITIONAL PROVISION

Article 93. When ratified by the parliaments or other appropriate constitutional organ of at least ten eligible states, four of which shall have a population of at least twenty millions, these ARTICLES shall take effect among the states so ratifying. Other eligible states may adhere subsequently by a similar act of ratification.

Article 94. Member states of the UNION shall adapt their respective constitutions and existing statute and other law to the provisions of these ARTICLES within a period of five years following ratification.

SECTION XV–AMENDMENT AND REVISION

Article 95. Amendment of these ARTICLES, in whole or in part, may be proposed by two thirds of the membership of Congress meeting as a single assembly; an amendment shall take effect when ratified by the parliaments of a majority of the member states among which must be included at least four states with twenty million or more inhabitants.

For the
Juridical Committee of the
Pan-European Conference:

FERNANDO DE LOS RÍOS
STEPHEN P. LADAS

For the
Research Seminar for
European Federation: New York University:

RICHARD COUDENHOVE-KALERGI
ARNOLD J. ZURCHER

New York, March 25, 1944

STATUTE OF THE COUNCIL OF EUROPE

London, 5th May, 1949

(*with amendments approved by the Committee of Ministers at Strasbourg in* 1951 *and* 1953)

The Governments of the Kingdom of Belgium, the Kingdom of Denmark, the French Republic, the Irish Republic, the Italian Republic, the Grand Duchy of Luxembourg, the Kingdom of the Netherlands, the Kingdom of Norway, the Kingdom of Sweden and the United Kingdom of Great Britain and Northern Ireland;

Convinced that the pursuit of peace based upon justice and international co-operation is vital for the preservation of human society and civilization;

Reaffirming their devotion to the spiritual and moral values which are the common heritage of their peoples and the true source of individual freedom, political liberty and the rule of law, principles which form the basis of all genuine democracy;

Believing that, for the maintenance and further realization of these ideals and in the interests of economic and social progress, there is need of a closer unity between all like-minded countries of Europe;

Considering that, to respond to this need and to the expressed aspirations of their peoples in this regard, it is necessary forthwith to create an organization which will bring European States into closer association;

Have in consequence decided to set up a Council of Europe consisting of a Committee of representatives of Governments and of a Consultative Assembly, and have for this purpose adopted the following Statute:

Chapter I

AIM OF THE COUNCIL OF EUROPE

ARTICLE 1

(*a*) The aim of the Council of Europe is to achieve a greater unity between its Members for the purpose of safeguarding and realizing the ideals and principles which are their common heritage and facilitating their economic and social progress.

(*b*) This aim shall be pursued through the organs of the Council by discussion of questions of common concern and by agreements and common action in economic, social, cultural, scientific, legal and administrative matters and in the maintenance and further realization of human rights and fundamental freedoms.

(*c*) Participation in the Council of Europe shall not affect the collaboration of its Members in the work of the United Nations and of other international organizations or unions to which they are parties.

(*d*) Matters relating to National Defence do not fall within the scope of the Council of Europe.

Chapter II

MEMBERSHIP

ARTICLE 2

The Members of the Council of Europe are the Parties to this Statute.

ARTICLE 3

Every Member of the Council of Europe must accept the principles of the rule of law and of the enjoyment by all persons within its jurisdiction of human rights and fundamental freedoms, and collaborate sincerely and effectively in the realization of the aim of the Council as specified in Chapter I.

ARTICLE 4

Any European State, which is deemed to be able and willing to fulfil the provisions of Article 3, may be invited to become a Member of the Council of Europe by the Committee of Ministers. Any State so invited shall become a Member on the deposit on its behalf with the Secretary-General of an instrument of accession to the present Statute.

ARTICLE 5

(*a*) In special circumstances, a European country, which is deemed to be able and willing to fulfil the provisions of Article 3, may be invited by the Committee of Ministers to become an Associate Member of the Council of Europe. Any country so invited shall become an Associate Member on the deposit on its behalf with the Secretary-General of an instrument accepting the present Statute. An Associate Member shall be entitled to be represented in the Consultative Assembly only.

(*b*) The expression 'Member' in this Statute includes an Associate Member except when used in connexion with representation on the Committee of Ministers.

ARTICLE 6

Before issuing invitations under Article 4 or 5 above, the Committee of Ministers shall determine the number of representatives on the Consultative Assembly to which the proposed Member shall be entitled and its proportionate financial contribution.

ARTICLE 7

Any Member of the Council of Europe may withdraw by formally notifying the Secretary-General of its intention to do so. Such withdrawal shall take effect at the end of the financial year in which it is notified, if the notification is given during the first nine months of that financial year. If the notification is given in the last three months of the financial year, it shall take effect at the end of the next financial year.

ARTICLE 8

Any Member of the Council of Europe, which has seriously violated Article 3, may be suspended from its rights of representation and requested by the Committee of Ministers to withdraw under Article 7. If such Member does not comply with this request, the Committee may decide that it has ceased to be a Member of the Council as from such date as the Committee may determine.

ARTICLE 9

The Committee of Ministers may suspend the right of representation on the Committee and on the Consultative Assembly of a Member, which has failed to fulfil its financial obligation, during such period as the obligation remains unfulfilled.

Chapter III
GENERAL

ARTICLE 10

The organs of the Council of Europe are:

(*i*) the Committee of Ministers;
(*ii*) the Consultative Assembly.

Both these organs shall be served by the Secretariat of the Council of Europe.

ARTICLE 11

The seat of the Council of Europe is at Strasbourg.

ARTICLE 12

The official languages of the Council of Europe are English and French. The rules of procedure of the Committee of Ministers and of the Consultative Assembly shall determine in what circumstances and under what conditions other languages may be used.

Chapter IV
COMMITTEE OF MINISTERS

ARTICLE 13

The Committee of Ministers is the organ which acts on behalf of the Council of Europe in accordance with Articles 15 and 16.

ARTICLE 14

Each Member shall be entitled to one representative on the Committee of Ministers and each representative shall be entitled to one vote. Representatives on the Committee shall be the Ministers for Foreign Affairs. When a Minister for Foreign Affairs is unable to be present or in other circumstances where it may be desirable, an alternate may be nominated to act for him, who shall, whenever possible, be a member of his Government.

ARTICLE 15

(*a*) On the recommendation of the Consultative Assembly or on its own initiative, the Committee of Ministers shall consider the action required to further the aim of the Council of Europe, including the conclusion of conventions or agreements and the adoption by Governments of a common policy with regard to particular matters. Its conclusions shall be communicated to Members by the Secretary-General.

(*b*) In appropriate cases, the conclusions of the Committee may take the form of recommendations to the Governments of Members, and the Committee may request the Governments of Members to inform it of the action taken by them with regard to such recommendations.

ARTICLE 16

The Committee of Ministers shall, subject to the provisions of Articles 24, 28, 30, 32, 33 and 35, relating to the powers of the Consultative Assembly, decide with binding effect all matters relating to the internal organization and arrangements of the Council of Europe. For this purpose the Committee of Ministers shall adopt such financial and administrative regulations as may be necessary.

ARTICLE 17

The Committee of Ministers may set up advisory and technical committees or commissions for such specific purposes as it may deem desirable.

ARTICLE 18

The Committee of Ministers shall adopt its rules of procedure which shall determine amongst other things:

(*i*) the quorum;
(*ii*) the method of appointment and term of office of its President;
(*iii*) the procedure for the admission of items to its agenda, including the giving of notice of proposals for resolutions; and
(*iv*) the notifications required for the nomination of alternates under Article 14.

ARTICLE 19

At each session of the Consultative Assembly the Committee of Ministers shall furnish the Assembly with statements of its activities, accompanied by appropriate documentation.

ARTICLE 20

(*a*) Resolutions of the Committee of Ministers relating to the following important matters, namely:

(*i*) recommendations under Article 15 (*b*);
(*ii*) questions under Article 19;
(*iii*) questions under Article 21 (*a*) (*i*) and (*b*);
(*iv*) questions under Article 33;
(*v*) recommendations for the amendment of Articles 1 (*d*), 7, 15, 20 and 22; and
(*vi*) any other question which the Committee may, by a resolution passed under (*d*) below, decide should be subject to a unanimous vote on account of its importance,

require the unanimous vote of the representatives casting a vote, and of a majority of the representatives entitled to sit on the Committee.

(*b*) Questions arising under the rules of procedure or under the financial and administrative regulations may be decided by a simple majority vote of the representatives entitled to sit on the Committee.

(*c*) Resolutions of the Committee under Articles 4 and 5 require a two-thirds majority of all the representatives entitled to sit on the Committee.

(*d*) All other resolutions of the Committee, including the adoption of the Budget, of rules of procedure and of financial and administrative regulations, recommendations for the amendment of articles of this Statute, other than those mentioned in paragraph (*a*) (*v*) above, and deciding in case of doubt which paragraph of this Article applies, require a two-thirds majority of the representatives casting a vote and of a majority of the representatives entitled to sit on the Committee.

ARTICLE 21

(*a*) Unless the Committee decides otherwise, meetings of the Committee of Ministers shall be held:

(*i*) in private, and
(*ii*) at the seat of the Council.

(*b*) The Committee shall determine what information shall be published regarding the conclusions and discussions of a meeting held in private.

(*c*) The Committee shall meet before and during the beginning of every session of the Consultative Assembly and at such other times as it may decide.

Chapter V

THE CONSULTATIVE ASSEMBLY

ARTICLE 22

The Consultative Assembly is the deliberative organ of the Council of Europe. It shall debate matters within its competence under this Statute and present its conclusions, in the form of recommendations, to the Committee of Ministers.

ARTICLE 23 [1]

(*a*) The Consultative Assembly may discuss and make recommendations upon any matter within the aim and scope of the Council of Europe as defined in Chapter I. It shall also discuss and may make recommendations upon any matter referred to it by the Committee of Ministers with a request for its opinion.

(*b*) The Assembly shall draw up its Agenda in accordance with the provisions of paragraph (*a*) above. In so doing, it shall have regard to the work of other European intergovernmental organizations to which some or all of the Members of the Council are parties.

(*c*) The President of the Assembly shall decide, in case of doubt, whether any question raised in the course of the Session is within the Agenda of the Assembly.

ARTICLE 24

The Consultative Assembly may, with due regard to the provisions of Article 38 (*d*), establish committees or commissions to consider and report to it on any matter which falls within its competence under Article 23, to examine and prepare questions on its Agenda and to advise on all matters of procedure.

ARTICLE 25 [2]

(*a*) The Consultative Assembly shall consist of Representatives of each Member elected by its Parliament or appointed in such manner as that Parliament shall decide, subject, however, to the right of each Member Government to make any additional appointments necessary when the Parliament is not in session and has not laid down the procedure to be followed in that case. Each Representative must be a national of the Member whom he represents, but shall not at the same time be a member of the Committee of Ministers.

The term of office of Representatives thus appointed will date from the opening of the Ordinary Session following their appointment; it will expire at the opening of the next Ordinary Session or of a later Ordinary

[1] As amended in May 1951.

[2] First sentence of paragraph (*a*) as amended in May 1951—The last two sub-paragraphs of paragraph (*a*) were added in May 1953.

Session, except that, in the event of elections to their Parliaments having taken place, Members shall be entitled to make new appointments.

If a Member fills vacancies due to death or resignation, or proceeds to make new appointments as a result of elections to its Parliament, the term of office of the new Representatives shall date from the first Sitting of the Assembly following their appointment.

(*b*) No Representative shall be deprived of his position as such during a session of the Assembly without the agreement of the Assembly.

(*c*) Each Representative may have a substitute who may, in the absence of the Representative, sit, speak and vote in his place. The provisions of paragraph (*a*) above apply to the appointment of substitutes.

ARTICLE 26 [3]

Members shall be entitled to the number of Representatives given below:

Belgium	7
Denmark	5
France	18
Germany (Federal Republic)	18
Greece	7
Iceland	3
Ireland	4
Italy	18
Luxembourg	3
Netherlands	7
Norway	5
Saar	3
Sweden	6
Turkey	10
United Kingdom of Great Britain and Northern Ireland	18

ARTICLE 27 [4]

The conditions under which the Committee of Ministers collectively may be represented in the debates of the Consultative Assembly, or individual Representatives on the Committee or their alternates may address the Assembly, shall be determined by such rules of procedure on this subject as may be drawn up by the Committee after consultation with the Assembly.

ARTICLE 28

(*a*) The Consultative Assembly shall adopt its rules of procedure and shall elect from its members its President, who shall remain in office until the next ordinary session.

[3] As amended in December 1951.

[4] As amended in May 1951.

(*b*) The President shall control the proceedings but shall not take part in the debate or vote. The substitute of the Representative who is President may sit, speak and vote in his place.

(*c*) The rules of procedure shall determine *inter alia:*

(*i*) the quorum;
(*ii*) the manner of the election and terms of office of the President and other officers;
(*iii*) the manner in which the Agenda shall be drawn up and be communicated to Representatives; and
(*iv*) the time and manner in which the names of Representatives and their substitutes shall be notified.

ARTICLE 29

Subject to the provisions of Article 30, all resolutions of the Consultative Assembly, including resolutions:

(*i*) embodying recommendations to the Committee of Ministers;
(*ii*) proposing to the Committee matters for discussion in the Assembly;
(*iii*) establishing committees or commissions;
(*iv*) determining the date of commencement of its sessions;
(*v*) determining what majority is required for resolution in cases not covered by (*i*) to (*iv*) above or determining cases of doubt as to what majority is required,

shall require a two-thirds majority of the Representatives casting a vote.

ARTICLE 30

On matters relating to its internal procedure, which includes the election of officers, the nomination of persons to serve on committees and commissions and the adoption of rules of procedure, resolutions of the Consultative Assembly shall be carried by such majorities as the Assembly may determine in accordance with Article 29 (*v*).

ARTICLE 31

Debates on proposals to be made to the Committee of Ministers that a matter should be placed on the Agenda of the Consultative Assembly shall be confined to an indication of the proposed subject-matter and the reasons for and against its inclusion in the Agenda.

ARTICLE 32

The Consultative Assembly shall meet in ordinary session once a year, the date and duration of which shall be determined by the Assembly so as to avoid as far as possible overlapping with parliamentary sessions of

Members and with sessions of the General Assembly of the United Nations. In no circumstances shall the duration of an ordinary session exceed one month unless both the Assembly and the Committee of Ministers concur.

ARTICLE 33

Ordinary sessions of the Consultative Assembly shall be held at the seat of the Council unless both the Assembly and the Committee of Ministers concur that the session should be held elsewhere.

ARTICLE 34 [5]

The Consultative Assembly may be convened in extraordinary sessions upon the initiative either of the Committee of Ministers or of the President of the Assembly after agreement between them, such agreement also to determine the date and place of the sessions.

ARTICLE 35

Unless the Consultative Assembly decides otherwise, its debates shall be conducted in public.

Chapter VI

SECRETARIAT

ARTICLE 36

(*a*) The Secretariat shall consist of a Secretary-General, a Deputy Secretary-General and such other staff as may be required.

(*b*) The Secretary-General and Deputy Secretary-General shall be appointed by the Consultative Assembly on the recommendation of the Committee of Ministers.

(*c*) The remaining staff of the Secretariat shall be appointed by the Secretary-General, in accordance with the administrative regulations.

(*d*) No member of the Secretariat shall hold any salaried office from any Government or be a member of the Consultative Assembly or of any national legislature or engage in any occupation incompatible with his duties.

(*e*) Every member of the staff of the Secretariat shall make a solemn declaration affirming that his duty is to the Council of Europe and that he will perform his duties conscientiously, uninfluenced by any national considerations, and that he will not seek or receive instructions in connexion with the performance of his duties from any Government or any authority external to the Council and will refrain from any action which

[5] As amended in May 1951.

might reflect on his position as an international official responsible only to the Council. In the case of the Secretary-General and the Deputy Secretary-General this declaration shall be made before the Committee, and in the case of all other members of the staff, before the Secretary-General.

(*f*) Every Member shall respect the exclusively international character of the responsibilities of the Secretary-General and the staff of the Secretariat and not seek to influence them in the discharge of their responsibilities.

ARTICLE 37

(*a*) The Secretariat shall be located at the seat of the Council.

(*b*) The Secretary-General is responsible to the Committee of Ministers for the work of the Secretariat. Amongst other things, he shall, subject to Article 38 (*d*), provide such secretariat and other assistance as the Consultative Assembly may require.

Chapter VII

FINANCE

ARTICLE 38 [6]

(*a*) Each Member shall bear the expenses of its own representation in the Committee of Ministers and in the Consultative Assembly.

(*b*) The expenses of the Secretariat and all other common expenses shall be shared between all Members in such proportions as shall be determined by the Committee on the basis of the population of Members.

The contributions of an Associate Member shall be determined by the Committee.

(*c*) In accordance with the financial regulations, the Budget of the Council shall be submitted annually by the Secretary-General for adoption by the Committee.

(*d*) The Secretary-General shall refer to the Committee requests from the Assembly which involve expenditure exceeding the amount already allocated in the Budget for the Assembly and its activities.

(*e*) The Secretary-General shall also submit to the Committee of Ministers an estimate of the expenditure to which the implementation of each of the recommendations presented to the Committee would give rise. Any resolution the implementation of which requires additional expenditure shall not be considered as adopted by the Committee of Ministers unless

[6] Paragraph (*e*) of Article 38 was added in May 1951.

the Committee has also approved the corresponding estimates for such additional expenditure.

ARTICLE 39

The Secretary-General shall each year notify the Government of each Member of the amount of its contribution, and each Member shall pay to the Secretary-General the amount of its contribution, which shall be deemed to be due on the date of its notification, not later than six months after that date.

Chapter VIII

PRIVILEGES AND IMMUNITIES

ARTICLE 40

(*a*) The Council of Europe, Representatives of Members and the Secretariat shall enjoy in the territories of its Members such privileges and immunities as are reasonably necessary for the fulfilment of their functions. These immunities shall include immunity for all Representatives in the Consultative Assembly from arrest and all legal proceedings in the territories of all Members, in respect of words spoken and votes cast in the debates of the Assembly or its committees or commissions.

(*b*) The Members undertake as soon as possible to enter into agreement for the purpose of fulfilling the provisions of paragraph (*a*) above. For this purpose the Committee of Ministers shall recommend to the Governments of Members the acceptance of an Agreement defining the privileges and immunities to be granted in the territories of all Members.[7] In addition a special Agreement shall be concluded with the Government of the French Republic defining the privileges and immunities which the Council shall enjoy at its seat.

Chapter IX

AMENDMENTS

ARTICLE 41

(*a*) Proposals for the amendments of this Statute may be made in the Committee of Ministers or, in the conditions provided for in Article 23, in the Consultative Assembly.

(*b*) The Committee shall recommend and cause to be embodied in a Protocol those amendments which it considers to be desirable.

(*c*) An amending Protocol shall come into force when it has been signed and ratified on behalf of two-thirds of the Members.

[7] 'Treaty Series No. 34 (1953),' Cmd. 8852.

(*d*) Notwithstanding the provisions of the preceding paragraphs of this Article, amendments to Articles 23-35, 38 and 39 which have been approved by the Committee and by the Assembly, shall come into force on the date of the certificate of the Secretary-General, transmitted to the Governments of Members, certifying that they have been so approved. This paragraph shall not operate until the conclusion of the second ordinary session of the Assembly.

Chapter X

FINAL PROVISIONS

ARTICLE 42

(*a*) This Statute shall be ratified. Ratification shall be deposited with the Government of the United Kingdom of Great Britain and Northern Ireland.

(*b*) The present Statute shall come into force as soon as seven instruments of ratification have been deposited.[8] The Government of the United Kingdom shall transmit to all signatory Governments a certificate declaring that the Statute has entered into force, and giving the names of the Members of the Council of Europe on that date.

(*c*) Thereafter each other signatory shall become a party to this Statute as from the date of the deposit of its instrument of ratification.

[8] The Statute entered into force on 3rd August 1949.

Index

HIEBERT LIBRARY
3 6877 00042 6089

Date Due

NOV 21 '62			

PRINTED IN U. S. A.